Finding Robert

Finding Robert

Robert J. Stevens and
Catherine E. Stevens, MS

SQUAREONE
PUBLISHERS

The information and advice contained in this book are based upon the research and personal experiences of the authors. They are not intended as a substitute for consulting with a health care professional. The publisher and authors are not responsible for any adverse effects or consequences resulting from the use of any of the suggestions, preparations, or procedures discussed in this book. All matters pertaining to your physical health should be supervised by a health care professional. It is a sign of wisdom, not cowardice, to seek a second or third opinion.

Cover Designer: Jeannie Tudor
Typesetter: Gary A. Rosenberg
Editor: Michael Weatherhead

Square One Publishers
115 Herricks Road
Garden City Park, NY 11040
(516) 535-2010 • www.squareonepublishers.com

Library of Congress Cataloging-in-Publication Data

Stevens, Robert J., 1961–
 Finding Robert / Robert J. Stevens and Catherine E. Stevens.
  pages cm
 Includes bibliographical references and index.
 ISBN 978-0-7570-0402-5 (alk. paper)
 1. Stevens, Robert, 1989 December 1—Mental health. 2. Child psychopathology—Chemotherapy. 3. Child psychopathology—Alternative treatment. 4. Exceptional children—United States—Biography. 5. Psychiatric errors—United States.
I. Stevens, Catherine E. II. Title.
 RJ499.S794   2015
 618.92'890092—dc23

                                                          2014038478

Printed in the United States of America

10   9   8   7   6   5   4   3   2   1

Contents

Acknowledgments

Tina (also known as Catherine) and I would be remiss if we did not express our deepest gratitude to friends and family. It goes without saying that this book—and more importantly, Robert's recovery—could never have happened without their support.

We would like to thank our friends Susan, Michelle, Philippa, Mike, Joanne, and Donna for their patience and time. They read and reread umpteen versions of this book, and offered unwavering encouragement and extraordinary support in helping to see it published. Philippa, you are missed.

We would like to thank the directors, teachers, coaches, aides, sitters, and health professionals for the love and care each gave our son. Kamau, Corinne, Martin (rest in peace), Ida, Hugh, Elisabeth, Joanne, Joan, Arlene, Dina, Lisa, Maryann, Barbara, Linda, Rima, Coach Larry, Sensei Mike, and Sensei David, know that you helped make Robert the wonderful person he is today. Many thanks also go out to our partners and colleagues. Avi, Vidya, Stephanie, Courtney, Amanda, Lauren, Chris, Theresa, Pennie, know that your support really makes a difference in this world.

Thank you, Rudy Shur, our publisher; Michael Weatherhead, our editor; and Square One Publishers, for helping us turn a diary into a real book.

Special thanks go out to our parents, without whom none of this would have ever been possible, and to our entire family, for its support, assistance, and inspiration.

Finally, I, Robert, would like to extend a personal note of appreciation to my wife, Tina. Thank you for your love, friendship, and belief in us and what we do.

Foreword

When a child is diagnosed with a learning, behavioral, or neurodevelopmental disorder, it is an extremely difficult reality to accept, not only for the child but also for the child's entire family. Such diagnoses bring with them a new world, complete with physical and drug-related therapies, educational evaluations, and a plethora of questions and advice. They are overwhelming. That is why I feel so strongly about this book, which gives you the tools you need to understand and help your child.

I came to know Robert and Tina several years ago through a mutual client who was then a student at the learning center where they worked. After going through my program and that of the learning center, this child showed remarkable improvement. I reached out to the Stevenses to learn more about their course. I learned that Robert and Tina had been working extensively with children on the spectrum since 1998. I was intrigued by and agreed with the holistic approach Robert and Tina took when treating these children.

Over and again, I have found that behavioral disorders may be caused by the unique way in which a child's genetics can interact with the environment. While most medications treat or suppress symptoms, leaving the underlying causes unaddressed, developmental professionals work towards understanding and treating the cause of a child's behavior. Moreover, when pharmaceuticals are used to treat behavioral disorders, they often exacerbate the problem. For instance, a child with ADHD is treated with Ritalin, to help him focus for a longer period of time during school. But Ritalin and similar amphetamines actually cause a decrease in the focusing ability of the eyes, causing blurry near vision and making desk work virtually impossible. The lesson here is that lifestyle choices play a significant role in a child's behavioral development.

Perhaps the most valuable aspect of this book's approach is that it does not fixate on the promotion of a single type of treatment for children afflicted with learning or behavioral problems. No one knows the exact causes of these disorders. Are they genetic? Are they environmental? Are they a bit of both? This lack of concrete knowledge leaves parents wondering what they can do about these problems. By publishing their family's harrowing journey through the world of developmental disorders, Robert and Tina hope parents dealing with these all-too-common issues will find much-needed empathy as well as fruitful information on alternative treatments. As they suggest in this book, potential causes of these problems may be avoided, and the right developmental and nutritional therapies may help undo some of the damage already done. Relying on a wealth of research and personal experiences, this book seeks to place both parents and children on the road to recovery.

Dr. Theresa Rua

Preface

It seems like a lifetime ago that I began writing this book. Where our son, Robert, is concerned, it was a lifetime ago. Almost from the time Robert could walk, he was trouble. He managed to annoy and frustrate every one of his activity group teachers and instructors, and at home, he was nearly unmanageable. He was overly active. He was overly physical. He was overly destructive. He was just too much. He was a maddening bundle of issues that would eventually lead to diagnoses of a number of learning and behavioral disorders, a few of which would be considered autism spectrum disorder today. Robert's disorders introduced us to the world of medical specialists, psychiatrists, psychologists, psychotropic medications, and special education. It was an upsetting and extremely intimidating world with which we had no previous experience.

Like any good parents, we searched for answers. We read, studied, and networked. We consulted specialist after specialist. Driven by our love and sense of responsibility, we did what the "experts" told us to do. We tried counseling, socialization classes, psychological therapy, behavior modification, and multiple-drug therapy, all with some small degree of initial success. These treatments, however, either failed to produce lasting results or simply made matters worse.

We needed someone who had been through this, someone who could help us navigate these waters. But, as we would come to realize over the years, we were on the leading edge of the autism spectrum disorder tsunami. What we experienced some twenty years ago was not then common—not like today, where one in ten children is considered to have an attention, learning, or behavioral disorder. In a very real sense, we were pioneers, forced to face our son's issues with little guidance and even less preparedness.

Growing desperate over Robert's lack of improvement and all the issues he continued to present, we began to question and then defy the dictates and directives of Robert's doctors and teachers. It was difficult to follow our hearts in the face of such opposition (and oftentimes, hostility), but there appeared little choice. Despite following the recommendations of Robert's doctors, we found that Robert's situation only seemed to grow worse. We were moving in the wrong direction, and we simply could not give up on our son.

Against Robert's doctors' advice, we began exploring alternative therapies. As we dug deeper, we discovered a wealth of information and research about which we had not been told. Much to our surprise, a lot of this research was antithetical to what mainstream professionals had been telling us about Robert's disorders and treatments. Of most concern was the information on the dangerous side effects of the "perfectly safe" medications we had been giving our son.

We tried different therapies, and Robert began to improve. We unearthed more and more research supporting our actions. Contrary to many professionals' assertions, we became convinced that children like Robert could be helped and essentially cured, and that the research supported the conclusion that the incidence of autism spectrum disorder might even be preventable.

When I first put pen to paper, my goal was to express one little boy's plight through his father's eyes. It was my intent to forewarn those who might face similar circumstances, to bring greater understanding to those who might be forced to endure that which we endured. I could do no more, for I did not know any better. I also must admit that putting our experiences in writing was a form of therapy. It helped me cope with our situation. As time passed and Robert began to improve with the help of alternative therapies, I had to revise the text. I greatly expanded the research section with all the new data and reports that seemed to provide ever more proof of just how right Tina and I were about Robert's treatment. After obtaining her master's in clinical nutrition and working with children with attention, learning, and behavioral issues, Tina was also able to help me draft an extensive section on diet and supplementation.

About a year ago, I shared the manuscript of this book with some parents at my workplace. They all but held a gun to my head to get it published—even if only through self-publication on the Internet. I spent six months adding more research to the text, and with the help of my sister, Susan, I prepared the book for self-publication. Then, just three days before I was planning on hitting the submission button online (I was going to publish on Robert's birthday), I came across a newspaper article about a local independent book publisher named Rudy Shur, who had overcome his own learning difficulty, dyslexia, to become a very successful business owner in a field defined by the printed word. *What the heck?* I thought. *I'll get in touch with him about the book. The worst thing he could say is "no."*

But he didn't. And my family could not be happier to share our story with you now.

Introduction

We were nervous. It was early November and time for the first parent-teacher conference of the school year. Tina and I were meeting our son's fifth-grade teacher to discuss his progress. I suspect that for most parents, parent-teacher conferences are fairly routine, but Robert had just been skipped a grade–from third to fifth–and in this challenging private school, we worried whether he was feeling overwhelmed as an "upper." Could he keep up with the demanding pace of instruction? How was he handling the increased workload? His homework had grown greater in both difficulty and length. He was completing his work in a reasonable time and without too much coaxing from us, but we wondered how he well he was doing in the classroom.

We worried about his emotional state as well. He had not yet celebrated his tenth birthday and was now the youngest child in his class. Moreover, skipping a grade had separated him from his fourth-grade friends. Was his behavior as expected? Was he making friends with the other fifth-graders? Was he happy? As we prepared to meet Mrs. Winkler-Brogan—an intelligent, quiet woman, whose calming temperament complemented our son's high-energy and intense personality—my thoughts slipped back to previous teacher-conferences. Would this one be any different?

She began by telling us of Robert's strengths. He was, as we already knew, highly intelligent. He kept up with the work. He participated in class discussions, and many times his comments were "pretty amazing." Academically, he was doing quite well. He even got an A+ on his very first book report.

"Was he paying attention?" we asked.

"Yes," she replied, although she noted that she let Robert draw during lessons. "I spot check him to make sure he's listening, and he's always right with us."

"Is he making friends?" we asked.

She admitted that Robert missed the children from last year. "He seeks them out at lunch and recess." But she noted that Robert got along well with the children in his present class. "They include Robert in their activities and some of the girls in the class seem to be keeping an eye on him." I smiled. "In fact," she said, "I noticed that, because of Robert, Robert's fourth-grade friends are starting to play with the fifth-grade kids in Robert's class."

So far, so good.

"I also want to address some things I think Robert needs to work on," she said.

Ah, here it comes.

"Robert really doesn't like to write. It's a struggle to get the work out of him. I know he's got the ideas in his head, but getting him to put those thoughts down on paper is rough."

Yes, we knew about that, and we were working on it. He worked better when he was able to use a word processor. The school gave all the "upper" students access to a portable one, and we immediately took advantage of the opportunity. Robert also used our home computer for word processing. Finally, we had made arrangements for another teacher at the school to tutor Robert in writing.

"Also," the teacher added, "he's very disorganized. He needs to write down his assignments and keep his books and homework better."

No argument from us there. We agreed to give him extra folders, and to review his assignments with him.

"What else?" we asked.

"That's it," she said.

"That's it?" we asked in disbelief.

"Yes, that's it. I am very pleased with Robert's progress this year. He's doing just fine."

We then spoke to Robert's Spanish teacher. She raved about how well Robert was doing in her class. The school director, Ida Edelman, gave us a similar report, remarking upon how happy she was with Robert's adjustment and progress. We were out of there in less than twenty minutes. I turned to Tina, "Did you ever think you'd hear 'pays attention' and 'Robert' in the same sentence?"

She was still shaking her head in disbelief. "Wow" was all she could manage.

I thought about Robert's other activities—ice hockey, piano, tennis, and karate. He was a busy little kid, but he was really starting to come into his own on all fronts.

The year progressed. My newly adopted career as a director of a small learning center was in full swing. Tina continued her part-time work as a catheterization lab technologist, and Robert and his sister, Kat, were joined by a new baby brother, Matthew. Before we knew it, "moving up day" at school had arrived.

We attended the ceremony, complete with the pomp and circumstance appropriate to the occasion. Afterwards, we met with Robert's teachers one last time before summer vacation. Mrs. Winkler-Brogan told us of his "wonderful growth" during the year and again commented on his "amazing" contributions to the class. Robert's Spanish teacher could not say enough about his enthusiasm. The art teacher bragged about Robert's projects, telling us how creative he was, how his work was some of the very best, and how Robert's classmates had come to respect his artistic talents. His writing tutor told us how Robert's work had become so much more intricate and expressive. She couldn't believe the progress he had made from the first time they had met. Mrs. Edelman summed it up when she stated that Robert had had a "truly wonderful year." We couldn't have been more proud of him.

I know what you must be thinking. "What's the big deal? You had a kid who did well in school and had an active agenda of extracurricular activities. So what?"

Consider this: By the age of four, Robert had been asked to leave a playgroup, nursery school, and a tee-ball clinic. He was a complete misfit in a skating program of four- and five-year-olds, and was unable to make friends. He couldn't sit still, and he couldn't finish anything. Tina could barely control him, and I was only marginally better at the task. And again, this was all by the age of four.

Before the age of five, Robert had been formally diagnosed with attention deficit hyperactivity disorder, possibly coupled with oppositional defiance disorder. The terms Tourette syndrome, Asperger syndrome, and dyspraxia (also known as developmental coordination disorder) would be bandied about by those who worked with Robert. By the time he was six years old, pervasive developmental disorder had been added to the list of diagnoses.

At the age of eight, clumsy and apparently bereft of any athletic ability whatsoever, he could not catch a ball thrown to him from a distance of three feet, hit a baseball, or track any object in motion. Doctors, teachers, and other professionals used words like "emotionally disturbed," "other health impaired," and "anxious and extremely fragile" to describe our son. He had underwent years of special education, complete with a one-to-one aide, behavior modification, individual and group counseling, and multiple-drug therapy, including the use of such psychotropic drugs as Prozac, Ritalin, Dexedrine, and Luvox. Mainstream public schooling was out of the question, and there wasn't a private school that would accept him. No one was sure whether Robert had a future.

That is how it all began. You may be wondering how Robert got from "impaired" to that glowing parent-teacher conference I mentioned earlier. As you will learn, it was an amazing journey of twists, turns, and false steps—a journey that, in the end, was worth it.

This book is not a textbook about children with emotional or psychological problems. Nor is it a guide to counseling, drug treatment, or nonmedical therapy. By anyone's standards, however, Robert made remarkable breakthroughs utilizing the treatments and methodologies described in these pages. While both Tina and I have worked extensively with children diagnosed with these problems, we are in no way offering blanket medical or dietary advice. While it is heartening to note that many of the approaches we utilized years ago are now being embraced by more and more medical professionals, we refer those interested in alternative courses of action to knowledgeable practitioners. Every child is different, and therapies have to be tailored accordingly.

Through these pages, we wish only to spread the word and share relevant information and research. Yes, you can certainly view this book as one that deals with autism spectrum disorder, the issues that go along with raising a child with such a diagnosis, and the potential of recovery, but I hope you think of it as much more. This is really a story about fighting the good fight and making a difference. Most importantly, it's about learning not to give up on something if you really believe in it. Robert is a testament to this truth.

This book focuses mainly on the story of my family. It begins with Robert's descent—his issues, his multiple diagnoses (which varied depending upon the particular professional with whom we met)—and goes on to detail our experiences with the medical treatments we tried, and the ways in which everything—from Robert's condition to our family life—seemed to spiral ever downward. Despite what we believed to be obvious problems, our personal observations and concerns were continually discounted or ignored by those who worked with Robert. In fact, when we actually had the temerity to question Robert's treatment, we were often subjected to what I can best describe as plain old bullying—not only by medical professionals but also by teachers, and, most surprisingly, by other parents of special needs children.

Eventually, one can take only so much. Tina and I took matters into our own hands. Completing our own research, consulting alternative practitioners, and trying new therapies, we saw an incredible change in Robert. Of course, some approaches worked better than others, but the fact is that it was the combination of our nonconventional efforts that brought about the miracle we see every day in our son.

This story is true, and told in a chronological format. It is a story of life experiences, of what was good and what was bad, of what worked and what didn't, of the decisions and problems we addressed—the stuff every parent with a special needs child should be aware of and expect, the stuff about which none of the experts ever really tells you. Ours was a journey filled with choices that took us in different directions to different destinations. Of course, you know, it's not about the destination but rather the trip itself.

After detailing our story, this book explains what we learned through our research and firsthand experience. It is information about which every parent should know. The appendix outlines the alternative theories in connection with learning, attention, and behavioral disorders, the treatments we attempted in regard to our son, as well as a great deal of research supporting these ideas.

Yes, we believe ASD can be treated. Perhaps more importantly, we believe it can be prevented. Now, will engaging in the remediation therapies or taking the types of preventive action described herein prevent or correct every instance of learning, attention, or behavioral disorder? Of course not. But that is no reason not to try, especially given the staggering number of children and families faced with such issues. Even if these methodologies are effective only some of the time, the number of positive results would be well worth the effort. Indeed, saving one child would be worth the effort.

At the very least, it appears that a little preventive action could greatly lessen the incidence and severity of these disorders. If we only knew then what we know now, our son's life– our lives–might have been very different. It is my deepest wish that you benefit from our story.

One last note before we begin. While I often use the word "I" throughout this book, this is a story of an entire family's struggles and efforts, and I hope I have honored the experience of each and every member of my family in these pages.

1

There Is Nothing Wrong with Robert

As the saying goes, "Man plans and God laughs." I used to have lots of plans. Do well in high school. Go to a great college. Get into a great law school. Become a lawyer, get married, buy a house, and start a family. It all seemed so simple. Thinking back, it seems I always wanted to be a lawyer. Even as a little kid, I saw myself in a suit, in court, passionately arguing my case. Not a cop with a gun or a fireman with an axe (although an astronaut or Batman would have been cool), I wanted to be a different kind of warrior—one who fought with words, intellect, and reason. My mom always thought my choice of profession was due to trouble I had witnessed her experience with a certain attorney when I was a kid. According to her, one day I suddenly declared that I would grow up to be a lawyer, and that I would be "nice" and "fair" to everyone. I don't remember this statement at all, but I do know that I had a penchant for debate, and that I was fascinated with the moral and philosophical underpinnings of the law. I even thought that, eventually, I would become a judge. I would listen to the intellectual debates of other attorneys and dispense justice for all. That's what I thought being a lawyer was all about: figuring out the law, knowing what was right under the circumstances, and engaging in arguments adjudicated by interested, informed, and intelligent people. I was going to help shape the very laws that formed the basis of our society. I would learn, unfortunately, that being a lawyer has more to do with being a hired gun, pushing papers, and letting economics dictate the outcome of a case than it has to do with any real sense of philosophical justice.

An overly serious student, I was a nerd before it became fashionable to be one. As a matter of fact, being short, skinny, and probably a bit obnoxious (it was my defense mechanism), I got picked on a lot. In today's world, it's called "bullying," but back then such treatment was considered simply a rite of passage. A classic overachiever, I graduated class valedictorian and was accepted at my first choice of college, Brown University. I graduated *magna cum laude* from Brown with a degree in political science and was then off to New York University School of Law. From there, it was on to a good paying job at a midtown Manhattan law firm. I had an office, a secretary, a 401K plan, and a lot of nice suits. So far, so good.

Catherine, whom everyone calls Tina, also had a plan. She wanted to work in the field of medicine. Exceptionally intelligent, she was accepted at Barnard, but went to NYU on a scholarship instead. She then transferred to Boston University, where she majored in biology. I'd like to think she made that move, in part, to be closer to me. After all, we were high school sweethearts. (In fact, as I am writing this, I'm staring at the picture taken of us behind the school after high school graduation. I had hair back then.) By the time she graduated from BU, Tina had decided against medical school. Instead, she attended Stony Brook University, where she earned a degree in cardiorespiratory science. She did her clinical rotations in several local hospitals and eventually took a position in Manhattan as a cardiac catheterization technologist at New York Hospital, now known as New York-Presbyterian Hospital.

After we had both taken up the reins of our respective careers, we married in our mid-twenties and lived in a small apartment on Bleecker Street. We shared a ride on the 6 train uptown, and on the rare occasion when I'd get out of work early, we'd share the same train home.

While my early career as an attorney meant doing a lot of research and writing in the law library, Tina's job was far more interesting and important. Working with individuals of all ages and all stages of cardiovascular disease, Tina found herself not only running the cath lab machines and recording data but also administering medicines, prepping patients, and even using the defibrillator to save a person's life on more than one occasion. Working side-by-side with doctors who often relied upon her input, she dealt with people's lives on a daily basis. Unfortunately, and more often than I would ever have imagined, she saw death there, too.

We had no complaints. Life was very good. But we also were looking forward to the day when we would start our family. We weren't really city people, and despite all New York had to offer, we stayed home most evenings, saving money for the home in which we would one day raise our children. After nearly a year of searching, we settled into a cozy brick house surrounded by flowers and trees in the suburbia known as Long Island. We were ready.

Within a year, our son Robert was born. The day of his birth was, without a doubt, the happiest of my life. I was a father and here was my son. In a way, it was much more than that. When I first laid eyes on Robert, an undeniable feeling of "rightness" swept over me. I truly believed that his birth was the moment for which I had been waiting my whole life, that I had been placed on this earth to be the father of this child, that it was simply meant to be. I could never imagine, however, quite how much Robert's birth would continue to redefine me in the years to come.

Determined to do things right, I took an unpaid two-month paternity leave from work so I could help care for Robert. Tina, just as committed to the task, left her position at New York Hospital to become a full-time mom. While she would miss the work, she had no regrets about leaving to raise our son. With both of us at home, and with Robert being the first grandchild on both sides of the family, our son would never want for attention. College fund begun, parenting books read, nursery furnished, decorated, and filled with safe (and sometimes educational) toys, we felt secure in the belief that we had everything under control. Everything was on course. The plan was working. We brought Robert to the pediatrician for all his well-visits, and, of course, Robert received all the required and recommended childhood vaccinations. We did not wish to leave anything to chance. We would follow his doctor's instructions to the letter. After all, this was our son.

In general, Robert's health was good. He was a happy baby, and was meeting all his milestones. Nevertheless, Robert had a few physical problems that doctors could not seem to explain. First, Robert's scalp was always very dry and flaky. His pediatrician called it "cradle cap." While not the most pleasant physical trait a child might have (it was kind of gross, and we used to refer to it as "cradle crap"), it didn't seem to cause Robert any discomfort, and it was not harming him in any way. We were told to, and did, rub mineral oil on Robert's scalp to stop the flaking. When we asked the pediatrician what caused "cradle cap," the doctor told us, "That's just the way Robert is. Some kids get it and some kids don't." In other words, he didn't know.

Frequently, Robert would vomit after feedings, and he was often colicky. He was about four or five months old when these particular problems began. In fact, they cropped up shortly after Tina had stopped breastfeeding him. Robert was breastfed for three months. He would have been breastfed beyond that period, except I had to return to work full time. Robert was a big kid with a big appetite. His feedings had been lasting longer and longer, and Tina simply could not keep up with everything while breastfeeding Robert all day long. We decided that it would ease our lives considerably if we switched him to formula, and with our pediatrician's blessing, we did so.

Robert ate well and continued to grow at an astonishing rate. We chalked up the colic to normal baby behavior, but we were still quite concerned about the recurrent vomiting. We asked our pediatrician if we should be worried. "No. That's just the way Robert is," he said. "As long as Robert is growing and gaining weight, there's nothing to worry about." Unfortunately, Robert also began to suffer from chronic ear infections. Although his doctor could not tell us what was actually causing the ear infections, he assured us that it was a fairly common problem that would correct itself with age. "Don't worry," he said confidently, "it's just the way Robert is."

Treatment consisted of placing Robert on a near continuous course of antibiotics. When the condition stubbornly persisted despite month after month of antibiotic use, we consulted an ear, nose, and throat specialist. He recommended that Robert have bilateral tubes placed in his ears to allow the fluids to drain properly. Robert was about two years old when the tubes were inserted, which did not seem to bother him. For a time, the ear infections stopped.

Colic, earaches, and antibiotics aside, it was around this time that we began to realize that Robert was "different." Growing into a handsome, affectionate little boy with the biggest brown eyes you've ever seen (he takes after his mother), Robert was the joy of my life. He made me prouder and happier than I had ever been. But he also made me angrier and more frustrated than I had ever thought imaginable.

At the time, calling him a handful would have been an understatement. My patience, temper, and parenting skills (to the extent that a new parent has parenting skills) were under assault nearly every minute I was with Robert, and my meager experience as a daycare volunteer was no match for this tornado. He was not only extraordinarily big (his height and weight were off the charts) but also very active. He never really crawled; instead, he started walking at ten months, and it seemed like he was running one month later. He also possessed a wicked sense of humor. Thus, almost from the minute he was mobile, he was getting into trouble. He was tall enough to reach things on countertops, and strong enough to mount chairs and climb towards whatever he could not reach. Nothing was safe from him. Childproofing our house was a never-ending battle of wits that resulted in locking away everything and anything that was remotely dangerous or could be broken. Mantles, tables, counters, and shelves were completely cleared. Child gates separated the rooms and stairways. Outlets were covered and cabinets were locked. We were at the mercy of our son's whims and curiosity.

And let's not forget that sense of humor. As if by instinct, Robert seemed to know how to push just about anyone's buttons, and with a smile on his face that stretched from ear to ear, he would gleefully push them over and over and over. We also noticed that he had a tendency to break things. Now, I know all children break things, but almost everything Robert got his hands on ended up in pieces, and quite on purpose. Like clockwork, Robert would tear a book apart, rip a cassette tape to pieces, or pull off the battery cover of the television remote control. Anything with a slot, including the VCR and computer drive, would be filled with toys or coins or marbles. When he played with his toys (the ones that survived the initial encounter), there would inevitably be some sort of crash—toy cars bashing into his tinker toys, toy trains smashing into one another to simulate a train wreck, the demolition of any structure I had built for him. In fact, one of Robert's favorite games involved me building towers for him out of Legos and other building blocks, the higher the better. As soon as one was built, Robert was on the spot, knocking it over. I built, he leveled. Faster and faster, I tried to build them. Faster and faster, he'd run over to knock them down to the last piece. At night, after Robert went to sleep, I would build a dozen towers in the basement, just so he would have a surprise waiting for him in the morning. Of course, I would always make one of them "Robert-proof," usually by interlocking Lego pieces as securely as I could. It was probably a little cruel, I admit, but Robert did get his sense of humor from somebody, right? Watching Robert trying to tear that one down was always interesting.

Even Robert's own creations were invariably the victims of his own destructive ways. He would line up his toy trains and cars and then demolish the line. Over and over. He would even destroy his own drawings and craft projects. Nothing was safe. You'd think that I would have known better, but Robert also had his way with my prized electric Lionel train set, which I had kept in mint condition for over fifteen years. Robert had always been fascinated with trains, and we indulged that fascination as much as we could by supplying him with toy push trains and train-related videos. It was the one thing that seemed to hold his attention and keep him still for more than five minutes. One day, I decided to set up my old Lionel train set for him. With me in the room, I figured it would be safe. I foolishly turned my back for two minutes and found the trains, which had been running smoothly around the track, in a heap, with Robert using the engine to pummel the other cars and screaming, "Train crash! Train crash!" (After spending over one hundred dollars to fix the engine, I decided to put the trains away until Robert reached a more appropriate age—say, twenty-one.)

Robert also liked to be physical—not in a mean, bullying way (there was no punching or biting), but he did like to wrestle, and hug, and kiss, and lick. While we didn't mind this kind of behavior (except, of course, the licking), it was very disconcerting to other children and their parents. He also was extremely tough to discipline. Demanding and stubborn, we used to refer to him as "el Exigente"—Spanish for "the Taskmaster." Everything had to be done on his terms, in his way. For Tina, he was almost impossible. He never seemed to listen to anything she said. It almost seemed like he purposely ignored her. I had more luck. I was firmer with Robert, and I could usually get him to listen. And when he didn't? Hey, he was just a baby. What was the big deal?

Tina didn't see it that way. She had to deal with Robert twenty-four hours a day while I "escaped" (her word, not mine) to the workplace. She was the one who was constantly trying to keep him occupied, trying to teach him, trying to get him to behave. She kept mentioning how active and physical and oppositional he was. She swore that none of the other children she knew were like that and feared that there was something "wrong" with Robert. I have two confessions to make at this point. First, I didn't think that commuting to Manhattan to do hours upon hours of mind-numbing, tedious paper-pushing was an escape, and I resented Tina's attitude. I was involved in very large document-intensive cases that dealt with the less-than-fascinating subject of corporate insurance. I sat with other attorneys and paralegals in a room filled to the ceiling with boxes of documents, each and every one of which had to be reviewed and catalogued. (The lawyer job was not really turning out quite the way I had planned.) As difficult as I thought Robert might be, I certainly wasn't having any fun. Second, I refused to take Tina's concerns seriously. To me, Robert was just a big, active boy. My mother said Robert behaved no differently than my brother, John, and I had behaved when we were young. (That should have been my first clue that something was amiss.)

The fact was that Robert was happy. He was always laughing, always smiling. He also was learning at a tremendous pace. He picked up things quickly, and language came easily. With his one-word greeting of "Hihowareya" and a smile, he was ready to take on the world. I assumed his behavior would get better with time. I was wrong.

Our beautiful baby girl, Katherine, whom we would call Kat, was born when Robert was about two and a half years old. Robert had become increasingly difficult. Even viewing the matter through my rose-colored glasses, I began to realize we had a problem. Robert's behavior was creating an atmosphere of increasing frustration and stress. Regardless of what I thought, Tina clearly was having a very difficult time. The tension in our home was palpable. We knew it was time for us to regain control of the situation (as though we ever really had any). We felt the first step was to be extra firm with Robert. I also wanted to take part in every aspect of raising my daughter, just as I had done with my son. Holding Kat in my arms somehow made my life that much more complete. I decided to take another unpaid paternity leave from work and help out at home.

From a practical standpoint, I realized that my help was needed around the house. Robert needed attention—and increasingly so. While I was on leave, things were manageable, but when I went back to work, the situation at home quickly deteriorated. Robert was now about three years old and his personality seemed to be intensifying. It appeared as if he was withdrawing into himself. While he was growing even more active and destructive—much to our amazement and disbelief—he was also becoming harder to reach. He barely listened to anyone. He could never sit still or maintain eye contact, even briefly. We noticed that Robert was becoming (or had always been?) sensitive to noise and touch. Loud noises seemed to bother him more and more. (Tina and I also learned not to whisper anywhere near Robert. He had amazing hearing and would often ask questions about our "grown-up" conversations, clearly demonstrating that he had heard every word we had said.) I also saw that if anyone, including his parents, initiated any physical contact, no matter how gentle, Robert would flinch and immediately pull away. Unless Robert offered contact, it was nearly impossible to touch him.

Meals became increasingly difficult. Although Robert always ate well, we couldn't get him to sit down or use utensils. Tina was reduced to following him around the house with a plate of food. Going out to dinner was a nightmare. We were constantly chasing Robert, half the time just trying to keep track of him, the other half trying to make sure he didn't break anything. Even playtime was frustrating. Robert could not play any one game for more than a couple of minutes. When he was in a group, he rarely did what any of the other children were doing. When he did take part in the group, everyone had to play his way. We did our best to make sure he shared and took turns, but it was always a struggle—much more of one than any other parent seemed to experience. (Although, we did observe that many parents took the easy way out by not even bothering to oversee their children's behaviors at all.)

Bedtime was the worst. Robert refused to dress or undress himself, and getting him into bed (and getting him to stay there) was nearly impossible. Couple this behavior with the fact that, by bedtime, Tina and I were exhausted and our patience long spent. Needless to say, the scene was often ripe for genuine unpleasantness. Then the tantrums started. If Robert didn't get his way, he'd throw himself on the floor kicking and screaming. Sometimes he would literally bang his head against the wall. Adding to our collective misery, the tubes in Robert's ears clogged up and fell out. Robert had to have the tube surgery again.

*   *   *

How did we deal with Robert's behavior? Very poorly, I'm afraid. We tried "time-outs" during which we would remove Robert from the entire area. This course of action was marginally effective, and then only when we physically held Robert close to us until he finally calmed down. We tried sending him to his room when he misbehaved. While this controlled the situation immediately in front of us, it did little to modify Robert's behavior. Also, this was only a viable option in our own home. Outside the confines of our house, we couldn't very well send him to his room. Robert was aware of this fact, and took advantage of it every chance he got.

I'm ashamed to admit it, but I even tried spanking Robert—over the knee, pants down, spanking. Thankfully, I regained my sanity quickly, and this atrocious practice ended abruptly. I hated spanking Robert, but at the time I truly felt there was no other choice. It seemed to work, and God knows nothing else we were doing was having any real effect. But Tina and I realized that there also was something terribly wrong about it. First of all, spanking was always a last resort. By the time Robert got a spanking, I was angry. So there I was, hitting my son in anger. Yes, he had done something wrong and deserved to be punished. Yes, it was the way I had been raised. But the fact remained that I was hitting my son. I always felt terrible about it after I had done it. Of course, so did Robert.

Eventually, whenever I warned Robert that he was about to be punished, he'd grab his butt and run away. He was afraid of me. That was something with which I could not live. I also wasn't absolutely sure that it was any more effective a deterrent than some of the other methods we had tried. He knew he was going to be spanked, yet he misbehaved anyway. Finally, worse than anything else, Robert soon started to hit other people (including us) when he got angry. Who could blame him? He was merely imitating his role models. There is no better way to teach someone a particular behavior than to model it for him. Robert had learned well from us, unfortunately. We were now in the ludicrous position of telling Robert that hitting was "bad," and then spanking him to drive home the point.

But what to do? Let Robert continue to misbehave? Ignore our responsibilities as parents? It was time to get creative. We stopped spanking and instead tried to make do with other forms of discipline. We continued to use "time-outs." We sent Robert to his room or an accessible corner when his room was not available. We began a "carrot and stick" approach. If Robert behaved, he received a toy or an extra privilege, such as watching television or playing video games. If he misbehaved, we took away a toy or a privilege. It wasn't a perfect situation, but it was the most effective means at our disposal, and it did, in fact, help.

*   *   *

Robert was getting close to the age of four by this time, and Tina was convinced that he was hyperactive. I disagreed. He could watch his train videos and play certain video games for relatively long stretches of time. If he could do those things, how could he be hyperactive? Unable to think of a reason for Robert's behavior, we thought experimenting with his diet might help. We began to monitor what he ate. We stopped giving him artificial snacks and drinks, instead offering him fruit, carrot sticks, and juices. Sweets and candies were completely forbidden, as was any drink that contained caffeine. We made sure that he ate well and ate healthfully, and we supplemented his diet with prescribed children's vitamins and herbal teas that claimed to be calming. We even had a four-hundred-dollar water filter installed in our house just to be safe. We had noticed that Robert drank a lot of water. He was always thirsty, and he urinated frequently. In fact, sometimes he'd urinate, and not twenty minutes later, he would have to go again! Robert's pediatrician assured us there was nothing wrong. "He's just a thirsty kid," he said. No change worth mentioning took place, so we ruled out diet as either a possible cause or a cure.

I then thought it might be video games. I liked playing video games (did I mention I was a nerd?), and Robert would watch and try to play, too. I discovered that video games could cause headaches or even seizures in some children. Indeed, many children feel tired, dizzy, and nauseated after even just fifteen minutes of exposure to video games, and many games come with warnings. I also know many people, including myself, get headaches from staring at computer monitors for extended periods of time. Maybe the video games were bothering him. Or perhaps Robert was just mimicking the nonstop action of the characters—after all, he would get very excited whenever he played. We told Robert that the video game machine had broken, packed up the games, and put them away. Again, this action produced no benefit worth mentioning.

The change in diet and removal of possible bad influences had not resulted in any substantial difference in Robert's behavior. I was forced to admit it: It had to be us. We weren't raising Robert properly. We had to be even firmer and more consistent. We set up special routines for morning, noon, and night. Robert had to do certain things in a certain order at meals and bedtime. We set forth specific expectations concerning his behavior. It was a battle, but things did get a little better. Nevertheless, it remained a terrible struggle. My father, God rest his soul, said Robert should be spanked. We consulted our pediatrician instead. He gave us the name of a child psychologist.

2

Coming to a Head

Although I realized Robert was difficult, I honestly didn't see the need for a child psychologist. Tina, however, was adamant about the idea. An appointment was made and we reported to the psychologist, but without Robert. The psychologist had explained to us that Robert was too young to evaluate. Besides, he believed "good parenting" was the key, and therefore wanted to discuss our situation as parents. We told him about Robert's behavior and our concerns. We asked what we should do to control his acting out. The psychologist agreed that spanking was inappropriate (and probably ineffective, in any event). He approved of our other forms of discipline, and he stressed that we must be "100-percent" consistent with Robert, always following through on all threats to remove a toy or a privilege. He also liked the idea of routines. He said that it would make things easier for Robert; he would always know what was expected of him, and habit would become an ally. He noted, though, that it was important for us to pick our battles carefully. It would be impossible to correct Robert's every misstep, and constant criticism, stress, and negativity would be detrimental to everyone. We were to concentrate on big behavioral problems. The small ones were not worth the effort, and, in his opinion, they would eventually take care of themselves.

The psychologist made one suggestion we thought quite novel. He told us to make a chart and give Robert a star whenever we "caught" him behaving. It was important not to use the stars as a bribe for good behavior (as we had done with the toys). Robert had to learn how to behave himself on his own. We would then "catch" him behaving and reward him for it—positive reinforcement of good behavior through reward. The psychologist stressed this idea over and over. We had to reinforce good behavior—look for it, recognize it, and then reward it. Many times, he warned us, parents only see and react to negative behavior. It was important for Robert and us to see and react to the good. We agreed to try this approach.

The discussion shifted to explaining Robert's behavior. Tina desperately wanted to know why Robert misbehaved to such a degree, and why he was so active. The psychologist seemed fairly sure that Robert was not hyperactive. Instead, he thought Robert was probably seeking attention. After all, we had just had a new baby. He didn't think there was anything to worry about. We shook hands, and Tina and I set off. I was completely satisfied; after all, the psychologist had told us we were basically doing everything right. What better testament to us as parents? Tina, on the other hand, was not so happy. She was still convinced that something was not "right" with Robert. I told her to relax. We'd try the psychologist's suggestions and take it from there. I was sure Robert would be just fine.

Things were a little better following our trip to the psychologist. I certainly felt better having had a professional agree with our approach to raising Robert. The psychologist had also given us some new tools with which to deal with Robert's behavior. Anything that might help was welcome. Indeed, much of my anxiety stemmed from my uncertainty towards what to do, and from my own severe critique of our actions. Of course, it also didn't hurt that the psychologist didn't think anything was wrong with Robert.

The star chart seemed to be fairly effective. Every time we "caught" Robert behaving, he would get a star. We began simply. Robert would get a star when he listened to us without constant repetition. He would get a star when he got dressed without too much fuss. Finishing a meal was also good for a star, as was sharing with Kat. Ten stars would result in a prize—some small toy or a special treat. Before long, Robert caught on to the game. He began doing good deeds whenever he wanted a toy. He would run from a room to tell us that he had been nice to his sister. "Do

I get a star for that?" Worse, whenever we'd ask him to do something, he would check to see if obeying would bring a star.

"Robert, please put on your coat."

"If I do, will I get a star?"

If we promised a star, he would do it. If we said he might get a star, he would be hesitant. If we said no, he wouldn't do it. He was bright, manipulative, and getting greedy. We knew the chart's days were numbered. Moreover, while the chart was an effective means of increasing desirable behavior, it did nothing in terms of decreasing undesirable behavior. When Robert earned a star, it was his—we did not take away stars for "bad" behavior. We thought, and the psychologist agreed, that if Robert knew there was a good chance he would lose a star, he might not even try to earn one in the first place. The psychologist referred to it as "setting him up to fail" because, inevitably, Robert was bound to misbehave. The past methods of discipline were still in full force with the same limited level of effectiveness.

It also was around this time that we enrolled Robert in a "Mommy and Me" class. For the uninitiated, "Mommy and Me" is basically an organized playgroup in which a parent, usually the mother, accompanies her child. We thought exposing Robert to his peers in a less familiar environment might help him grow up a little.

Robert was a terror. He never did anything the class did, choosing instead to pursue his own interests rather than participate in the group. Completely content to run amok, Robert stood out like a sore thumb. While the rest of the children sat in a circle, quietly listening to stories, Robert could be found tearing through the toy shelves. While the other children ate their snacks, Robert ran laps around the classroom. He was also intimidating the other children. His size (he stood a full head taller than any other child in his class), independence, constant motion, and tendency towards physical contact were unsettling. Tina continually got dirty looks and overheard the not-so-whispered comments of the other mothers, especially when Robert attempted to play with their children. (Robert and Tina got the same treatment at the local playgrounds.) I dismissed it, thinking these ladies were being overprotective, snooty, or just plain unfriendly. Robert wasn't hurting anyone; he was just trying to be friendly. I just thought Robert was being independent. Certainly, there was nothing wrong with that. Maybe he was just bored. Besides, he was only three and a half years old; he didn't know any better.

Tina, thinking that the "Mommy and Me" classes would afford her a break, came home exhausted, flustered, and embarrassed. I didn't yet realize how much Robert was affecting her life. I didn't realize how much effort Robert truly required.

*   *   *

Although the class didn't exactly work out as well as we had hoped, Robert made it to the end of the semester. We decided that "Mommy and Me" had at least been a step in the right direction. The next move was to see how Robert would fare in a class without either of us present. An added benefit to this arrangement was the fact that it would give Tina the break she so desperately needed. Although she loved him dearly, Tina needed some time away from Robert. "Mommy and Me" did not supply it, and she was having a harder and harder time dealing with Robert's behavior. It was not only mentally exhausting but also physically trying. At the conclusion of "Mommy and Me," we enrolled Robert in a play-group for three- and four-year-old children. He attended this group without his mother.

We began receiving phone calls about Robert almost immediately. It started with the fact that Robert could not sit still in class. He also had an extremely hard time moving from one activity to another. His teacher said he had trouble with "transition," that is, Robert could not easily stop one activity and then switch to another. And, of course, there were the usual complaints.

"Robert won't listen."

"Robert is too aggressive."

"Robert is disrupting the class."

Much to the teacher's apparent surprise, Robert was perfectly fine in one-on-one situations. In fact, she went out of her way to explain how pleasant Robert was apart from the group. The problem was that she simply could not devote so much time exclusively to Robert. We were told that something needed to be done. I was quite taken aback by all this. I strongly suspected that the teacher was exaggerating, and I didn't understand what they wanted from us. I told her to deal with it—after all, wasn't that her job? I added that I didn't appreciate hearing that the group leaders couldn't "devote so much time" to Robert. What were we paying these people for anyway?

Another week or two passed after this conversation. Finally, the ultimatum came. We would either have to stay with Robert during the time he was with the playgroup or take him out of the class completely. I couldn't believe it. I went to class to see for myself. I immediately felt a tension in the room. The teacher wouldn't even acknowledge my presence. She had had it with Robert and wanted him out of the class, period. I watched from a corner of the room. Objectively speaking (to the extent that I can be objective), Robert behaved no worse than the other children, except for one incident.

Robert and another boy got into a fight over a toy. Robert lost control. He did not hit the other boy or throw a tantrum, he just became extremely agitated. He would not listen or look at anyone, including me. He kept trying to get the toy despite anything anyone said. I had to pick him up and physically remove him from the class. Once outside, it took me a full five minutes just to "reach" him. He wouldn't even look at me. I had to hold his head still in an attempt to make eye contact and communicate with him. Even then, he kept shifting his eyes away.

After he was under control, we returned to the classroom where I noticed something else. Every once in a while, another child would take something from Robert or hit him. Robert would retaliate loudly, at which point the teacher or aides would notice a problem and invariably catch Robert doing something inappropriate. Robert would receive the "time-out" or the "talking to." I also saw that the teacher's voice would become noticeably harsher when she spoke Robert, and that she was quicker to take things away from him than from the other children.

Furious, I spoke to the program director. I told her I didn't care for the teacher's attitude, and I didn't like her picking on my son. I then noted that, other than that one previously mentioned incident, Robert's behavior was no worse than that of the other children. The director agreed that Robert had behaved—that day. She said, however, that this was unusual, and attributed it to the fact that I had been present. Then she focused on the moment in which Robert had lost control. I pointed out that he had settled down once I'd taken him outside the room for a few minutes. She agreed. She told me that there was never a problem with Robert one-on-one. But they had neither the staff nor the time to commit to Robert. She really didn't have much to say concerning my complaints about the teacher's behavior.

"Fine," I thought. I disliked his teacher (or maybe I was just disappointed in her), and if the program didn't have the resources to deal with my son, I didn't want him there anyway. We withdrew Robert from the class. Tina was very shaken by this incident. Despite what I said out loud, deep inside, I, too, was concerned. Robert really was out of control. I had never seen him like that before. We returned to the child psychologist—again, without Robert.

*   *   *

We sat down with the psychologist and explained what had happened. He still did not seem concerned, and he still thought Robert was too young for a full-scale evaluation. He honestly felt that if we were patient, consistent, and encouraging, Robert would be all right. He stressed the importance of being strict and having definite and certain consequences for "bad" or "inappropriate" behavior. He didn't believe that Robert was hyperactive; he felt that Robert just needed more time. In contrast to my feelings after our first meeting, I left the psychologist's office somewhat discouraged. We gave Robert more time, and we did our best, hoping that, sooner or later, his behavior would improve. We made sure that we gave both him and his sister lots of love, encouragement, and attention.

At a little over four years of age, Robert weighed about forty-five pounds and stood about an inch shy of four feet tall. His physical growth was off the charts, and he looked a whole lot older than he really was. That was a problem, especially when others had to deal with him. They saw a big kid, and expected him to act the age they thought him to be.

We enrolled Robert in nursery school. This time, everything started out well. We grew optimistic. Maybe we were finally over the worst, but then again, maybe not. We started getting calls about Robert. It was the same story.

"Robert can't sit still."

"Robert has trouble with transition."

"Robert doesn't listen."

"Robert is too aggressive."

Robert also turned into quite the instigator. Whenever Robert engaged in some sort of disruptive behavior, like running to the window in the middle of class or breaking the circle the children were sitting in, the other children would follow his lead. While I secretly applauded his leadership qualities, I knew this had to stop.

Robert also was having trouble socializing with other children. It wasn't that he was mean or unfriendly to them. In fact, he was just the opposite. Robert went out of his way to say hello to other kids, ask their names, and ask if they wanted to play or come to his house. He'd share his toys and was friendly. But his inability to stick with any particular activity for more than two minutes, constant motion, and intensity continued to scare some of the children. Others simply lost interest in playing with Robert, since he couldn't play or converse about one particular subject for any amount of time.

Of course, one-on-one, Robert was fine. Robert's nursery school teacher thought he was very sweet, quite bright, and a good learner. She was, however, quite blunt about the fact that she felt Robert had a "real problem" and should be evaluated. She mentioned hyperactivity. She also mentioned something called "attention deficit disorder." I remember Tina's face vividly upon hearing this said out loud. It was a strange mix of relief and concern—relief that she had found someone who agreed with her and offered a plausible reason for Robert's behavior, and concern for the well-being of her baby.

I steadfastly refused to believe this opinion. I thought Tina was simply seeking an explanation for Robert's behavior and was happy to hear that someone agreed with her suspicions. I did not feel I could trust Tina's instincts (big mistake). Instead, I chose to continue in my blind belief that Robert was just a big, active boy. Indeed, I argued that he was supposed to be difficult. I began making excuses for him. Maybe he's too young for this. Maybe he's bored. Maybe the teachers are just too damn lazy to deal with him. And what's this about hyperactivity? We had already discussed the matter with the psychologist. He didn't think Robert was hyperactive. I wasn't about to heed the unsolicited opinion of a nursery school teacher. Attention deficit? I had never heard of it before, and the teacher's description of the disorder was very vague. I dismissed it completely. We left Robert in the nursery school for the time being.

*   *   *

The tubes in Robert's ears clogged-up and fell out again. And by "fell out," what I really mean is that Robert was sitting in my lap in tears from the pain in his ears. I tried my best to console him. There wasn't much I could do. I remember administering ear drops recommended by Robert's doctor, but they had little, if any, effect. Suddenly, my lap was wet. I knew it wasn't from his tears alone. I picked Robert up and noticed fluid running from his ear. His eardrum had popped and fluid was pouring out. Robert ended up having ear surgery again.

We asked both Robert's pediatrician and his surgeon what they thought might be causing these chronic ear infections. Although we had done no independent research on the subject, we had heard that diet might have some connection to the problem. They both told us, in no uncertain terms, that diet had absolutely nothing to do with the infections. "It's just the way Robert is," they said. This time, though, the surgeon recommended that Robert have his adenoids and tonsils removed. He told us that although there was nothing wrong with Robert's adenoids and tonsils, per se, there might be some connection between the adenoids and tonsils and the constant ear infections. Since they were going to put in the tubes, they might as well take out the adenoids and tonsils while they were there. We consulted another doctor who confirmed the possible connection between adenoids and ear infections, though he disputed the idea that tonsils had any proven relationship to the issue. In fact, he cited research that suggested tonsils play a role in the body's immune system. So, we allowed the surgeon to remove Robert's adenoids only.

*　　　*　　　*

I love hockey, although I have never played (mostly because I cannot skate). At the time, Robert seemed to enjoy hockey, too. He'd watch the games with me on television. (Well, sort of—he'd watch a few minutes, run around the room, play with some toys, look up when someone scored, and, for reasons still unknown to me, cheer, "*Hot dog! Hot dog! Hot dog!*") He also knew which team to root for (my favorite team, the Islanders), and which team to boo (Tina's favorite, the Rangers, of course). We played floor hockey indoors and outside.

Tina and I thought Robert might like to learn the game. We also thought that another structured activity with other children his age couldn't hurt, especially one in which the children were supposed to be moving around a lot. We enrolled Robert in a skating class, which lasted exactly one day. He was terribly excited by the prospect of learning to skate, until he hit the ice, literally. After falling down the first time, he refused to pay attention or try anything. He cried a lot, and despite his inability to move on the ice, still found ways to be disruptive. We withdrew Robert from the class.

We then found a hockey school that had a class for children aged four to six. Both the coaches and the facilities came highly recommended. It didn't work out well at first. Although Robert enthusiastically attended the initial session and seemed to do well, he lost interest soon after. It then became a battle of wills just to get him to class. Once there, the battle would continue as we tried to get his equipment on. He would fidget, he would complain, he would fight with us. He wouldn't wear his gloves. He wouldn't carry his stick. He was no better once he was dressed and on the ice, but then he was a problem for the coaches. And what a problem he was. All Robert wanted to do was be pulled around by the coaches. He wouldn't listen to them at all. He wouldn't do what the other children were doing.

While eighteen children skated clockwise around the rink, Robert skated counterclockwise. While eighteen children went one way down the ice, Robert went the other way. While all the other children practiced, Robert stood by himself and stared at the lights, leaned up against the boards looking for the Zamboni, or just lay down on his back in the middle of the ice as everyone skated around him. Then there was the scrimmage. The rink became a mass of happily squealing children all vying for the puck—all except Robert, who was sitting in the net or skating off in the opposite direction. Even when the coaches purposely passed the puck to Robert, he would skate right by as if he hadn't seen it.

At worst, Robert would take off his equipment and throw it onto the bench because he wanted to come off the ice. Sometimes he'd kick the boards and scream until someone let him off. Not once during his first set of classes was he able to stay out on the ice for the entire hour. It wasn't long before everyone knew who Robert was. All anyone ever heard from the coaches was "Robert, get over here! Robert, get up! Robert, skate in this direction!" Robert was oblivious to it all.

It was frustrating. It was disappointing. It was embarrassing. It killed me inside. Why was my son the only one who didn't listen? Why was my son skating left when everyone was going right? Why was my son lying in the middle of the ice? Of course, I wanted Robert to do well in sports. He was certainly big enough and strong enough. I remember when I was a kid; I was small and not naturally athletic. Needless to say, I was never a star athlete, and no one ever fought to have me on a team. I hated it. So, here was my son, given the physique and size I never had, not listening and not trying, and I could only sit on the side and watch. I honestly didn't care if he couldn't do it; it was his complete lack of effort and stubborn opposition that bothered me. I guess, like most fathers, sometimes I forgot my son wasn't me.

We tried everything to get Robert to pay attention and participate. It wasn't that he didn't like hockey; he never actually complained about going. We couldn't figure out what the problem was for Robert. We encouraged him. We took him ice skating on the weekends. We bought him inline skates and practiced skating in the street whenever we could. We even tried bribery, promising him a toy if he stayed out on the ice the entire time. We also tried the reverse; we threatened to punish him if he quit halfway through. Nothing worked.

Everything came to a head one day during a scrimmage. Robert wouldn't listen to the coaches. He refused to go on the ice or to get off the ice when he was supposed to, and he was disrupting the game for the other children. The other parents were getting upset and frustrated. The coaches were getting upset and frustrated. I completely lost it. During one shift, I picked Robert up by his jersey, hauled him out of the rink, and started yelling at him. "What are you doing? Why won't you listen? What's the matter with you? All the other kids are listening and playing; *Why can't you?*" I was so angry. I couldn't believe he was behaving like this. I couldn't figure out why.

After that incident, Tina and I talked for a long time about taking Robert out of the hockey program. In fact, we talked about all the activities in which we had attempted to enroll Robert. I'm sure it sounds like we were overdoing it—too many activities, too young, too much, too fast. Perhaps we were. Perhaps we had made the rookie mistake of expecting too much from our son. But we were desperate to get Robert into some kind of activity with other children. He needed friends. He needed to learn to get along with other children. And, God knows, we needed a break. Besides, we truly thought hockey would be good for him. Robert had the opportunity to learn at an early age. How many of us wish we had learned a sport or some other type of athletic or creative skill when we were young? How many of us wish we'd stuck with something? Of course, we were going to expose Robert to other sports, activities, and interests, including music and art. But for now, it was hockey.

But was it worth the aggravation he put us through? Was it worth the effort it took to get Robert to the rink and dressed to play? Was the nagging and yelling with which we and the coaches bombarded Robert doing more harm than good? What about Robert? What was he getting out of this anyway? When he really tried, he could do it, and believe it or not, each time he went, he got a little better, in spite of himself. Still, we felt like we were forcing him to do something that maybe he didn't want to do, as though we were imposing our values upon him. We agreed, however, that prodding him was what we were supposed to be doing.

I mean, if it had been up to Robert, he wouldn't have done anything. He wouldn't have even gone to school. But we made him go. We also made him pick up his toys, brush his teeth, and be polite. What was so different about this? It was good for him. It forced him to socialize with other boys his age. In fact, many of his cousins and friends played hockey. It was good exercise, and he was growing stronger and more coordinated. He was learning something different. And thank goodness for the coaches. They were terribly patient, and they genuinely liked Robert. They just kept saying, "Give him time; he's young yet." We would. We had no other choice.

We decided to keep Robert in hockey. We also signed him up for tee-ball. Unfortunately, the tee-ball coach was not nearly as patient as Robert's hockey coaches. This disaster didn't even last one day. Unlike hockey, tee-ball involves a lot of standing around doing nothing. It also involves a lot of sitting and waiting for one's turn. Well, we should have known what would happen. Robert was his usual self. He wouldn't listen to the coach. He wouldn't wait his turn. He went out of his way to push the coach's buttons. The coach got angry. He turned to Tina, told her flat out that he couldn't handle Robert, and asked her to take him out of the program before the first session was over. Tina left in tears with Robert in tow.

3

Trouble at Home

Robert may have just needed more time to mature, but the fact was that we were growing more and more frustrated and impatient. While we encouraged him and rewarded him anytime he behaved, we continued to have an extremely hard time dealing with his oppositional tendencies. That he rarely sat still was also becoming increasingly discouraging. I can't begin to count the times I tried to watch television with him or play a game with him. I couldn't understand why Robert refused to do any of these things with me, and it hurt. Robert simply wouldn't stay focused, and it bothered me that we couldn't spend some quiet time together. Also, all our tricks for dealing with his behavior were losing their effectiveness. We started to have long talks with Robert about what we expected of him. (Having adult heart-to-hearts with our baby boy—what was I thinking?) Unfortunately, Robert bore the brunt of our frustration. Tina and I grew quicker to lose our tempers, quicker to yell at him, and quicker to punish. (I was beginning to understand the struggle through which Robert had put his playgroup teacher.) Moreover, even though we had done away with spankings, there was still the rare occasion on which Robert received a good swat on the behind, and there was more than one time when he was "physically persuaded" to behave after I had completely lost patience.

Even my family was having problems dealing with Robert. My father could not accept Robert's poor behavior, and I'm sure, but for the fact that we told everyone that we do not punish our children by hitting them, Robert would have been over his grandpa's knee many a time.

31

Even Robert's younger cousins had problems with him. Although Robert loved their company, he managed only to annoy them. While he might initially join them in a game they were playing, he would inevitably lose interest and want to do something else. Of course, the other children wanted to finish what they had started, so Robert would constantly interrupt their games in order to get their attention. The others would get angry with Robert, a fight would ensue, and we would be forced to remove our son from the area. Or, realizing how excited Robert could get, the children would purposefully agitate him just to get a reaction. Sometimes they even hid from Robert. Kids can be mean.

It broke my heart. I always ended up playing with Robert. Whether playing with action figures, pushing toy trains around, or dressing up like his favorite superheroes and fighting the bad guys (with his sister as his ally), I was the one to whom Robert looked for companionship. It was obvious that I was his best friend—perhaps his only friend.

The strain created by the situation with Robert was taking a toll on all of us, both individually and as a family. Combine that fact with the necessities of keeping up a household and taking care of our daughter—not to mention my late working hours—and our home life was quickly deteriorating. Tina was having an especially rough time. It certainly didn't help that I was less than sympathetic when she complained about how Robert never listened to her. I could get Robert to listen, sort of, most of the time. On the occasions that I couldn't, he was still young enough to be made to behave. I really thought she just didn't know how to handle Robert, and, therefore, had caused some of the problems. This garbage about something being "wrong" with Robert (and I honestly felt it was garbage) was nothing more than an excuse to explain her inability to handle the situation. Not very understanding of me, I admit, but it's what I believed. Although I had sense enough not to voice my opinions at the time, my attitude showed. Quite justifiably, Tina resented it. Moreover, it was easy for me to come home from work right before Robert's bedtime, play with him and his sister, and help put them to bed. After all, he had to behave for only a short time with me. Besides, Robert really didn't have to behave that much when I was around. I was the fun one—we spent most of our time together playing.

Our many talks with Robert's nursery school teacher only added fuel to Tina's argument. She wanted Robert evaluated. "You see; it's not just me. Someone else thinks there's something wrong with Robert."

I continued to disagree. "There's nothing wrong with him. He's just being a boy. You have to be firm with him."

When she pointed out that I was refusing to face reality, my long hidden prejudices erupted to the surface. I accused her of not being strict enough with Robert. I told her she was inconsistent, that she let him get away with too much. I felt she simply didn't know what she was doing. "If he doesn't do what he's told, make him do it," I told her. "You're the parent, damn it!" We had many a fight in that vein.

Tina and I have known each other for a long time. We first met in seventh grade. Due to our last names both starting with the letter "S" (her maiden name is Sabat), I often sat right behind her in our classes. She was tall and pretty, and it was hard for me not to notice her (especially when I couldn't see the blackboard over her head of beautiful, dark hair). I was kind of short back then—I had yet to hit my growth spurt—and Tina was at least a head taller than I was. While we traveled in the same group of friends for many years, it wasn't until our senior year in high school that we began dating. We've been together ever since. I attribute this connection to the fact that we share the same core values and beliefs. Now, I'm not saying that we see eye to eye on everything, especially concerning TV in the bedroom (she's pro, I'm con), hockey teams, watching football, and my driving skills, but we have never really argued about the big, important, life-defining things. We love each other, and I have a deep and profound respect for her.

Of course, over all these years, we have had our fair share of fights. What couple hasn't? But now it seemed as though we were fighting more frequently and over nothing. Our patience with each other seemed to have worn thin. We were tired. We were cranky. We were on edge. Little things that had not mattered before, or to which I had never even given thought—like failing to pick up the laundry or turn off lights—were now reason enough to pick each other apart, to yell, to scream.

Being married isn't easy. At the very least, it requires significant effort. Caring for someone always does. When you're married, you have to compromise. That can be tough, but you want to be fair to your love. You have to be considerate. You have to recognize that you are not the only one who matters, that there is someone else who must matter even more. You give up a piece of yourself, but in the end, you realize you are giving up that piece to share in a whole that is far greater than either you or your partner is alone.

Then you have a child. For the first time in your life, you truly understand what the word "precious" means. And you give. You give till it hurts, but you don't even think about it. None of it is easy. It all takes time, energy, and effort. You realize that the more people with whom you share yourself, the greater the cost. If something unwanted and unexpected makes your day-to-day life harder, starts to sap your energy and effort, causes disagreement and discord—if things aren't going the way you'd planned—there grows disappointment, frustration, and anger.

Robert's situation was our "something unwanted and unexpected." It was something that was making our day-to-day life harder, something that was sapping our energy and effort, something that was causing disagreement, something we didn't want, something for which we hadn't planned, something so very disruptive, something that was taking us off our intended course. We never really fought about Robert, but we surely fought because of him. On some level, I recognized that Tina was having a hard time with Robert, but I refused to give that difficulty legitimacy. Why? What was I feeling? In retrospect, I think it was a bad mix of disbelief, anger, and upset. First, I still would not allow myself to believe that there was anything wrong. Robert was healthy, happy, and intelligent. Other than his "hyperness," there were no obvious physical manifestations of any problem or disorder. As long as I didn't acknowledge a problem, there couldn't be one, right?

Now, if there wasn't anything wrong with Robert, then what was Tina complaining about? I felt that Tina should have been handling the situation better. She was home. She had time. We had money. Get a sitter, call a friend, and be tough. It's a mentality: Don't complain; just deal with it. Really, how hard could it be?

I also was under a lot of pressure at work. As the firm's head partner constantly reminded us, as lawyers we would be defined by hours billed.

Bluntly speaking, a lawyer's worth to the firm was directly and inextricably twined to the number of hours billed to the client. The more we worked, the more we were worth. And I was working a lot. Twelve-hour days were not uncommon, and I felt like I should have been working more. A lot of other attorneys were out-billing me. Didn't Tina know the kind of pressure I was under?

What's more, I was never one to multitask. I do one thing at a time, almost to the point of obsession. I needed to be focused on work. Nothing else. I was more than happy to help out at home when I could, but I truly believed that Tina should be taking care of things there. I had enough on my plate. More than anything, I was upset. This was not the way it was supposed to be. Robert was supposed to be a perfect little boy who brought only joy into our lives. We were supposed to be perfect parents that raised him the right way and enriched his life. We were supposed to be nothing more than a happy family. Why wasn't the plan working out? Was there really something wrong with Robert?

I know Tina felt the same way. Taking care of a family, a house, two kids—one, an infant, the other, an oversized toddler with "issues"—she worked from sun up till sun down. It was never enough. And Robert was her baby. In a quiet moment, she told me she thought she should be able to handle things. She thought she should be able to take care of Robert. She was overwhelmed and felt like she was failing us all.

Finally, I began to doubt myself. If Robert was having problems, maybe it was because I wasn't a good enough parent. Maybe I wasn't around enough. Maybe I played too rough with him. Maybe I let him watch all the wrong things. Maybe I wasn't a good father.

*   *   *

It wasn't long before all our friends and family members realized what a handful Robert was. They made all sorts of useful observations.

"He's hyper."

"He must be eating too much sugar."

"I just knew you shouldn't have let him play all those video games."

Along with the observations, Tina and I also got plenty of advice, whether we asked for it or not.

"He needs quiet time."

"Don't play so rough with him."

"Enroll him in martial arts classes; the discipline will do him good."

"You need to be firmer with him."

Aunt Sophie even gave us gemstones that were supposed to have a calming effect on Robert. They didn't. Of course, there were many inquiries as to whether we had ever considered having him evaluated just to make sure nothing was wrong. *Not yet*, I thought. *Not yet*.

Meanwhile, back in nursery school, the situation continued to worsen. Robert's teacher told us that Robert was getting nothing out of the class. She also was getting closer to delivering the "I can't handle him" speech. Worse, the other children realized that they could get Robert riled up and in trouble, and so they did. Robert was having a hard time, and it hurt us to see it. Constantly suggesting (and probably hoping) that we might want to take Robert out of her classroom, Robert's teacher was convinced our son had a problem. She urged us to have him evaluated. Even our pediatrician, based partially on observing Robert in his office during regular office visits, suggested we have him evaluated.

Eventually, we were forced to take Robert out of the nursery school. It was then that we thought long and hard about having Robert evaluated. Well, I thought long and hard about it. As I mentioned, Tina was already convinced that Robert needed to be evaluated. So far, Robert had been asked to leave a playgroup, a nursery school, and a tee-ball team. He was a complete misfit in his hockey program, and unable to make friends. He couldn't sit still, and he couldn't finish anything. Tina could barely control him, and while I might have had a bit more luck getting him to listen, I have to admit this task was far more difficult than it should have been. A teacher, a doctor, and numerous other people had suggested there was a problem and that we ought to look into it. "Okay," I said, reluctantly.

4

There Is Something Wrong with Robert

Looking back, Tina was absolutely correct to insist upon an evaluation of Robert, and I was foolish not to agree to it sooner. I wrongly ignored her feelings on the matter, yet who knew our son better than she? Like a man who refuses to see a dentist despite the fact that his jaw is swollen shut and the mere thought of eating is sheer agony, I guess I just did not want to admit anything was wrong. Instead of confronting our problems and taking action, I did nothing, hoping they would go away on their own.

They didn't. For all I know, my period of denial might have actually made things worse. My inflexibility might have robbed us of valuable information and precious time. These were, after all, Robert's formative years—months could make an enormous difference in his development. While there is something to be said for not overreacting, all the signs pointed to a problem. Knowing what I knew—Robert's difficulties in school and extracurricular programs, the recognition of disturbing character traits in Robert by those who interacted with him, Robert's frustrating behavior at home—I should not have waited so long to act.

Indeed, there had been reason enough for Tina and me to see a child psychologist about Robert twice. While I can probably be forgiven for not having Robert at the first meeting, how I ever thought it would be enough merely to talk to the psychologist about parenting without having Robert examined in person is beyond me. How could I have relied on the judgment of someone who had never even met Robert? Had this been a physical problem, I know I wouldn't have waited to bring Robert to a doctor. Whenever Robert's ears bothered him, we rushed him to the pediatrician. Why did I hesitate to do so where Robert's mental well-being was concerned? Were physical problems simply more acceptable to me? Could I acknowledge an earache but not hyperactivity? Besides, when it came to getting Robert evaluated, what would be the downside? If the doctor said something we didn't like, we could ignore him, or, at a minimum, get a second opinion. At least he would be giving us some information—something to go on.

Case in point: One of my relatives told me that she, too, had had her son evaluated—after her son's private school teacher all but demanded he be "checked." The teacher had grown frustrated with the boy's day-dreaming as well as his slowness in the completion of tasks. One day, she bluntly communicated to the boy's mother that something was "not right." She was convinced the child was learning disabled. Although the boy's mother had never dreamed anything was seriously wrong with her son, the teacher's harsh words and insistence had unnerved her. Anxious and afraid for her child's well-being, she immediately brought him to a private specialist, who, after extensive testing, told her there was absolutely nothing wrong with the boy. Realizing the problem was the school and not her son, she transferred her child to a different private school—one that dealt with children on a more individual basis. At this new school, it was discovered that her son was, in reality, exceptionally bright. He merely approached problems in a very different manner—one that his previous teacher failed to recognize. When taught by caring teachers willing to take the time necessary to connect with him, her son excelled. Can you imagine being told your child has a learning disability, only to find out, in reality, he is gifted?

*   *   *

The question before us was: Who would evaluate our son? Tina learned we could either have Robert evaluated through our local school district or consult a private physician for an evaluation. While regulations vary according to locality, generally speaking, preschool children are entitled to early intervention services from their local school districts. Of course, the services available will depend upon the child's age and the actual issues presented. The point is that consultation with a trusted physician and the local school district are generally good first steps for those unsure of how to obtain information and proceed.

Tina contacted the school district and received the relevant information, including a list of state-approved evaluators. She then began the arduous task of compiling as many referrals as she could through friends, neighbors, relatives, teachers, and other doctors. These people, in turn, introduced us to an amazing network of similarly situated parents. In time, we would learn a lot from these parents. They would provide us with a wealth of information and support.

Now, should Robert be evaluated privately or through the school district? Either way, the school district informed us that if we desired any sort of special services for Robert (a summer program, special education placement, or even a classroom aide), he must qualify for such services. In other words, to take advantage of these services, an evaluator would have to come to the conclusion that Robert had a disability that made it difficult to learn in a mainstream or unrestricted environment. Of course, this conclusion would also mean Robert would be classified, or labeled, on his permanent record. We were assured that such classification would be kept strictly confidential.

If we had Robert privately evaluated, however, we could avoid the label. We would also have a greater choice of doctors, and a private doctor might be more sympathetic to our own opinions regarding Robert's status. We probably could, if we really wanted to do so, influence a private evaluator's decision to reflect what we ultimately wanted to hear. In addition, we obviously could do what we wanted with private test results, and no one would be the wiser. If we did not agree with the results, we could toss them in the trash, or we could get another opinion. If a problem was found to exist, we would have the option of seeking private therapy, and the school district would know nothing about it, once again leaving Robert's permanent record unblemished. Finally, even if we used a private evaluator, we were still not precluded from seeking services through the district. (Of course, doing so would mean turning over Robert's records to the district.) The downside to going private? A private evaluation would cost a few thousand dollars.

Given our particular situation, the concerns that made a private evaluation more attractive were moot. First, we were sure that Robert would need special services of some sort—ideally, an individualized program that would address attention-related issues. Robert simply was not functioning well in a mainstream environment, as evidenced by his involuntary departure from nearly every program in which he had been enrolled. Thus, the "label" issue was not foremost in our minds. While no parent would be thrilled by the prospect of having a child branded as disabled, it was critically important to us that Robert receive the services he required. If a label had to appear in order for Robert to receive help, then so be it. It was a necessary evil. Whether the label came from a private physician or an evaluator paid for by the district made little difference. (At that time, it had never dawned on us to consider private non-special education schools. The ones with small classes that boasted "individualized attention" were very expensive. And quite frankly, we weren't sure that Robert would fare any better in those schools than he had in the programs in which he had already been placed.)

The list of approved evaluators from the school district was more than adequate. In fact, one of the leading hospitals in our area was on the list. The choice was easy and, therefore, not an issue. Finally, Robert obviously fit the profile of a child in need of special services. We seriously doubted, given Robert's track record, that we would have to influence someone to diagnose what surely existed. And even if the school district evaluator failed to find a problem, we always had the option to fight for classification legally. While it was not an option I wished to exercise, I found that through legal maneuvering, many parents had managed to have a substantial portion of their children's tuitions—a few of which had ended up costing tens of thousands of dollars—paid for by the state. The routine was as follows: Parents who wanted to place their children in specialized centers or very expensive private schools would get private diagnoses of disability for their kids and then argue that such specialized schools were the only "appropriate" options for their children. If the school district balked, the parents would retain a lawyer familiar with the system to achieve their goal. Manipulate the system correctly and the district would pay.

*   *   *

A few months shy of his fifth birthday, Robert was evaluated at a highly recommended children's hospital through the school district. We completed a stack of questionnaires requesting information on Robert, our backgrounds, our family life, and our family history. Robert's nursery school teacher was asked to complete a set of questionnaires. These questionnaires were filled out prior to Robert's actual examination and would form part of Robert's overall evaluation.

Tina and I were interviewed by a social worker, a medical doctor, and a psychologist. Each asked questions about our family life, our family history (medical, emotional, and social), and Robert's behavior, as well as general questions regarding Robert's health and habits. Robert was then interviewed and given a series of tests by these same three individuals. The testing was done over two sessions. The results stated that Robert was a likable and pleasant little boy, extremely bright, and in possession of language skills of which a seven-year-old would be proud. There was no question in the evaluators' minds that Robert had attention deficit disorder (ADD) coupled with hyperactivity, resulting in a diagnosis of attention deficit hyperactivity disorder (ADHD). The experts also suspected the presence of oppositional defiance disorder (ODD).

Tina and I discussed the results with the psychologist. We told him we had heard of ADHD but did not know what it was exactly. We then confessed that we had never heard of ODD before. He told us we had a child who, as a basic part of his personality, was oppositional. It had nothing to do with how we were raising Robert. It turns out that some children are born with this particular predisposition. I was a bit skeptical. I thought all children were born with this predisposition—the ones that didn't grow out of it were called "brats." I had never imagined there was a psychological term for it. The psychologist, however, was more concerned about the ADHD. He explained that there is a part of the brain that enables a person to concentrate and control impulsive behavior.

In the brains of those with ADHD, this part is understimulated. Individuals with ADHD physically lack the ability to stay on task and control their own impulses.

Again, I was skeptical. "What about the fact that Robert is able to play video games and watch his favorite movie? He certainly concentrates then. He's not constantly running around or being hyper," I said.

The psychologist told me this was not unusual. When there is a separate motivating factor, that is, when a person with ADHD is internally motivated, concentration is not a problem. It is a problem, however, when a task is externally imposed. While a person who does not have ADHD can force himself to complete externally imposed tasks, people with ADHD simply cannot. Moreover, in reaction to such a situation, people with ADHD will fidget, run around, and flit from one thing to another.

I asked about the "hyperactivity" label. I told him of the first psychologist's opinion that Robert was not hyperactive. He shrugged his shoulders and said that the other psychologist had obviously never seen Robert. He also added that hyperactivity in a child like Robert was not unusual. He noted that children with attention deficit disorder are often hyperactive. Moreover, he told us that many children with ADHD tend to have problems learning since they cannot pay attention to what is being taught in school. Others suffer from actual learning disabilities— even if they could pay attention, their learning abilities are impaired. Finally, he warned us that if ADHD is not treated at an early age, the constant punishment, criticism, and rejection a child with ADHD frequently endures because of poor behavior and performance may create low self-esteem, depression, and a host of social problems.

"Well, if all this is true," I asked, "why is Robert okay one-on-one and not in a group? And why can I sometimes handle him?"

Again, the psychologist had answers. He felt that Robert must be easily distracted by the other children. He also noted that a classroom filled with toys could distract almost any child. "Think what it does to a child who cannot control the impulse to jump out of his seat," he said. As to why I had more control over Robert than anyone else, he said that Robert listened to me because I was his "buddy" and he didn't want to upset me. Again, it was a matter of internal motivation—Robert didn't want to disappoint his friend. It had very little to do with Robert's ability, or lack thereof, to listen and behave.

Although I didn't say so then (that stubborn part of me was still having trouble admitting that anything was wrong), some of what the psychologist said made sense. I remember one incident in which I came home late from work after a week of late nights. I had promised Tina that we'd go out to dinner without the kids. Robert had a fit when he found out he wouldn't be coming. He hadn't seen me all week, and he cried his eyes out when he found out we would be going without him. I explained that it was a "big people" restaurant. He promised he would behave.

Tina and I looked at each other in mutual resignation. "Okay," we said, "but, if you don't listen to us, even one time, we are not taking you out to 'big people' restaurants again."

We went to the restaurant. In all my life, I have never seen a person— adult or child—exercise such self-restraint. Robert was literally shaking in his seat. He wanted to get up and run around, but he knew that doing so would mean the end of dinner. I was never so proud of him, nor so upset. I could not believe the effort required for Robert to control himself—an effort so great that he was physically quivering.

Despite this experience, however, I still wasn't completely convinced that ADHD or ODD was real. "I have trouble concentrating," I explained. "I have trouble doing things that I don't want to do. Everyone thought I was hyperactive when I was young, but I wasn't asked to leave program after program, and no one said anything about ADHD. My brother was the same way."

The psychologist explained that disorders such as ADHD had only recently begun to be identified, recognized, and diagnosed. He also said that there was a good chance that I or someone in our family also had ADHD, since it is believed that heredity plays a role in the matter. Deciding to swallow this idea for the time being, I asked, "Okay, so let's assume that Robert has these disorders. What do we do?"

The psychologist said there were two ways of dealing with these disorders: behavior modification and medication. Behavior modification involved parenting skills. We would have to establish a very strict, consistent, highly structured environment at home that provided constant positive reinforcement. Other necessary components of behavior modification included counseling for Robert, counseling for us, and enrolling Robert in special education. Medication would involve taking one of a number of stimulants, the most widely prescribed of which was Ritalin.

I wasn't sure I had heard the psychologist correctly. "Did you say 'stimulant'?" I asked. He had. He explained that Ritalin stimulates the part of the brain that helps concentration. Thus, it actually calms children like Robert.

"Side effects?" Tina and I asked.

There were some, but usually nothing serious. As with all stimulants, Ritalin might cause a loss of appetite and sleeping problems. It might also slow Robert's growth. Although, once off the medication (the psychologist was always careful to call it a medication and not a drug), if Robert's growth had been affected, he would catchup to where he would have been but for the Ritalin. Facial tics and mood swings were more severe side effects, but we were told these were rare, and that if they appeared, there were other medications available to treat them.

I didn't like the idea of giving Robert a stimulant at all. I was absolutely sure he didn't need anything so drastic. There was some disagreement on this point.

The medical doctor who had taken part in Robert's evaluation made no bones about it. She thought Robert should be placed on Ritalin right away. When I explained that I didn't like the idea of putting my not-yet-five-year-old son on drugs, I was told that Ritalin was "perfectly safe" and had proven to be very effective on children with ADHD. "Besides," she asked, "if your son had diabetes, you'd give him insulin, wouldn't you?" The analogy was lost on me. Insulin does not alter one's mind. You can physically test insulin levels and know when someone is lacking in insulin. There are no substitutes for insulin. People can die without it. Last time I checked, Ritalin was not a naturally occurring substance in the body, and my son was not going to become viciously ill without it. Needless to say, I was dead set against the idea. There was no way in hell I was going to allow anyone to start pumping mind-altering drugs into my son. Tina wasn't happy with this prospect, either, but I knew she wasn't nearly as opposed to it as I. The psychologist said he understood how I felt, and if Tina and I were uncomfortable with the idea of administering medication, we could try behavior modification and special education first. If those options didn't work, Ritalin was always available.

We left Robert's evaluation with very mixed feelings. On the one hand, we were upset that there really was something wrong with Robert. On the other hand, Tina was relieved—relieved that she hadn't been imagining that Robert was different, relieved that his behavior wasn't her fault.

*   *   *

I wasn't sure I believed any of it. I had a very hard time accepting that Robert suffered from genuine disorders. First, there were the inevitable comparisons to my brother and me, who, like Robert, had been called "hyper" when we were children. "You were just like Robert," my mother would say. "You turned out okay. You didn't have problems in school or making friends." I've heard the same story countless times from other adults who were very active as children—unable to concentrate, always in trouble—and who eventually grew out of it. And what about all the other "hyper" little boys I was seeing out there? Did each and every one of them have a discernible, diagnosable disorder? Surely that couldn't be the case. Maybe this was just a phase Robert was going through. Maybe he just needed a chance to mature.

More than anything else, I could not accept the fact that a person might not be responsible for his own behavior. Robert knew right from wrong, and there was no denying his intelligence. If he did something on purpose that he knew he should not have done, punishment should follow. No excuses.

Robert's symptoms made any diagnosis difficult to take seriously; they were so vague, varied, and contradictory. For example, we were told that children with ADD cannot stay on task or control impulses. But, if interested in what they were doing, these same children could continue an activity for hours. Sometimes these children had learning disabilities. Sometimes they did not. Some ADD children were prone to depression, while others could become anxious, frustrated, or hyperactive, or any combination of these emotions. Some ADD children seemed impossible to deal with on any level. Others, like my son, appeared impossible to deal with in certain situations, but were merely difficult the rest of the time.

I wondered why I had never heard of these disorders before. Why was ADD suddenly all the rage? A hot media topic, there was no shortage of articles and television programs about ADD. *Time* had published a cover story on attention deficit disorder. *Newsweek* had published a cover story on Ritalin. ADD had been a featured topic on *60 Minutes*. Oprah Winfrey had done numerous shows about it. Attention deficit disorder was even being debated in letters to Ann Landers. For better or worse, it seemed that many people shared my initial feelings about these so-called disorders: that they really didn't exist. The media seemed to reflect this general disbelief. The debate on Oprah was rather heated, with many people in the audience expressing the opinion that there was nothing wrong with children supposedly suffering from ADD that couldn't be fixed with a little discipline. *Time* bluntly asked of the disorder, "Is it for real?"[1] *Newsweek* asked, "Are we overmedicating our kids?"[2] What made matters worse was the fact that disorders such as ADD were being overdiagnosed. Many parents with "difficult" or "spirited" children were, in fact, not practicing good parenting skills, and were quick to jump on the ADD bandwagon.[3] ADD offered a convenient excuse for their unruly children.

More alarming was the fact that many teachers were beginning to do the same. Confronted with unruly, disruptive children, some teachers started suggesting the possibility of ADD to parents. They would then urge parents to medicate their children, hoping to no longer have to deal with "problem" children, whether the children truly had medical issues or not.[4] Among several pediatricians consulted by Ann Landers, "attention deficit disorder had become a fashionable catch-all for children with behavioral problems."[5] *Newsweek* noted that ADHD had become America's number one "childhood psychiatric disorder," affecting more than two million children.[6] According to a report issued by the Institute of Medicine, 7.5 million children had "psychiatric disorders."[7]

One clinical psychologist wrote that it was his belief that ADD was being terribly overdiagnosed, having become a label often used by parents and those who were "poorly trained" to explain behavior they didn't understand or for which they did not want to take responsibility.[8] He described ADD as the "perfect American diagnosis: superficial, biological, blameless and readily curable by drugs." While this psychologist reluctantly admitted that, "[i]n some cases, medication is necessary and helpful," he refused to believe that ADD symptoms could be the result of a neurological problem (absent any mental deficiency). He claimed the misdiagnosed child's problems arose from problematic familial interactions—for example, a twelve-year-old boy who was misdiagnosed with ADD also had an "overbearing, self-centered, intrusive mother," and a father who was "in orbit around Mars."

Was he describing us?

*   *   *

When we told my parents about the diagnosis, they thought it was ridiculous—especially my father. In fact, they couldn't even understand why we had had Robert evaluated in the first place. I got the "He's just like you were when you were a kid, and you turned out okay" speech again. "Just be firm with him, that's all," was my father's advice. I admitted that that's what I thought, too. But then I did a reality check. Robert was an inordinate amount of trouble at home, and nothing we had tried had resulted in any positive effect on the situation in the long-term. Robert had been asked to leave three programs and was having trouble in another, didn't have any real friends, had been refused acceptance into a private kindergarten program, and was thought to have a problem by Tina, two teachers, and his pediatrician. He had been given a thorough evaluation by specialists, including a child psychologist, a social worker, and a medical doctor, each of whom had confirmed that there was a problem. I had to admit it. Something was not exactly right. What it was or how bad it was, we could debate. But something had to be done. My parents just shook their heads.

Then I mentioned medication. They were horrified. "You wouldn't!" they said.

No, we wouldn't—at least not yet. I swore to Tina that I would try to keep an open mind about the matter. In the face of all the disbelief and rationalization, it was going to be difficult. Diagnosis in hand, we needed to determine an appropriate course of action. How would we deal with this situation, however, when there was already disagreement among the experts from whom we had sought advice and guidance? The medical doctor was telling us to medicate Robert. The psychologist was suggesting behavior modification.

A more immediate and pressing concern was the need to place Robert into some type of special education program. We contacted the school district and were put in touch with the Committee on Preschool Special Education (CPSE). We were, of course, immediately inundated with paperwork. There were more forms to fill out and more meetings to attend. We were handed one-hundred-page booklets, innumerable pamphlets, and scores of hand-outs that explained how special education worked, who was eligible, what our rights were, etc. We were also asked to send Robert's test results and reports to the CPSE. Of course, we were assured that the file would be kept strictly confidential. Unless we released it, only the school, the CPSE, and we would have access to the file. Also, since this was preschool, it would not be released to elementary schools without our permission.

Finally, a date was set for a meeting. We would present our case to the CPSE in person, and the CPSE would determine the type of education to which Robert was specifically entitled. Tina was nervous about the meeting, and I was prepared for a fight. Together, we would see that these people did right by our son. Present at the meeting were the director of the program, the state representative, a school psychologist, a parent-member, and the social worker who had performed part of Robert's evaluation. Copies of Robert's evaluation, tests, and reports sat before the committee members.

As it turned out, we had absolutely nothing about which to worry. The CPSE was extremely sympathetic to Robert's situation and our plight. Robert was clearly a bright little boy who needed some special attention to ensure that he got off on the right foot. Judging from the sympathetic nods we received when we talked about how difficult Robert was at home, it was apparent that the CPSE would do its best to place Robert in a program as soon as possible.

The standard classification for all preschool children in need of special services was "preschooler with disability." Thus, Robert's first label was somewhat nondescript. As this classification would be kept "strictly confidential," I didn't have a problem with it. Tina, however, did. The reality of Robert being labeled hurt her, even though we had both known it was coming. She fully understood that it was simply a matter of falling within a category that would qualify Robert to receive state-funded special services, and that the category was basically meaningless. Nevertheless, understanding did not make her happy. "How will this affect him later on?" she asked. "How is this going to look on his records?"

I didn't know it then, but Tina was right to be concerned. Despite the many assurances of confidentiality, the truth was that most of the schools to which Robert would later apply would request Robert's previous records and teacher evaluations. Once Robert made the move to another school, his status as a special education student would be out of the bag. His label would be known. While the CPSE would not release Robert's records without our approval, we would soon find we had no choice but to give such approval. The confidentiality of Robert's records was, for all intents and purposes, illusory.

There also was talk of placing Robert on medication. We got the "Ritalin has been wonderfully effective on some children" and "If your son had diabetes, you'd give him insulin" speeches. But I remained adamantly against the drugs. I wanted to give Robert as much of a chance as possible to get through this without resorting to them. Maybe the special education program would prove effective. It was worth a shot. If special education didn't help us achieve our goals, we would consider the use of Ritalin. Although no one outwardly disagreed with me, I got the distinct impression that many of the members of the CPSE thought I was being narrow-minded. At best, they thought I was merely postponing the inevitable. I was willing to wait and see.

*   *   *

Having received state approval to place Robert in special education, we had to find a school that was appropriate and had an opening. The CPSE began contacting state-approved schools with special education programs both inside and outside our district. We set up appointments to check them out. We also began our own networking, initially with the teachers and professionals who had seen Robert, and then with other parents who had faced similar situations. I lost count of the places we called and the people with whom we spoke—all dead ends. We were told either that the classes were full, or that Robert wouldn't fit in. It seemed that most of the schools were intended for children with separate and distinct learning disabilities in addition to or apart from ADHD. Since Robert did not appear to have a learning disability, and since his test scores indicated that his intelligence and ability to learn were above average in most respects, placing Robert in many of these programs would not have been in his best interests. Indeed, it could have done more harm than good.

The irony of the situation was apparent and painful. Robert did not fit into the mainstream public schools because of his special concerns. But his ability to learn and natural intelligence—qualities that would make him an ideal student—made him an inappropriate candidate for the specialty schools. With that avenue of inquiry closed, we proceeded to look at smaller private schools in the area. Most of them readily admitted that they had neither the expertise nor the services necessary to handle children with ADHD or ODD. One that did seem equipped for the task was prohibitively expensive, and we simply could not consider it at the time. We did, however, find one highly recommended private school whose teachers assured us they could teach Robert. It was their experience that "difficult" children needed only to be approached differently. Given this school's small classes and expertise, it appeared as though Robert would fit in fine. But these people had not yet met our son.

We brought Robert to the school and received a tour. The teachers felt that Robert was bound to do well. They emphasized that finding success was just a matter of discovering the way in which Robert learned. At the end of the tour, Robert was asked to sit in with the other kindergarten children. We waited in the director's office. Within ten minutes, the director of the school was called to Robert's classroom. She came back with

Robert in tow. We knew what was coming. They couldn't (didn't want to?) handle him. We were extremely disappointed. We had told them about Robert before making the appointment to see them. Why raise our hopes? Why subject Robert to this experience if they were just going to reject him?

Unfortunately, this would not be the last time a school would react to Robert in such a way.

5

Special Education

Having ruled out private schools, the only avenue left seemed to be public school special education. Although Robert obviously needed special attention, the idea of placing him in special education still troubled us. I remembered these schools from when I was young. I recalled (hopefully incorrectly) that the only children in special education were noticeably handicapped or not terribly bright. Robert was neither. Did we really want our son there? Moreover, even if my perception of special education was completely wrong, it was still the one shared by most people I knew when I was a kid. If it had not changed, how would the mainstream children treat Robert? What kind of impact would it have on his self-esteem, his confidence, his life? The old questions began to swirl anew in our minds. Were Tina and I jeopardizing Robert's future? What effect would Robert's placement in special education have on his acceptance to mainstream schools in later years? Were we wrongly placing a stigma on our child? What were we going to tell our friends and neighbors when they asked where Robert was going to school?

It was readily apparent that I held some prejudices towards special education programs. I realized I would need to get over them quickly, as Robert was certainly going to be enrolled in one.

*   *   *

The first public school we contacted was within our district. We were directed to the special education kindergarten program. We sat in on a class and became so upset by what we saw that we had to leave. The children in the class were so visibly . . . different. Several of the children were obviously medicated—they sat nearly motionless; their little faces were devoid of expression. One child, who did not appear to be medicated, spent most of his time in the corner because he could not sit still. The rest of the children seemed lethargic and uninterested. The teacher also seemed unengaged. Although teaching in a perfectly competent manner, she looked as if she were merely going through the motions. If this was her level of enthusiasm when parents were present, what on Earth was she like when she was alone with the students?

We met with the school psychologist afterwards, and she asked us how we liked the class. Clearly upset, we told her that Robert did not belong there. She asked why we felt that way, and we told her that if she knew Robert, she would agree with us. We could not, and in any event, did not want to, articulate our reasons—we did not wish to speak disparagingly of the program. She sort of nodded, obviously realizing we were not fully expressing our thoughts. We were utterly depressed and discouraged when we left.

We visited several other schools and programs, first within our district and then outside it. We had no luck. None of the schools were, in our opinion, appropriate for Robert. Most were depressing, quiet places of apparent inactivity. Where was the noise, we thought? Where was the energy, the laughter? Where were the happy faces? When asked, we were hard pressed to point to any particular fault or inadequacy—we were going on our gut reactions to the schools and students. We were not happy with what was available.

We were directed to an out-of-district special education elementary school that catered to children with disabilities, from mild impairments to the most severe. The school was instituting a special six-week program for several children with problems similar to Robert's. It was a half-day program run five days a week and designed to introduce these children to the school system. Ideally, the program would help the children with their socialization skills and behavior. It was not, in any sense, an academic program. After all the problems we had endured, we couldn't believe the timing of this program. It sounded perfect!

Nevertheless, we had some major concerns. First, the school was outside our district and a one-hour bus ride from our house—and that wasn't including traffic or stops. We didn't like the idea of Robert traveling so far for so long. Also, because the school was outside our district, it would be more difficult to take advantage of the extracurricular programs available in our own neighborhood. Furthermore, going to this school meant Robert would have no contact with children near our home aside from immediate neighbors. It was important for Robert to make more friends. We were counting on the fact that he would make friends at school. Now, he undoubtedly would make friends, except they'd all be an hour or more away. Finally, this entire school did nothing but special education. Thus, some of the most severely challenged students would be in attendance. But we were desperate and went to see the school.

It was beautiful! It was open and airy. The halls were brightly decorated and bustled with activity. The teachers and staff were polite, helpful, motivated, and interested. Most importantly, the children were happy. We met with the principal and began our interrogation. What would Robert's class be like? What did she know about ADD? ODD? Hyperactivity? What will he be taught? How does this place compare to "regular" school? If we enrolled Robert, would the other children in his class have similar problems, or would he be placed with children with more severe disabilities? We felt that placing Robert in an environment with children who were more severely challenged emotionally, socially, or intellectually would do more harm than good. I know it sounds selfish and hypocritical (what right did we have to be so picky?), but, like all parents, we wanted to ensure that Robert would be placed in the best possible environment. We were concerned about the type of influence Robert's peers would have on him. (I have since learned that our thinking on this last point was only partially correct. Children with differing temperaments and abilities can be placed in the same environment with wonderful results for all the children, when done correctly with the proper mix of students, outstanding teachers, and adequate support.)

The principal understood our concerns. She told us that they were familiar with the disorders that we had mentioned and were learning more about them all the time. The teachers were all certified in special education, and there were several child psychologists on staff. Class sizes varied, but they were all noticeably smaller than regular school classes. In addition, by and large, the curriculum taught in the school was the same as the one followed in regular public schools. Of course, variations arose according to the needs and abilities of the children.

Regarding the composition of the classes, the principal told us that "higher functioning" children were generally grouped together. In addition, given the extremely generous teacher-to-student ratio (no more than ten to twelve children per teacher, with an additional aide or two), each child received individual attention. Each child was taught on his own level, at his own speed. Thus, if Robert excelled academically, he would be taught at a pace commensurate with his skills. Although we continued to be somewhat uneasy about the situation, the school really did sound great. We enrolled Robert and kept our fingers tightly crossed.

*   *   *

While the long bus ride was a problem, the school, the program, and especially Robert's teacher, Mrs. Aronowsky, were terrific. No, not everything was perfect, but Robert liked his school, Tina was afforded some relief, and we knew this was one place that wouldn't kick Robert out.

Robert's progress was slow at first. He was often in his own world, paying little attention to what he was told. He also wanted everything his way. He had to be first, the children had to play what he wanted to play, and everybody had to do whatever he wanted to do. Mrs. Aronowsky called it "Robert's world." She was determined to bring him out of it. We were determined to help.

We met with Mrs. Aronowsky and the school psychologist many times. We wanted to know exactly what they were doing with Robert. What was his class like? What were they teaching him? How did they motivate him? How was he disciplined? We shared how we motivated Robert and disciplined him, what seemed to work and what did not. We sat in on his class several times. We offered our opinions on how the class was run, and on Mrs. Aronowsky's demeanor. Many times, we were critical. It wasn't that she was ineffective or uninterested. To the contrary,

Mrs. Aronowsky was extremely competent and truly cared. That being said, she did some things we thought would be better done in other ways.

I would be lying if I said Mrs. Aronowsky and the school psychologist readily agreed and gratefully accepted our suggestions. At first, we felt their attitude was "Thanks, but we know what we're doing." For example, when we first met the school psychologist, he was prepared to explain Robert's problems to us in simplified terms, and then he was going to "sell" us on the school by telling us how well it would deal with Robert. After five minutes, it was perfectly clear that we already knew an awful lot about Robert's situation. We certainly didn't need anything sugarcoated.

Once the school psychologist realized that we had invested a lot of time and energy in learning about Robert and were genuinely concerned and interested, he took us more seriously. In time, he seemed to listen gladly to what we had to say, and would act upon our suggestions.

Our experience with Mrs. Aronowsky was much the same, although I think it took her a bit longer to warm up to us. We sensed the same "I know what I'm doing" attitude, only worse. We weren't surprised, though, since she bore the brunt of our critique. She was the one in direct and constant contact with Robert; she was the one to whom we looked to care for our son. We wanted daily reports about Robert's progress. We wanted to know if Robert was having any specific problems, either in terms of behavior or with tasks he had been asked to perform. We wanted to know what we could do at home to help. We would visit the classroom and talk to Mrs. Aronowsky about her technique. We would call if we did not receive a progress report. We would call if the report worried us. We would call if the report surprised us. We would call if we disagreed with something Mrs. Aronowsky had done. In other words, we were complete pains in the ass.

Although I'm sure she would deny it, there was no way that Mrs. Aronowsky could have expected our level of involvement. We eventually realized that many of the other parents at that school could not or simply chose not to get as involved as we did. Also, I doubt that many were quite as assertive as we were. In fact, Tina downright scares me when she is protecting Robert. I could be wrong, but I don't think Mrs.

Aronowsky liked us at first. I couldn't blame her. Would you like someone who was constantly telling you how to do your job?

*   *   *

The summer wore on, and Robert's six-week program became a twelve-week program. Progress was being made on all fronts, although more slowly than we had hoped. Robert was, in fact, doing terrifically. His behavior and temperament were getting better each day. Tina and I were even getting along very well with Mrs. Aronowsky. We had learned to trust each other, and the lines of communication were open. We spoke with each other frequently, exchanging ideas, stories, and our feelings. We grew to appreciate Mrs. Aronowsky's dedication and professionalism. I think she grew to appreciate how much we cared. There is no doubt in my mind that Robert was the one who ultimately benefited from this interaction.

Of course, Mrs. Aronowsky eventually raised the subject of medication. Once again, we were told how Ritalin had helped so many children like Robert. I told her that I preferred to avoid it if at all possible. She replied with the "If Robert had diabetes, you'd give him insulin" speech. (I am convinced that Ritalin comes with a brochure with this suggestion on it: "In case of reluctant parent, immediately state the analogy 'If [fill in child's name] had diabetes, you'd give him insulin.'") I countered this line of reasoning by noting that Robert had made substantial progress already. I was determined to give him every opportunity and as much time as possible to get his act together without resorting to medication. Besides, the mere thought of having to medicate my baby was devastating to me. Did he really need it? What would it do to him? Would it change him? Would it hurt him? I didn't know the answer to any of these questions.

Tina, on the other hand, was ready to give Ritalin a try. Although she liked the school and Robert's teacher, she wanted Robert in a mainstream school close to home as soon as possible. She was concerned about Robert's current bus ride. She was concerned about Robert not having any friends in the neighborhood. She was concerned about the influence of his peers, and of any possible stigma special education or Robert's classification might carry. She also was concerned that one day Robert would realize that there was something different about his school and the children in it. Robert was a bright, sensitive little boy. It would not take him long to figure out why he had to take a bus to school while the other children in the neighborhood did not, or why he was in summer school and the other children were not, or why the children that attended his school behaved differently from the neighborhood children.

In addition, while things at home were easier with Robert in school, they were far from perfect—or even tolerable. Our daughter, Kat, clearly a spirited child in her own right (exceptionally strong-willed with a bit of a temper, she is just like her mom), was demanding more and more attention, and Robert was still a handful from the time he got off the bus until he finally fell asleep. Tina thought that if Ritalin could get Robert to behave even a little better while he was home, it would be worth it. While I shared her concerns, I still wanted to wait. There was still time.

*   *   *

Summer came to a close and we found ourselves preparing for a meeting with the Committee on Special Education (CSE)—not the CPSE, since this time it wouldn't be for preschool placement. Robert would be going to kindergarten in September. Naturally, a whole host of problems were associated with this next step. First, according to the cut-off age of the private schools in our area, as well as that of the overwhelming majority of public school districts in our state, Robert would be one month too young for kindergarten. In our district, however, he was eligible to enter kindergarten. We thought it a good idea, however, to keep him back a year. If placed in kindergarten, Robert would be one of the youngest children in his class. Add that to the fact that boys are relatively immature at any age (or so they say), and it just made sense to keep Robert in pre-K one more year.

We also wanted to give Robert one more year in which the demands on him weren't so great, one more year where he could grow up a little and learn to concentrate just a bit better. We knew that once he was placed in a more demanding environment in which academics played a major role, he might have a more difficult time, and we might be forced to use medication. We wanted the luxury of one more year to decide exactly where he should go to school, and whether he really required medication.

All we learned was that you cannot fight City Hall. Or maybe we just didn't fight hard enough. While the CSE director was sympathetic, we got nowhere. She told us that a lot of parents want to keep their children back a year believing that it will give their children an advantage. One more year of maturity, one more year of growth, and their children might have a leg up. There simply was nothing she could do. Besides, she thought it would be better to place Robert ahead. Intellectually, Robert was more in line with the older children. Indeed, based on the CSE's observations, Robert was likely intellectually ahead of the children with whom he was to be placed. How could we hold him back if he was academically advanced? Robert would be bored. That certainly would not help his disposition, behavior, or his ability to stay on task. Finally, she thought that older children would provide better role models. If we wanted Robert to mature, why not place him with the more mature children?

I had to admit, there was logic to her reasoning, and it made me somewhat unsure of our position. There were, of course, advantages to letting Robert enter kindergarten. We agreed, the more mature children in kindergarten (everything is relative) might have a good influence on Robert, and academics might stimulate his interests and enable him to focus better. We also worried that Robert might stick out a lot in pre-K. He was still very big for his age (over four feet tall), and he was often mistaken for a child two or three years older. He also possessed extremely good language skills—again, two to three years ahead of the norm. In fact, these two factors only added to his socialization problems. People looked at Robert and expected him to behave with more maturity. He never did. In any event, if it were necessary, we could always place Robert in private school, we thought. A private school would hold him back a year if we wished.

The next issue was more serious. At the CPSE meeting that we had attended several months prior, we had been forewarned of the label

Robert would likely receive as a school-age child. Like pre-K, Robert had to be categorized with a disability in order to qualify for state funded special services. Unlike pre-K, where all children in need of special services were categorized as "preschooler with disability," in our school district, school-age children in need of special attention were placed within at least one of thirteen distinct categories. "Child with ADD/ODD/hyperactivity" was not one of them.

There was no question Robert needed special attention, but his particular problems were not a state-defined category of disability, so Robert would have to be shoe-horned into a different category—most likely "emotionally disturbed." Even though I knew it was only a label designed to ensure Robert qualified for special services, and even though I knew it would remain confidential, I had a hard time dealing with the fact that Robert was going to be deemed "emotionally disturbed" on his permanent school records. It bothered me; it killed Tina.

We asked the CPSE why there wasn't at least a category for ADHD. So many children had ADHD; it was obviously affecting so many lives. With all this supposed awareness of the problem, why must our son get thrown into the "emotionally disturbed" group? Although everyone on the CPSE agreed that the categories needed to be changed, no one had any real solutions at the moment. The CPSE kept assuring us that the label was a means to an end. We understood, but wasn't it bad enough that Robert had such problems? Wasn't it bad enough that very few people really understood what these problems were or the impact they were having on our son? Now we would have to call him "emotionally disturbed"? Would the person who picked up Robert's record in the future comprehend why Robert had been classified as such? Would this label affect the way people treated Robert?

Dragging this emotional baggage, we attended the CSE meeting. Present, among others, was the school psychologist that we had met after sitting-in on the special education kindergarten in our school district. We didn't know it yet, but she would be a Godsend.

The meeting started with a review of Robert's reports (the dissemination of which to the CSE was previously approved by us). Everyone noted how bright Robert was. They all acknowledged that Robert had excellent strengths and showed good potential. Addressing Robert's individual education program (IEP), it was decided that Robert was to receive group counseling and speech therapy. The former was to aid Robert in his socialization, the latter to help Robert maintain a conversation with someone.

The discussion then turned to placement. The director asked us whether we would consider moving Robert to the special education kindergarten in district. We just shook our heads, at which point the school psychologist looked at us and said, "Now that I see Robert's test scores, I can understand why you were so upset about that class. Robert clearly doesn't belong there." There was some debate about other state-approved placement options, but in the end, we told the CSE that, despite the busing situation, we were happy with the school Robert was presently attending. It was decided that he should stay there.

The committee then took up the issue of how Robert should be categorized for the record. We were prepared for the worst, and indeed, our expectations were met when the director said, "Because there is no category for children like Robert, we'll probably have to place him under 'emotionally disturbed'." Imagine our surprise when the school psychologist picked her head up from Robert's papers with a jerk and exclaimed, "What? Robert's not emotionally disturbed. How about 'other health impaired'?"

We seized the opportunity. "Yes," we said in unison, "we can live with that!" The director shrugged her shoulders; there was no opposition from anyone on the CSE. It was done. We finally left one of these meetings smiling. Imagine being happy that your son is being considered "other health impaired."

6

More Trouble at Home

We were sure Robert was going to do well at school. We were already familiar with Mrs. Aronowsky, and Robert's class was extremely small—only six little boys. They were great. All of them were sweet, active, happy children who were very similar to Robert in behavior and temperament.

Things at home, however, were not going well. I daresay that they had gotten worse. While the diagnosis had made us more understanding and, in some ways, better able to deal with Robert, his constant activity, disruptiveness, and unmanageable behavior were still causing problems within our family. It also didn't help that I was having a hard time at work. The firm was demanding more and more of my time (not to mention the fact that I had to make up for all the time missed traipsing from one doctor to the next, and from school to school to school with Robert), and I was becoming more and more disenchanted with my chosen profession. And let's not forget Kat, who was giving new meaning to the expression the "terrible twos."

It was one of my life's low points. The tension, frustration, and disappointment accumulated. Nothing was working out the way I had planned. Let's start with work. Being a lawyer was not at all what I had thought it would be. I am not by nature an aggressive person. Surrounded by brilliant and often times highly opinionated coworkers, I admit I felt intimidated and kept many an opinion to myself. Additionally, I am a perfectionist who is never 100-percent sure of himself, and the nature of the practice, in any case, made it difficult to be. When was enough research really enough? What was the right course of action? What was the most persuasive argument to pursue? Nothing was black and white. Nothing ever seemed simple.

While I enjoyed the intellectual exercise involved in researching, writing, and discussing case law with my fellow attorneys, I also discovered that nearly every piece of work I produced was subject to scrutiny. You could not write a paragraph that would not be subject to review. Of course, the other attorneys made their edits, positive that the new wording was better, and that the new approach was more appropriate. Revision, upon revision; research, piled on top of research; always afraid of using the wrong word, or of missing a single, relative case; it was a miracle that anything ever got finished. If it weren't for deadlines, nothing would ever be considered good enough. Worse, with the advent of word processors and Fed Ex, you could work nonstop, right up until the very last minute. And we all did.

And the hours. Oh, the hours. With briefs due and deadlines approaching, you could easily stay at work for ten to fifteen hours, or even pull an all-nighter. There was more than one occasion on which I literally slept at my desk. Long hours were expected. I wasn't happy, and I was literally making myself sick trying to do a good job. Why? Well, it's like I said earlier, I consider myself an overachiever. I am not the quickest or the brightest, but I make up for these shortcomings through sheer brute force. (I play sports the same way. I may not have the most natural talent, but you will never outwork me, and I will never, ever give up.) I wanted to succeed as a lawyer, and if that meant working through the pain, then so be it.

Amazingly, I had the distinct impression that some of my coworkers didn't think I was working enough! I was often out of the office dealing with Robert's issues, and even though I tried to make up the time, I simply could not match many of my coworkers reported billable hours. And the work? Can you say b-o-r-i-n-g? The vast majority of my time as an attorney was spent reviewing and cataloguing documents, and researching and writing briefs on the language used in insurance contracts. I was getting physically ill—all related to the stress under which I was putting myself. I even had a full-blown panic attack, complete with a trip to the emergency room . . . while I was still in the office. I was beginning to wonder if I had wasted my time in college and law school. I wasn't really happy at work, and it was starting to show.

At home, things weren't getting any easier. When I walked in the house, I was often greeted with what seemed like a laundry list of complaints about what had transpired during the day. Tina was still having a difficult time. She was a full-time mom, having given up her career to raise the children, and dealing with them twenty-four hours a day was taking its toll. She complained that I never helped around the house. She complained that she never got to see another adult. She complained that our children were trouble from the minute they woke up until the minute they fell asleep. She complained that I wasn't doing enough to help out. She was also angry that I didn't spend more time with her. "Sure," she would say, "you make an effort to play with the kids, but it's always at my expense."

Intellectually, I understood her distress. Unfortunately, by now I was taking it all very personally. In my mind, her complaints became accusations, and I resented them. Wasn't I the one who missed work to accompany her and Robert to the testing, the schools, and the examinations? Wasn't I the one taking flak from coworkers about all the time I was missing? Wasn't I the one who had to put in extra hours at the office to make up for the time I had taken off? Who was the guy who straightened out the house every night? Who helped bathe and dress the children for bed? Who entertained the children when no one else was around to play with them? Who gave up his free time so that he could spend more time at home?

And what about her spending more time with me? She was always angry, upset, or tired. I missed her as much as she missed me. She was having a hard time, but damn it, so was I! While I thought I understood and appreciated her problems, staying calm and not getting upset, hurt, angry, or defensive under the brunt of what I perceived to be daily assaults was quite another matter. Of course, the stress just increased over time, with each bad situation feeding off the last. Things never got better, only worse. It was getting to the point at which I didn't want to come home from work. If Tina merely looked at me funny, I immediately took it as some sort of criticism, snapping at her, and the fighting would start anew.

Now, in retrospect, I was being a tad unreasonable. Tina was raising our two children almost single-handedly, and I guess I neglected to recognize how much work it was keeping the house and family together. At the time, all I saw was her frustration. I was hurt that despite all my effort, I could not seem to make her happy, and I deeply resented the fact that she seemed to take it all out on me. Tina, no doubt, was just trying to convey her frustrations, just needing to vent. But it sounded to me like she was very unhappy with our lives, and that was enough to make me very unhappy.

Yet, none of this was my fault, was it? Was it my fault I had to put in so many hours at work? Was it my fault that Robert was giving Tina a hard time? Was it my fault that Tina didn't have any time for herself, or that she found trying to keep up with the house and kids so overwhelming? I was doing everything I could. I was miserable and sick, and yet Tina was still unhappy. On some level, I felt like Tina was blaming me, that somehow I was supposed to fix everything, that I wasn't doing my job. I was failing her.

If ever asked on an interview what my greatest strength is, I would say that I make things better. I fix things. I keep everyone happy. I have a knack for seeing problems, boiling them down to their simplest manifestations, and then addressing the core issues. But if I was so good at fixing things and keeping everyone happy, why couldn't I do these things at home? I doubted myself as an attorney, a husband, and a father.

I was doing the best I could muster, yet I was failing. I should be able to fix this, I thought. It's my job. I should be succeeding at work. That's my job. Tina should be happy. That's my job. Robert should be healthy and strong. That's my job. Moreover, Tina and I were both spending so much time with Robert that we had little time to spend with Kat and no time to spend with each other. While we each did our collective best to give Kat the attention she needed (although I'm sure she could have used more), Tina and I never made time for each other. I was living for work and the children; Tina was living for the house and the children. When we found ourselves finally alone, usually late at night after we'd put the children to bed, we were either exhausted or in very foul moods.

I was feeling the strain of being pulled in too many directions. I resented the demands placed upon me. I was always tired. I was irritable. I was also withdrawing—I went about my business as if in a daze. I stayed in my office and worked by myself during the day. I hardly spoke to Tina when I was at home.

So, with all our plans gone awry, pressures from within and without, and no time for each other (or for ourselves), things changed between us. With all that tension, anger, resentment, and disappointment simmering below the surface, is it any wonder we fought? Is it any surprise that every gesture and every word was misinterpreted as an attack? Of course, our fighting led to further problems with the children. Fighting made me angry. Try as I might to avoid it, I would inevitably vent some of my anger on them when they misbehaved. No doubt, part of the venting was a reaction to Tina's complaints. I reasoned that if the children behaved, she wouldn't be in a foul mood when I got home from work. To me, keeping the children in line became a matter of self-preservation. Thus, there were many times when the kids were punished for the slightest misstep, even though, under more normal circumstances, they probably wouldn't have been punished at all.

*   *   *

Clearly, something had to change. We examined what was important to us and made decisions that were not entirely popular with our families or my coworkers. First, we thought it would be good for Tina to get out of the house once or twice a week—perhaps even go back to work, taking a part time position in her field. We could hire someone to babysit and clean the house while she was out.

Tina resisted this idea. She was reluctant to work, even on a part-time basis. She wanted to be home with the children. She didn't like the idea of a stranger looking after Robert and Kat. Tina also reiterated her belief that she should be able to stay home and deal with the situation, and that leaving the house would prove her failure. I assured her that such thoughts were ridiculous. We were doing our best, and she was, in fact, pretty amazing. We just needed to make some adjustments for sanity's sake. We were faced with a difficult situation that called for different thinking, that's all—this was not an issue of failure. Besides, I knew she enjoyed her work and that she needed to be out of the house for a little while and in the presence of adults.

She took a job, returning to the catheterization lab on a part-time basis after many years of being a stay-at-home mom. It broke her heart to leave the kids, even for just a few hours. Crazy, isn't it? Weren't they the same two children that were driving her nuts? A part-time job for Tina, however, addressed only part of the problem. I still needed to help around the house, and more importantly, I needed to take care of Robert when he exhausted Tina's patience. I required more time, but my job did not allow me this luxury. In fact, as each month went by, my responsibilities grew, and with each new responsibility, my hours got longer. I knew my firm offered part-time status to women who had had children. They could work four days a week with a corresponding 20-percent pay cut. No man had ever asked for this arrangement, but there's a first time for everything (I just love being a trendsetter). Tina and I discussed the matter at length. We both knew the pay cut would be large and tough to swallow at first, but we also agreed that, with a little budgeting, we could manage. Besides, what was my time worth, anyway?

My career would suffer. There was little doubt in my mind that this move would probably be the end of my career. I wouldn't be around the office as often. I would have to pass up certain assignments. It would appear as though I wasn't totally committed to the profession. My male coworkers warned me against my decision (although, I must note that my female coworkers strongly supported me). They did not even take me seriously. "Why would you do such a thing?" and "Can't your wife handle things at home?" and "Just hire some help"—I heard it all. "Don't jeopardize your position," they said. "How can you give up the money?" they said. My father said much the same.

Moreover, the timing of this decision couldn't have been worse. My firm was in the process of cutting back on costs and expenses and had already let some people go. Employees were concerned about keeping their jobs. Benefits, including part-time status, had come under heavy scrutiny. Also, I had finally found my niche. We had extremely large document-based cases that were staffed with numerous paralegals and attorneys at every level. Indeed, we had cases with teams of up to ten paralegals and just as many attorneys. Most of the time, these cases were complete chaos. That's where I would come in. I found I was very good at managing such teams. I was starting to be placed in charge of important projects on a regular basis. Powerful people at the firm were taking notice of my work. The fact that there was a decent chance of actually receiving some monetary recognition for my performance made the idea of taking a substantial pay cut especially hard to swallow. Nor was it the time to start turning down work. It hurt. I had worked and sacrificed for years to get to where I was. I identified with my profession. As much as I was dissatisfied with my job, and as ridiculous as it sounds, my sense of self-worth was tied to my success as an attorney.

I wondered why I couldn't do both. Why couldn't I work full time and be a good husband and father? Other people did it. Was I a failure? Was it possible that I did not have what it takes to be a success? Then I thought of Tina and how she needed me, of how my daughter and son needed me. I thought of how I couldn't be at work twelve, thirteen, fourteen hours every day, sleep, eat, help around the house, play with the kids, be a loving husband, and have time for myself. Time was precious, and I couldn't put a price tag on it. You can make up for lost income; you can't make up for lost time.

Although I didn't realize it, my son was leading me down a path I had never intended to travel. Through him and because of him, I was learning what was important in my life, and it wasn't a title, a promotion, recognition from people who hardly knew me, or an excess of money. I soon found myself spilling my guts to John, a senior partner at the firm and the individual in charge of deciding whether my application for part-time status would be approved. I told him about the problems I was facing at home, Robert's diagnosis, Tina's new job, and the constant fighting caused by overwhelming stress. I explained that I simply had to be home more often.

Much to my surprise and everlasting appreciation, John was extremely sympathetic. (His was definitely an anticlimatic response, but not disappointingly so.) We worked out a part-time schedule that involved some telecommuting (technology is wonderful), and I would, of course, take a pay cut of 20- to 25-percent, depending upon how many hours I ended up actually working. While this arrangement clearly hurt my career, and though there were times when Tina and I definitely missed the money, I was growing happier and certainly more content with life.

7

Robert and Ritalin

We attempted to get our lives in order, and Robert seemed to be doing better—at least in school. His behavior had improved greatly (his class was extremely structured, which helped Robert tremendously), and he was doing well academically. In fact, at five years old, although he wasn't even halfway through kindergarten, Robert was already performing at a first-grade level in certain subjects. His ability to concentrate, however, was showing absolutely no signs of improvement. We met with Mrs. Aronowsky and the school psychologist to discuss the matter.

I wasn't the least bit surprised when they strongly urged us to put Robert on medication. While they were both very happy with Robert's progress, they were sure that medication was necessary in order for Robert to reach his full potential. Mrs. Aronowsky, in particular, was sure Robert would do well. "Soar" was the word she used. She even suggested that, on the right medication, Robert might be mainstreamed within a year.

Robert learned as if through osmosis. He absorbed information like a sponge, but you would never know it. During class, he would stare at the ceiling or out the window. He would interrupt the proceedings constantly. He would fidget. He never seemed to pay attention, yet when Mrs. Aronowsky would ask him a question about the lesson, he would always know the answer. Nevertheless, Mrs. Aronowsky noted that they would eventually study things requiring greater concentration. It would be a disaster if Robert couldn't focus and lost interest.

It was obvious to me that Mrs. Aronowsky was frustrated. She told us Robert could do everything asked of him, but that he refused to do tasks as well as he could, or at all. There's only so much of this behavior a person can take without becoming critical. (I knew what she was talking about; I frequently helped Robert with his homework. Talk about trying one's patience. What should have taken ten minutes to complete often took well over an hour. You try to be patient and understanding, but it's not easy.) The constant prodding and criticism couldn't be good for Robert. We were all worried about his self-esteem.

It was difficult to dismiss what we were being told. I didn't want Robert to become lost. I wanted him to soar. But I was still reluctant to medicate him. First, everything I had read about Ritalin stated that this drug was not typically prescribed to children under the age of six. Robert was just five. There also were the potential side effects we had discussed with the psychologist who first evaluated Robert. Moreover, could Ritalin end up producing negative side effects in the future, even if Robert would no longer be taking it? Could it hurt him?

I was also uneasy about the specific effects Ritalin would have on our son. This drug would change the way Robert felt, the way he acted, the way he behaved. Unlike aspirin or an antibiotic, this medication would change who Robert was, not just take care of some ache or pain. I feared it might interfere with a gift we all knew Robert had: his ability to absorb information so readily. Robert was incredibly observant. He saw and remembered details of events that passed everyone else without notice. I even relied on him when I had forgotten where something was, what someone's name was, or what Tina had told me to buy at the supermarket. By forcing Robert to focus his attention, would the Ritalin destroy his ability to observe and absorb so much? Would this effect be a necessary trade-off?

Speaking of trade-offs, I once read about a writer who had attention deficit disorder. She claimed that while Ritalin did, in fact, help her to concentrate better, it also robbed her of her creativity. She refused to use the drug after noticing this outcome.

Robert had a great imagination. Was it really possible that Ritalin took away one's creativity? Was this a sacrifice that we were willing to make? Other parents complained that their children were subdued on Ritalin, that they lost a certain spark while on the medication. Now, don't get me wrong, Robert certainly needed to take it down a notch, but did he really need to be subdued? And did we even have the right to do such a thing? What if Robert was meant to be some sort of gifted visionary? Would we be spoiling the plan by giving him Ritalin?

I started to get angry. I was angry about the fact that we were being asked to medicate Robert— a charming, creative little boy with a proven ability to learn—just so he would be able to sit still in a class with twenty five other "regular" children and learn the way everyone else was supposed to learn. He was the square peg being forced into a round hole. Why? What's wrong with being different? Some of the greatest people who ever lived were different. History suggests that Thomas Edison, Ben Franklin, and even Albert Einstein experienced similar difficulties. Indeed, Thomas Edison's situation was so bad that his mother resorted to home schooling. There was no doubt in my mind that these people achieved greatness because they were different, not in spite of that fact.

Why did we have to change our son? And change him into what? What was "normal" anyway? I saw lots of children who, at times, behaved just like Robert. Robert was sweet-tempered, sensitive, thoughtful, and polite. He was frustrating because he didn't listen, but he was never openly defiant or nasty or bratty. I knew lots of parents who wished they could say such things about their children. Who's to say exactly how Robert was supposed to act?

Why weren't there schools where Robert could get the attention, treatment, and education that he needed and deserved? I was sure he would do well. I did not want to worry that I'd forced something on him that robbed him of some special talent. Deep down inside, I kept thinking that maybe Robert really didn't need to be medicated. Maybe in time, he'd learn to control himself enough to get by. I mean, Ritalin was a mind-altering drug. How could we give it to our baby? But things were what they were, and Robert was who he was. The ideal school existed only in my imagination, and Robert showed no signs of being able to control his behavior well enough to function in a regular school. Society wanted him to be a round peg for that round hole, at least until he reached college, where he could be as different as he liked. We were told that Robert would have to be a round peg (or a reasonably close facsimile) or he would never make it to the point where he would be allowed to be a square peg. But I was growing fearful of breaking that square peg by trying to force it into a round hole.

I was beginning to succumb to the pressures surrounding me. I no longer trusted my instincts. I wasn't sure I could trust them given my prejudices against medication. I was starting to listen to those who I hoped knew better than I, and rationalized this potential course of action by telling myself that it was for Robert's own good.

The perceived (and real) intolerance of those who worked with Robert and of the education system was forcing me to do things I had never dreamed of doing. First, I had allowed my son to be labeled. I had then separated him from the neighborhood by placing him in a special education school far from his home—putting him on a bus for an hour and twenty minutes twice a day! Now I was going to medicate him.

I wasn't happy with our options, but I was surrendering to what I perceived to be the inevitable. Tina did her best to ease me into it.

"You're imagining the worst," she told me.

Well, yeah, I knew that already.

"What if it works? What if Ritalin does exactly what it's supposed to do? Maybe we're hurting Robert by not giving it to him," she said.

I looked at Tina. She wanted to do it. She was sure it would help. Maybe she was right. Maybe I was hurting Robert by denying him medication. Maybe I was depriving him of something that would make his life better.

I began thinking about what it would be like if the Ritalin really worked. I wanted to believe it would. I really did. What would it be like to be around Robert without anger and frustration? Maybe I could play ball with him, teach him how to catch. Maybe we could spend some quiet time together. Maybe he'd finally be able to sit with me and watch an entire movie. Maybe I would be able to read a book to him. Maybe he'd be able to play hockey like the other children, or even just play a board game. Maybe he would be able to be mainstreamed at a school near our house. Maybe he would make some friends.

Was it possible that one little pill was the answer? We made the necessary appointments.

*   *   *

Two months later (it took us that long to get an appointment), we we're meeting with a popular, highly recommended neurologist. For the sake of this book, we will call him Dr. Lakeville. He interviewed us. What was Robert like? What did they say about him at school? What had Tina and I been like as children? What did we expect from Robert? What had we tried? How had we been disciplining him?

We talked about Ritalin. I told him I was hesitant about the whole thing. I didn't like the idea of giving my son a drug—"medication," I was corrected—that could change his personality. I didn't understand how it worked. Would Robert lose anything by taking it? What about its possible side effects: loss of sleep, loss of appetite, nervous tics, mood swings, stunting of growth? What about the fact that Ritalin was not recommended for children under six? Were there any long-term problems known? How long would Robert be on the medication?

I refused to ask what would happen if it wasn't effective. Just accepting the possibility that Robert should be on medication had taken too much out of me. The last thing I wanted to hear was that there was a chance it wouldn't work. Dr. Lakeville began by saying that he did not easily prescribe medication (every medical doctor we'd met had also said that). Therefore, if he thought Robert did not need Ritalin, or that Ritalin would be ineffective, he would not prescribe its use. He told us that the side effects were very rare, but if they were to develop, we might have to try a different, albeit similar, medication. He assured us that Robert's personality would not change; all that Ritalin did was enhance a person's ability to concentrate. In fact, by allowing Robert to control himself better, his "true" personality might finally emerge.

He said he was not sure how long Robert would need medication. Circumstances varied from individual to individual. He may need it for just a few years, or for the rest of his life. He did say that prolonged use would probably suppress Robert's growth slightly. This came as a tremendous blow. I fully expected, based on Robert's growth to date, that he might end up being well over six feet tall. What an athlete he would be! Dr. Lakeville shook his head. "Do you really expect him to be a professional athlete?" he asked us. "Look what you and your wife do. Look at your backgrounds. Do you see a career in sports for your son?"

"You never know," I said. I had my hopes.

"I wouldn't worry about it," Dr. Lakeville replied. "Besides, when he is off the medication, his body will make up for any loss of growth he might have experienced."

We were to take him off periodically. The doctor called these periods "med-vacations." "At worst," he said, "use of this medication may stunt his growth about an inch. Which would you rather have, the inch or a happy, well-adjusted son?"

When he put it that way, I suppose I saw his point, sort of. On the age issue, he said it was true that the use of Ritalin was "counter indicated" for children under six, but that was only because there had yet to be long-term tests on children who had used the medication prior to that age. He explained that Ritalin had been thoroughly studied and tested, and that it was perfectly safe. In fact, Ritalin had been prescribed for children under the age of six "without incident" for years.

He did say, however, that he would not prescribe Ritalin to children under the age of five. The reason? He stated that something happened to children once they hit the age of five. Whatever it was, they automatically responded better, both to counseling and medication. In other words, he didn't like to prescribe Ritalin to children under the age of five because it had been his experience that it did not work well for them. He ended the discussion with the now nauseating refrain: "If your son had diabetes, you'd give him insulin, wouldn't you?"

He called Robert into his office, and Robert was in rare form. He didn't want to be there, and he certainly didn't want to have anything to do with this doctor. Eventually, the doctor was able to complete his examination. It was, to us, surprisingly quick and superficial. His evaluation started with the doctor asking Robert to name different parts of the body. The doctor then did a quick physical exam—heart rate, blood pressure, vision, etc. He then asked Robert to close his eyes and touch his nose, walk heel to toe, and jump up and down on one foot. That was it. Robert was excused from the office.

The first thing Dr. Lakeville did after Robert left was point out that Robert had misnamed two parts of the body. I had noticed the mistakes as well, although I hadn't thought anything of them. After all, Robert was only five years old, and he obviously hadn't been paying much attention. Dr. Lakeville, though, thought that Robert might be suffering from yet another psychological problem in addition to the ones that had already been diagnosed.

Was this a joke? He had seen our son for maybe five minutes, and based upon the fact that Robert—a hyperactive five-year-old boy with an apparent attention issue who clearly did not want to be there—had mis-named two body parts, he was now ready to diagnose Robert with yet another disorder? I was dumbfounded and speechless. All I was able to do was assure Dr. Lakeville that Robert had merely been confused. He raised his eyebrows, looked at me as if to say, "Don't say I didn't warn you," and scribbled something on Robert's file. I shook my head in wonder. Do doctors just try to find something wrong? Do they not feel as though they've done their jobs if they cannot find a disorder or two? Do they automatically assume that something must be wrong just because you're there? In our case, maybe he thought this diagnosis was what we wanted to hear.

I don't make these accusations lightly. Another doctor had seen Robert for an unrelated matter and had told Tina he thought Robert might have Marfan syndrome. This doctor had never seen Robert before, and his pronouncement had been based entirely on the fact that Robert was so tall, and his arm span so big. There had been no other physical examination, no genetic testing, no blood work, and no history done prior to offering the opinion that Robert had a disorder that could prove fatal when Robert hit his twenties! In a panic, we would take Robert to another doctor for a second opinion. Robert, thankfully, did not have Marfan Syndrome.

Dr. Lakeville quickly moved on. He pulled out a chart that explained how to build up dosages of Ritalin over a two-week period. I was taken aback.

I stopped him. "So, I assume you think Robert needs the Ritalin."

He looked at me like I had two heads. "Robert?" he said. "It's a no-brainer."

Yes, those were his exact words.

Dr. Lakeville suggested we start Robert on Ritalin over winter vacation, so that Robert would be fully acclimated to it by the time he returned to school. Also, we'd get a chance to see how it affected him, and could place him on the medication without his teacher knowing. The idea behind the secrecy was to ensure we got completely objective observations from Robert's teacher. If she noted a marked change in Robert's behavior, then we'd know for sure that the Ritalin was having an effect.

Dr. Lakeville wanted to begin with a low dose and gradually build it up to 20 mg a day. He explained that this was the dosage at which he usually started children. We could adjust the dosage later according to Robert's reaction. He also explained that there were two ways of administering the medication. We could give Robert two doses during the day, one 10-mg dose in the morning, and another 10-mg dose in the afternoon. The reason for two doses was the fact that Ritalin took effect quickly, usually within thirty to forty-five minutes of ingestion, and was effective for only three to four hours. A second dose at lunchtime was, therefore, necessary in order to get through an entire school day.

The other method of administering Ritalin was via a single sustained-release dose of 20 mg taken each the morning. Dr. Lakeville favored this method because it was obviously easier. He also felt it would be better for Robert, as it meant he wouldn't have to go to the nurse in the middle of the day and be placed in the position of explaining the medication to his friends. We opted to go with the 20-mg sustained-release tablet. "After all," we reassured each other, "Dr. Lakeville must know what he's doing."

*   *   *

Now, how were we to explain all this to Robert? He knew something was going on, but we made it a point never to talk about his "issue" in front of him. We couldn't tell him there was something "wrong" with him. We couldn't tell him he had ADD or ODD or was hyperactive; he was far too young to understand. We certainly couldn't tell him he wasn't like other children. How were we going to explain the Ritalin?

I then thought of something. The tablet was going to be his "special vitamin." It was going to help him in school. I thought he would like that idea, and, in fact, it was the truth. This "special pill" was going to help him concentrate better in class. We just needed to stress that we were in no way upset with or disappointed in Robert. He was not getting a "special vitamin" because he had misbehaved or because he wasn't doing well. It was simply something that would help him do better.

Of course, I was elected to give Robert his first dose of medication. Although I thought I had prepared myself for this occasion, that I had convinced myself it was the right thing to do, when it came right down to giving Robert Ritalin, I didn't want to do it. I held those pills in my hand for the longest time, fighting off a sick feeling in my stomach. Robert, on the other hand, was fine about the whole thing. In fact, Robert was excited about taking his "special vitamin."

I took it out, gave it to him, and gave him a glass of water.

I felt awful. It's hard to describe. Here was my little boy, all excited about a pill. I had no idea what he thought it was going to do for him, but he obviously thought it was going to do something wonderful. I didn't tell him otherwise. I felt I had lied to him. Worse, I was doing something to his head, something that I didn't entirely understand or trust, but I was doing it anyway, partly because everyone had told me he needed it done, but also because we needed it done. I felt powerless.

I also felt selfish. Was I doing this for Robert or for us? What was it going to do to him? Was he going to have side effects? Were we hurting our son? Were we doing the right thing?

The two weeks over which Robert acclimated to Ritalin were two of the worst weeks of my life. During the first week, Robert frequently became nauseated, and he looked awful. Moreover, aside from making Robert ill, the low dosages he received during the first week had absolutely no effect on his ability to concentrate. Any miracle expectations Tina and I had entertained were completely dashed.

To make matters worse, when we called Dr. Lakeville to ask about Robert's nausea, we were told that the doctor was very busy, and that we would have to call him back the next day after office hours. Our son was pale and vomiting, and Dr. Lakeville was too busy to speak with us. I yelled at the secretary, my anger compounded by the feeling that I had made a huge mistake in allowing myself to be talked into medicating Robert in the first place.

Dr. Lakeville took my call. He told me that the Ritalin was not causing the nausea. He thought it was probably nothing more than a flu bug. I wasn't so sure—there had been no flu bug in my neighborhood, and obviously the timing of the nausea was suspect. In any event, he assured us, there would be no problems once Robert became acclimated to the medication. (If it were the flu, then why did we have to wait for Robert to become acclimated?)

During the second week, we began to notice significant changes in Robert's behavior. His attention span was getting longer. He was listening better and staying on task longer. And the vomiting stopped. Our hopes began to rise, but quickly fell. As we continued to increase the dosage to the recommended 20-mg sustained-release tablet, matters became worse. Robert's eyes became black and hollow-looking. He was pale. And he was extremely serious. He was concentrating better than we had ever seen him concentrate before, but even when playing, he was completely without joy. He had changed from an active, happy, laughing little boy to a quiet, solemn, serious little man.

And the mood swings. He would get angry—no, furious—over nothing when the medication began to wear off. He had uncontrollable screaming, hitting, and snarling fits. I'm no doctor, but I was pretty sure this was not supposed to happen. My doubts about medicating Robert returned stronger than ever. Even administering the sustained-release pill was a problem. Robert would chew it, getting entirely too much medication too quickly. Of course, he wasn't supposed to chew it, but try getting a five-year-old to swallow a pill.

His behavior became worse than we had ever seen or imagined it could be. He was utterly and completely uncontrollable—threats and punishment had no effect. He was nasty and obsessive. He kept repeating how he hated everyone.

This was insane. I hated this pill. I hated what it was doing to our son. I was ready to call off this whole fiasco and take my chances with special education programs and behavior modification to help Robert attain control. Nothing was worth putting our son through this—nothing was worth seeing him in this state! But Dr. Lakeville talked me out of it.

"Robert hasn't become acclimated to the Ritalin yet," he explained. "Give him time, he'll get used to it. If necessary, we could always tinker with the dosage. Robert will be fine."

We could only hope he was right.

*   *   *

The two-week acclimation period finally ended and it was time for Robert to return to school. Against Dr. Lakeville's orders, we informed Mrs. Aronowsky and the school psychologist that we had started Robert on Ritalin. How could we chance Robert having problematic reactions without his caretakers knowing that he was on medication? Mrs. Aronowsky and the school psychologist were grateful for our openness. What's more, they were absolutely mortified by the fact that Dr. Lakeville had specifically instructed us not to tell them. Dr. Lakeville's objective of obtaining completely unbiased observations paled in comparison to the school's concerns. Anyway, given Robert's extreme changes in behavior, it was pretty obvious that he was on some kind of medication.

After we got Robert to swallow the 20-mg tablet, the change it had over him was remarkable, but it was not necessarily the change for which we had hoped. Clearly, he now concentrated better than anyone ever imagined he could. Mrs. Aronowsky raved about how well his studies were coming along, how he listened intently and behaved, and how he even waited his turn—a feat he had never before accomplished. While this was all well and good, we noticed that Robert was becoming much more withdrawn and quiet. Yes, he concentrated better, but he also seemed to have lost his personality. He was extremely serious. He rarely smiled and never laughed. Even a game would be treated as a job that demanded 100 percent concentration—a demanding task that needed to be done.

He wasn't as lively and energetic either. Don't get me wrong, Robert clearly had to tone down those aspects of his personality, but now they were completely gone. I really didn't recognize him anymore. I missed the old Robert. I missed my son. When the effects of the medication began to wear off, Robert would become extremely emotional. The littlest thing would send him into a fit of anger or a bout of sadness that often ended in out-and-out bawling. He still got dark circles under his eyes, and he looked ill in general. The doctors and teachers had not told us this could happen. All we had ever heard about were the wonders of this medication. Side effects, if any, were supposed to be exceedingly rare.

Perhaps Robert was being overmedicated. We contacted Dr. Lakeville. We wanted to take Robert off the single sustained-release tablet and instead give him two separate doses of less than 10 mg twice a day. Dr. Lakeville didn't like the idea.

First of all, Dr. Lakeville thought it better to have to take only one pill a day. Robert would not have to visit the nurse during the day for a second dose. Dr. Lakeville thought this important for Robert's self-esteem since, if he were to be mainstreamed into a regular school program, he would not be singled out as the "kid on drugs." Moreover, the smallest sustained-release tablet available was 20 mg. It therefore followed that we should try 20 mg a little longer in the hope that it would work. Tina and I thought this recommendation made no sense at all. Clearly, 20 mg was too much. So, despite his advice, we arranged for Robert to receive two doses, each containing less than 10 mg of Ritalin. Dr. Lakeville wrote the appropriate prescriptions, and a physician's note was delivered to the school nurse, authorizing her to administer Robert's afternoon dose.

Mrs. Aronowsky immediately noticed a change. In fact, she wrote in Robert's journal, "The old Robert is back! He's lively again!" She also noted that Robert was concentrating as well as ever. I began to feel a little better. I was glad that Robert was feeling better, and glad that we had taken a stand that had obviously helped our son.

*   *   *

With the exception of looking for a new doctor to monitor Robert's medication (we had had it with Dr. Lakeville), the next few months were pleasantly uneventful. I have to admit, when the Ritalin worked, it was wonderful. Robert made tremendous progress. At school, he tore through his studies like a buzz saw. He no longer frustrated everyone who worked with him. He waited his turn, sat in his chair, and paid much closer attention to his teachers. They all told us how far he had come.

His transformation at hockey was even more remarkable. He willingly went to practice without a fuss. He sat still while we dressed him. In fact, he even helped us get his equipment on, thus turning what used to be a half-hour ordeal into a ten-minute breeze. He even grabbed his stick and ran—yes, ran—to the ice. And on the ice, what a difference! Robert actually did what all the other children were doing, and did it well! He no longer stared at the lights, or looked for the Zamboni, or kicked the boards because he wanted to get off the ice. We no longer heard the coaches yelling, "Robert, pay attention! Robert, get over here! Robert! Robert!" The coaches couldn't believe it. "It's like night and day," they told me.

When I told Robert's coaches of Robert's diagnosis, one coach who had experience with special needs children said that he had suspected Robert had a problem. Based on Robert's tendency to make strange noises ("rat noises," I called them) and yell for no apparent reason while on the ice, he had actually suspected Tourette syndrome. *Would anyone else care to diagnose our son with a problem?* I thought.

It was strange seeing Robert on Ritalin. I wasn't used to him being so passive. I had grown used to this little person for over five years, and now he was different—not different "bad," but different nonetheless. I wondered where the Ritalin ended and Robert began. Of course, we still had bad days—days when Robert was just too wound up or in a foul mood and the Ritalin didn't seem to help. (It was almost cyclical. He would have a couple of good weeks, and then a really bad week, and then he would be all right again.) He was not on Ritalin all day, though (we tried to limit it to when he was attending school or at hockey), so we still had to deal with Robert when he was not on medication. That did not get much easier. In fact, knowing how well he could behave when he was on medication made it more difficult for us to be patient with Robert when he was not on Ritalin. But that's the choice we made. We'd just as soon not have Robert on Ritalin every waking moment.

The worst days were when Robert would tell me he didn't need his "special vitamin" and practically beg us not to give it to him. What was he thinking? Obviously, on some level the Ritalin bothered him. Was it a physical discomfort? Was it something emotional, something less tangible, but nonetheless disturbing to our son? Or did he think there was something wrong with him? Did he think we were angry with or disappointed in him, and that we gave him his "special vitamin" so that he would live up to our expectations? Was it punishment to him? We told him that we never thought such things. We told him how proud we were of him, and that it was okay to need to take his "vitamin." We tried to comfort and reassure him.

He would often say he didn't like taking the "vitamin." He didn't like the way it made him feel. He couldn't tell us anymore than that. It hurt me so much to force him to take that pill on those days. There were times when I just couldn't. Most times, though, I told myself it was for his own good—that he needed it. Sometimes, he would cry.

8

A New Diagnosis

lthough we had only worked with Dr. Lakeville for a short time, we had already grown to dislike the man. We thought his examination of Robert had been superficial. We did not appreciate being told to call back after office hours as we watched our son vomit. We did not like how he had ignored our concerns over the 20-mg pill when it seemed so clear that Robert was overmedicated. We switched to a child psychiatrist. We'll call him Dr. Schneider. Dr. Schneider was a leader in the field of treating children like Robert. We would find out sometime later, unfortunately, that he strongly believed in psychopharmacology—treating neurological disorders with drugs.

We started nearly from scratch with Dr. Schneider. There was another pile of forms to complete. There was the obligatory parent interview, and, of course, Robert was interviewed as well. In addition, Dr. Schneider gave Robert a physical examination that included a blood workup. He wanted to rule out any other possible physiological causes for Robert's behavior, such as lead poisoning or thyroid problems. He was shocked (or at least pretended to be) when he found out that Dr. Lakeville hadn't performed one before prescribing Ritalin.

He had us schedule Robert for a series of tests that would help establish Robert's IQ and determine whether, in fact, Robert had any learning disabilities. He sent biweekly progress charts to Robert's teacher for her to complete, and asked Tina to keep a daily journal of Robert's behavior at home. Clearly, this man was going to monitor Robert's progress closely. Finally, he asked us to join a behavior modification training group. We would be meeting with doctors and parents of children Robert's age to discuss proven methods of behavior modification. He assured us that it would help us (and Robert) tremendously.

He then spoke with us about medication, consistent discipline, encouragement, and understanding. We had heard it all before. He also stressed that none of this situation was our fault. It wasn't what Robert ate. It wasn't how we were raising him. It wasn't video games. It wasn't his teachers, his sister, or our family and friends. He told us we were good parents. We were doing the right things. Robert, he said, has a physiological disorder. His brain chemistry was off, we needed to fix it, and the only way to fix it was through medication. It was that simple.

I was pleased with our switch. Obviously, this doctor was listening to us. In fact, through this doctor, I felt that we were more in control of the situation, until our second visit.

*   *   *

We thought Robert was doing so much better. Although he wasn't yet ready to be mainstreamed, Robert was making positive strides. His teachers were thrilled with his progress, his coaches were happy, and while far from perfect, things were going a little better at home. We even started to wonder if we could cut back on the amount of medication Robert was taking; he still looked so awfully pale. Also, he continued to have emotional swings when the Ritalin wore off. He could still be oppositional and obsessive—he would lock onto a particular subject or desire and refuse to let go of it for hours. Something simply wasn't right. We thought Robert might still be overmedicated.

Imagine our disbelief and disappointment when Dr. Schneider recommended that we increase the amount of Ritalin Robert was taking each day by almost 66 percent!

Why?" I asked. "He's doing great! I don't want to give him more. Besides, Robert was awful on higher dosages."

Based on Robert's teacher's evaluations and our reports of his afternoon mood swings and obsessive behavior, Dr. Schneider told us he wanted to increase Robert's present medication or switch to another similar medication. He suggested a drug called Dexedrine. I couldn't listen to this. It was hard enough to place Robert on Ritalin—supposedly the safest (or at least the most tested and widely prescribed) of the medications used to treat children like Robert. How could we switch? I did not want to increase the dosage either. I remembered how Robert had changed when he took that much Ritalin. Yes, it had made him more manageable, but it had also made him a zombie. I didn't want a zombie; I wanted my son.

Tina grew upset listening to me. "The doctor thinks it will be better," she tried to reason with me. "Maybe Robert will be easier to deal with—maybe he will concentrate better. Maybe we can think about mainstreaming him sooner—bring him closer to home. Maybe, it will be better. We should at least try this route."

Indecision overwhelmed me. What could I say? I certainly had no better idea, and after all, this doctor was renowned in his field throughout the world. We followed his directions and increased Robert's medication. Now, I'm not one to say, "I told you so," but . . .

I was disappointed but not surprised when the increased dosage of Ritalin did not work as planned. Robert became better able to stay on task, but his "bad" traits seemed to intensify. At home, he was very serious again. He got angry easily, and he stayed angry for a long time. He was also overly emotional and extremely oppositional. He had to be first all the time. When he didn't get his way, he would have a tantrum, physically throwing himself about. He became more obsessive—constantly repeating himself, constantly harping on the same thing over and over again.

In addition, we noticed that Ritalin was having a pronounced effect on Robert physically. As I mentioned before, Robert had always been sensitive to noise. Loud noises bothered him, but he could tolerate them. On Ritalin, however, any noise, such as the roar of the crowd at a ball game or even the band at assembly, would reduce Robert to tears. He would cry inconsolably, his hands clasped over his ears. He also developed a facial tic. More disturbing, we noticed a heightened sense of anxiety in Robert when he was on the medication. His hands were always in motion. His fingers moved nervously. He was jittery.

After a couple of weeks of these effects, we contacted Mrs. Aronowsky. If Robert actually was doing better at school, then perhaps it might be worth it to stick to the plan. It seemed, however, that Mrs. Aronowsky was having just as hard a time with Robert as we were. Robert wasn't listening to her. Robert threw fits when he didn't get his way. In fact, one time several of the children, including Robert, were sent to the nurse in the afternoon for their medications, and Robert demanded he get his first. It seemed comical until Robert had a fit, threw himself over, and whacked his head on a chair. Mrs. Aronowsky didn't know what to do. She admitted that Robert had become so frustrating over the past week that she had been forced to leave him with the aide. We assured her that we understood.

She also told us that Robert was behaving just as he had when he had first come to her over the summer. She felt he had regressed. It was "Robert's world" all over again, with one exception. He was doing phenomenally well in his studies. In fact, he had completed the first-grade curriculum in math. He wasn't nearly through kindergarten yet. His teacher asked why we had increased his medication; she thought that he had been doing quite well on the lower dose. This came as a complete surprise to me. I told her that it was mostly because Dr. Schneider hadn't been happy with her report about Robert.

She was shocked. "That can't be," she said. "He must have misunderstood what I wrote." I didn't doubt her. We had heard enough. We decided to put Robert back on the lower dose. We attempted to contact Dr. Schneider about this change. He was out of town. We took Robert back down to his original lower dose, administered twice a day, and things were soon back to "normal." Of course, when Dr. Schneider called back and found out what we had done, he wasn't happy. "You can't switch his dosage like that. He has to be monitored. You have to talk to me about these things."

When Tina told him we had tried to contact him before reducing his medication, he got defensive. He got downright nasty when we told him we'd spoken to Robert's teacher, who had been surprised to hear that the higher dosage had been prescribed due, in large part, to her report. Dr. Schnieder said we had biased her, that we could no longer be sure she was being objective.

This incident greatly bothered Tina. Confronted by the doctor, she began to question our actions. He could be very intimidating, and given our insecurity, we were easy targets. I tried to assure her we had done the right thing. The higher dosage wasn't working. Dr. Schneider was probably bothered because our actions were outside his methodology. He was likely even more upset because we hadn't consulted him first. Perhaps he wasn't used to parents who questioned him.

I, too, was bothered by what had transpired, but in a completely different way. I had thought (perhaps "hoped" is a better word) the drug therapy we had undertaken was a fairly precise practice that employed reliable assessment tools, which would, in turn, dictate definitive, effective treatments. Instead, we were witness to reports and forms Robert's teacher could not understand, a possible misreading of his teacher's report, and a very defensive practitioner who was, for all intents and purposes, experimenting with different medication dosages on our son. I probably shouldn't have been so surprised. After all, they don't say that doctors "practice" medicine for nothing.

The doctors and teachers never told me how much of their jobs was pure guesswork. While I recognized that Tina and I had a significant role to play concerning Robert's treatment, I was only now appreciating just how important that role truly was. All along, I had hoped to find an omniscient expert who would provide us with a concrete answer. It would never be that simple. There was nothing about Robert or the prescribed therapies that was precise, automatic, or assured. Although I had hoped otherwise, we could not simply rely on Robert's teachers and doctors to know what was right and what should be done always. They were guessing as much as we were. We would have to assert ourselves. The only problem was that we had to assert ourselves in a field in which we knew next to nothing.

Was I deluding myself? Did I actually believe we could contribute to or, in fact, contradict an expert psychiatrist's treatment of our son?

*   *   *

We attended the next scheduled appointment with Dr. Schneider. He was ready for battle. He made it clear, in no uncertain terms, that we should not have reduced Robert's medication. First, he was adamant that we should not alter Robert's medication without his approval. Second, it was his opinion that Robert needed more Ritalin, not less, and even possibly a second medication.

I received a lecture about my "anti-medication" attitude. "Less is not better," he said. "In fact, if Robert doesn't get enough, he may suffer all the side effects associated with Ritalin without any of the benefits. It's just like an antibiotic. If you don't take enough, it won't cure you even though you'll probably still get the upset stomach."

I admitted we preferred to use as little medication as possible, but in all honesty, it seemed to us that Robert was doing well on his current reduced dosage. Dr. Schneider disagreed. "Just look at the way he's acting in the office," he said. "He slammed the door when he was told to wait outside for us."

He told us how his assistant had to get extra toys and mentally prepare herself for Robert every time we visited Dr. Schneider, despite the fact that she was used to dealing with children. Robert was the only one with whom she ever had a problem. She had told Dr. Schneider that she simply could not handle Robert. "If that's how he acts on a reduced dosage, it's clearly not enough," Dr. Schneider said.

We pointed out that whenever Robert came with us to the doctor, he was angry about being separated from us and then asked to sit out in the hallway with a stranger for forty-five minutes. Also, Robert was never on medication during his office visits, as by then his noon dosage had long since worn off.

Dr. Schneider was surprised but not dissuaded. He went straight to the teacher's reports and told us that, based on the scores, Robert was not doing well, even on medication. I countered with the fact that Robert's teacher had not fully understood the forms. Moreover, it had been her opinion that Robert was doing much better on the reduced dosage. We then explained that the extra Ritalin was causing side effects that were quite noticeable, not only to us but also to his teacher. Maybe our dosage wasn't enough, but the drastically higher dosage he had recommended was unacceptable, and we simply could not continue down this path.

At this point, he backed down. He explained that his goal was to get Robert mainstreamed as soon as possible. We had to get the ADHD under control so we could work on his other behavior problems. To do that, we had to do look at his medication. He asked about the small dose he had suggested Robert take after school. Tina told him she had stopped giving it to him at the same time we had reduced his medication. The doctor asked why. Tina explained that she and Robert had a routine after school, and that Robert wasn't that much of a problem then. The doctor persisted. "If Robert's even a little better for having had a small dose of Ritalin after school, he should have it."

"Why?" we asked. "If he's doing okay, why give him more medication?"

We had to get off this "anti-medication thing," Dr. Schneider told us. It was simple; if Robert needed more Ritalin to behave properly, he should get it. Tina didn't agree. "Our routine is good, and dealing with Robert is becoming less of a problem. Why do it?"

"If it helps Robert behave even marginally better when he's at home, it will be worth it," was the reply. "Robert will be under less stress, and so will you. You'll spend more time enjoying his company rather than disciplining him. That would be good for him as well as you. And don't forget how much more tolerant you are with Robert. Other people, including his future teachers, won't be."

He then told us about an experienced special education school-teacher who had taken part in an experiment. She had been asked to handle a group of young children for an entire day. Unbeknownst to her, one of the children was hyperactive. She handled the class well, but it was obvious from her behavior towards the hyperactive child that she steadily developed a strong dislike of that child throughout the day. In fact, by the end of the day, she didn't even want to see him.

I immediately thought of Robert's playgroup teacher, the one who had harshly scolded him, who had had nothing nice to say about Robert, and who hadn't talked to me during my visit.

Tina grew visibly agitated. She fumbled with her wedding band and her voice began to shake as she tried to defend our position.

I spoke up. I told the doctor that we weren't convinced that Ritalin was 100-percent safe. Robert had developed a facial tic. He had suffered drastic mood swings after receiving mere milligrams too much. His appetite had become suppressed. And who really knew what the long-term effects of this drug were? This was our son we were talking about.

He told us, again, how well tested and widely used Ritalin was. He asked what he could do to convince us that Ritalin was safe. I shook my head. With all the problems we had experienced, I said, "I'm not sure you can."

"You have to trust me," he said. "I'm on your side."

He began to talk about how untreated children like Robert fared, as a group, over time. It was not a pretty picture. Since they cannot sit still long enough to make friends or interact on any meaningful level, these kids have trouble socializing. Moreover, they miss subtle social cues. "For example," he said, "Robert's demeanor could make another child uncomfortable. While you or I could tell that the child was uncomfortable just from that child's body language, Robert would never know it. So, instead of backing off, Robert might continue to upset the child."

The doctor also said that children like Robert tend to have difficulty in school and are often labeled "trouble makers" because of their impulsiveness and inability to sit still. Many have problems learning and do poorly academically simply because they can't concentrate long enough to learn. He said, by and large, these children get yelled at more, punished more, and hit more. They don't listen, and parents—especially fathers—have difficulty tolerating disobedience. It makes them feel impotent.

I began to squirm. All those little whacks on the behind I had given Robert when I just couldn't deal with his behavior. I remembered all the screaming and yelling.

Dr. Schneider continued. As these children get older, they have a high dropout rate, especially by eleventh grade. They tend to get in trouble with drugs and the police. As adults, they have trouble with relationships. They have trouble holding jobs.

My brother. He was describing my brother, John.

I saw Dr. Schneider's lips moving, but I wasn't listening. John had had so many problems growing up. He had always been a good person, bright, naturally athletic, artistic, creative, outgoing, and charismatic. He had always had so much going for him, and yet he could never get his act together. He was just like my son.

As a child, John was always active and a little wild. (To this day, he has trouble sitting through a movie in a theater.) He could get extremely angry and obsessive, just like Robert. Even though he was bright, as he grew up, he had trouble in school. He was labeled a troublemaker. He didn't do very well academically, except in math.

Math was Robert's favorite subject, too, and he had also been labeled a troublemaker.

My brother even dropped out of high school for a few months, though to his credit, he went back and got his diploma. After school, he switched jobs every few months. He was never fired, though. In fact, he always did a tremendous job at each place of employment. He just lost interest and quit after a period of working.

I've lost count of his girlfriends—no relationship ever seemed to last very long. And he was always getting in trouble—sometimes pretty nasty trouble. My father couldn't understand it.

I vividly remember one conversation with my dad. I was working the summer in a factory that manufactured lamps. My father was vice president in charge of production, and he would often take me to suppliers so I could learn the routes and see the business from the bottom up. No cushy job at the showroom for his son. I got to work at 6:30 AM, punched in with everyone else, swept out trucks, took out garbage, and ran errands for the factory foremen and repairmen. Picking up parts and supplies was part of the job. I came home covered in dust and dirt nearly every day.

One day, my father took me to a factory in Brooklyn that manufactured glass. Out of the blue, he started talking about John. John had gotten into some trouble, and my father was beside himself with anger, pain, and self-doubt. "What am I going to do with him? We raised him just like the rest of you. I've tried bribing him, punishing him, grounding him, threatening to throw him out. What am I doing wrong?" he said.

We sought blame in our family. My father was too hard on him. My mother was too soft. I even thought it was my fault. Maybe I wasn't a good older brother. Maybe I should have been more of a friend to him, helped him more, encouraged him more, and spent more time with him.

But what if the problem wasn't my parents' fault, my fault, or even my brother's fault? What if it was merely a chemical imbalance?

There were echoes of my brother John in my son. Robert was bright, likeable, and had so many things going for him, but why couldn't he behave? We tried everything, too. We bribed, we threatened, we yelled, and we even spanked. Nothing seemed to work, and we continually blamed ourselves. I didn't want Robert to go through what my brother had gone through. I didn't want to go through what my parents had gone through.

My mind returned to the conversation with the doctor in front of me. Dr. Schneider had begun talking about other, alternative drugs. "But," he added, "if you don't like Ritalin, you're really not going to like the others. They haven't been nearly as well tested." Then he looked me right in the eye and said, "I also think Robert needs something else."

"What?" I asked.

He began talking about using other medications that he thought should be tried in conjunction with Ritalin. One was clonidine. He told us that this medication would help the Ritalin work more effectively. He also told me that Robert seemed to be very "anxious," "awkward," and "odd." (Yes, these were the exact terms he used.) He was concerned that Robert would not be accepted by his peers. Moreover, he thought that Robert was extremely eager to please others, even to the point of being overly worried about what others thought of him. It was his opinion that Robert suffered from pervasive developmental disorder (PDD). I rolled my eyes. What on Earth was this man talking about now?

The doctor explained PDD as a condition in which several areas of a person's development are seriously impaired. While Robert was developing academically, his maturity level, physical skills, and especially his social skills, unfortunately, were not. Simply put, Robert was developing emotionally and psychologically at far different rates. Although it was clear he was intellectually ahead, his emotions and behavior were lagging far behind.

Robert's new diagnosis was serious. It suggested PDD—a condition now considered part of the autism spectrum.

"Robert," Dr. Schneider explained, "is not simply ADD or ADHD. Robert has serious emotional and behavioral problems that must be addressed."

He also noted Robert's extreme sensitivity to Ritalin. It was clear to Dr. Schneider that Ritalin compounded Robert's anxiety and awkwardness. (We didn't tell him that Ritalin also compounded Robert's sensitivity to noise.) Something needed to be done to address Robert's newly diagnosed problem as well as the side effects he was experiencing as a result of taking Ritalin.

"Robert should be on Prozac," the doctor said.

I was speechless. What was going on here? We had entered his office secure in the belief that Robert was improving. Now, despite what we thought and what Robert's teacher had said, according to Dr. Schneider, Robert was doing poorly. In fact, in Dr. Schneider's opinion, Robert was worse than we had been led to believe, suffering from a disorder far more disabling than we could have imagined.

Instead of reducing his medication, we were told to increase it. Moreover, we were told we had to give Robert two additional medications of a far more serious nature. Completely unprepared for this, thoughts and doubts raced through my mind. Is all this really necessary? Maybe Dr. Schneider was seeing something that wasn't really there. I mean, what did he have to go by anyway? How accurate a reading of Robert's emotional state could he have gotten from biweekly report forms and office visits with Robert once or twice a month? If I were going to trust anyone's judgment, other than our own, it would be Robert's teacher's judgment. She saw him every day. But then again, what did she know about psychological disorders and medication?

Needless to say, I felt the same way about this as I had the first time Ritalin was mentioned. Unlike Ritalin, Prozac I had heard of before, and what I had heard wasn't all good.

Dr. Schneider told me it was perfectly safe.

"Yes, we've heard that before," I said.

"And," he added, "if your son . . ."

I interrupted him. "If I hear the diabetes analogy from one more person, I'm going to pop someone."

I explained to Dr. Schneider that I was having enough trouble with one medication. I couldn't imagine doubling or tripling drugs—at least not yet. I argued my case. Perhaps Robert's anxiousness was the result of immaturity. He wasn't even six years old yet! How could we know his behavior and disposition wouldn't improve in time? (I know, I had said the same things when Ritalin was first suggested.) But I had to admit that maybe the doctor was right about the anxiety. Maybe that was why there were days when Robert didn't want to take his "special vitamin." Maybe it made him uncomfortably anxious. I kept this thought to myself for the time being. I really wasn't in favor of giving Robert Prozac, and I didn't want to give Dr. Schneider more ammunition.

In the end, we compromised. We agreed to increase Robert's Ritalin dosage slightly, but we simply could not handle the idea of additional medications at this point. We promised to reconsider our position if we found Robert truly needed the extra medications. It was déjà vu.

*   *   *

The extra dosage of Ritalin helped in some ways, but it was obvious that something was still amiss. Tina couldn't put her finger on it, but she wasn't satisfied. On the one hand, Robert was excelling academically, and his behavior reports from school were progressively more favorable, and for the time being, he was not suffering from any severe side effects. Encouraged by his progress, we enrolled him in a karate class, and Robert even began piano lessons. Although not the most complaisant or attentive of students, Robert was able to undertake these new challenges fairly successfully while on medication. Joan, his piano teacher, was exceptionally patient with both Robert and us. Under the extremely kind and competent hands of Sensei Mike and Senpai David, the instructors at the karate dojo, Robert earned his yellow belt in no time at all—an event which forced me to choke back tears. Robert was so happy, and I was so proud of him. Deep down inside, I had wondered whether he would ever be able to attain even this simple goal.

On the other hand, it was clear, at least to Tina, that Ritalin wasn't doing everything it was supposed to do for Robert. She insisted that

Robert, by force of will alone, could overpower Ritalin's effectiveness. She noticed that Robert was still easily distracted. She also was sure that Ritalin's effects weren't lasting long enough. Each dose seemed to allow Robert to, more-or-less, maintain control for about two or three hours, not the four or five hours the doctors had expected. Tina thought maybe Robert's psychiatrist might be right. Maybe Robert needed clonidine to increase Ritalin's effectiveness, or maybe Robert needed an increase in Ritalin, with Prozac to counter the side effects.

I could not deny the fact that Ritalin clearly bothered Robert. He was now constantly asking us not to give him his "special vitamin," although he could not articulate why he didn't want it. All he would say was, "It isn't working," and he "didn't feel right."

We noticed that Robert never seemed happy when he was on Ritalin. As he had been before on the much higher dosage, Robert was subdued and nervous. It was telling to us that Robert's most strident protests came on days when there was a party or get-together—days when Robert knew he was supposed to have fun. It was clear the Ritalin was doing something that made him uncomfortable.

There was one last reason to consider trying a second medication. We were growing dissatisfied with Robert's placement in special education, and perhaps a second medication would enable Robert to be mainstreamed sooner. While we loved Mrs. Aronowsky, we were increasingly upset about Robert's hour-and-twenty-minute bus trip twice a day. Robert was growing antsy on the bus, and he was now beginning to cause trouble, and of course, the district bus personnel were of absolutely no help. Our suggestions and pleas to reduce the number of stops the bus made and thus shorten Robert's time on the bus went completely unheeded at all levels.

In addition, Robert's socialization skills were still well behind expectations. Indeed, new, disconcerting quirks began to appear in Robert's behavior. While he didn't do anything bad, he was engaging in behavior that was increasingly inappropriate. Even his language skills were deteriorating. I know every little boy goes through periods like this, and that fact didn't bother me. What bothered me was the fact that Robert did these things because other children in his class did them.

Robert also began to complain that the other children were upsetting him—class was "too noisy" and he couldn't work. We took this comment with a large grain of salt, although we knew Robert was not prone to exaggeration.

We sat in on his class and were not happy with what we saw. The class was far wilder than even Robert had described. Not riotous or violent—just loud, distracting, and chaotic. The children were constantly shouting at the teacher and each other during lessons. They engaged in rampant name-calling—something we knew truly bothered Robert. No one stayed in his or her seat. The aides were constantly reprimanding their charges (and there were three aides in the class, two with individual charges). A string of "bad behavior" marks were etched next to most of the children's names on the blackboard. Two children were removed from class that day because they were completely uncontrollable.

It clearly was not the teacher's or the aides' fault. They were doing their best. Short of sending the children out into the hall or down to the doctor's office, there didn't seem to be much they could do. We later found out that several of the children were experiencing very difficult times at home and, as of late, had begun to act up. In fact, one child had been suspended indefinitely.

How Robert's teacher could teach in this environment was an amazing tribute to her patience and skill. How Robert managed to learn anything was beyond belief. We were disappointed and extremely upset. We wanted Robert's classmates to be role models for Robert, not the other way around.

Our family began to pressure us into moving Robert out of special education and into a private school. Now in first grade, Robert had his sixth birthday. We threw him a party inviting not only the neighborhood children and family but also all the children from Robert's class. A couple of Robert's classmates were unmanageable—fighting with each other, throwing kicking and screaming temper tantrums whenever they didn't get their way. Some of his other classmates were highly and obviously medicated. The contrast between the kids in Robert's class and the neighborhood children was startling.

The severity of the problems Robert and his classmates faced was brought home with even more force by the parents of these children. They were grateful that we'd do something like this and invite their children. They were genuinely thankful that their children had someone with whom to play and somewhere to be invited as part of a group.

I felt horrible. Tears rolled down my aunt's face. It was a happy occasion for the children but not for us. My friends and relatives wondered why Robert was part of this world.

9

Chocolate-Covered Prozac

Robert was now several months into first grade (still in the same special education school), and we set up a meeting with his principal, his teacher, and the class psychologist to discuss our concerns over Robert's current placement. They all still thought this was the best class available for Robert. We were assured that Robert was with the very brightest students, and we all agreed he had a wonderful teacher. They thought the class an appropriate setting for Robert.

While we strongly disagreed with their assessment that the class was an appropriate place for Robert, we recognized that our choices were limited, and everyone agreed that it could hurt Robert to switch him into another classroom, as the school year had already started. We felt we had little choice but to leave him where he was, otherwise we would have to transfer him to another school entirely—perhaps even a mainstream private school with smaller classes.

Mainstream private school, however, was not an option at this point. Something needed to be done about Robert's medication, and a second medication might be in order as well. But before we would agree to use Prozac on our son, we insisted on a second opinion.

After discussing the matter with the teachers and staff at Robert's school, we arranged to have Robert evaluated while he was actually attending class. The evaluation would be performed by a highly regarded child psychiatrist in private practice who frequently worked with the school district. We'll call him Dr. Parker. We thought this the most logical way to proceed, since school was the environment about which we knew the least, the one that put the most demands on Robert, and the one that presented us with the most concerns.

The evaluation turned out to be a bit more serious than we had expected. The meeting in which we were to discuss the results of Robert's in-school evaluation was attended by a host of people—Robert's teacher, Robert's speech therapist, Robert's class psychologist and counselor, another school psychologist responsible for Robert's testing, a social worker, and, of course, Dr. Parker. We learned that we were lucky to have arranged this evaluation at all. Apparently, it was highly unusual for Dr. Parker to see a child who, like Robert, had already been evaluated. It was even more unusual for him to see a child who, like Robert, was under the care of another physician. He asked why we had requested the conference.

I told him of our concerns regarding Robert's progress in school. I told him that Robert's psychiatrist had also recommended a second medication (although I was careful not to mention what that medication was or why it was being recommended). We were looking for a second opinion. Dr. Parker asked if we had informed Dr. Schneider of this consultation. When we said we hadn't, the consultation almost ended before it had begun. It seemed this psychiatrist was extremely reluctant to share his opinions with us after discovering that Dr. Schneider had not been informed of our actions. He mumbled something about "professional courtesy" and told us he didn't think he could talk to us.

I couldn't believe my ears. "I'm sorry," I said "are you seriously telling me that you're not going to give us your opinion?"

"Well sir, would you like it if, unbeknownst to you, one of your clients went for a second opinion?" he asked.

"That would be his right," I snapped. "It wouldn't bother me in the least. I work for him, not the other way around."

"These things just aren't done," he insisted. "There are certain rules of professional courtesy and . . ."

I cut him short. We all knew damn well what was going on here. This guy was scared that his opinion wouldn't match Dr. Schneider's. He wanted to know what Robert's doctor had said before he would say anything. He was more concerned about covering his ass than he was about our son.

"I don't really care about professional courtesy," I said. "This is our son we're talking about." I barely kept the anger out of my voice. "We are the ones who have to make the decisions. We are the ones who need this information. We asked for this meeting. The only concern you should have at this moment is for Robert."

Dr. Parker shifted somewhat nervously. I'm sure he wasn't expecting any of this, and he clearly didn't know what to do. The rest of the room was dead silent.

"Of course, I'm concerned about your son," he began, "but it really would be best if Robert's doctor knew about this meeting."

I calmed down a bit. "If it will make you more comfortable," I said, choosing my words carefully, "I will call Dr. Schneider right now and let him know we are meeting." I had given the doctor an out.

"I think that's fine," he said.

We left a message with the doctor's secretary (it turns out he was unavailable anyway) and avoided disaster. Our meeting began in earnest. Despite our rocky start, it turned out that Dr. Parker was pleasant and extremely professional. Nothing he said surprised us. We had heard it all before, months ago, in fact, from Dr. Schneider. It didn't hurt any less hearing it again. Dr. Parker told us that Robert was an "extremely fragile" little boy. Robert was "anxious" and "nervous." He appeared "odd" when under stress. He could not maintain eye contact. He fidgeted, made faces (facial tics), and babbled on and on about nothing. He thought Robert had emotional problems. "Robert is not merely ADHD," Dr. Parker said.

We already knew that.

Dr. Parker also told us that Robert was "defenseless," and that he had yet to mature enough to deal with any unfairness or teasing that would undoubtedly come his way. Worse, he felt that Robert lacked the "emotional brakes" necessary to deal with everyday problems.

"Take, for example, the problems we had when we first started talking. I could tell you were angry, but you were able to maintain your calm and work out a solution. Your son could not have controlled himself," he said. "If your son were in a mainstream class of twenty-five to thirty kids, they'd eat him alive." Those were his exact words, and no one in the room disagreed with his evaluation.

He then told us that mainstreaming Robert was obviously out of the question. He said we needed to get Robert's anxiety under control.

"You know how horrible it is for an adult to feel anxious?" he asked. "Imagine how Robert must feel all the time. Now, you didn't tell me the second medication Robert's doctor prescribed, but I'm sure it is something along the lines of Prozac."

Very perceptive, I thought. "Yes, it is Prozac as a matter of fact."

"Well, then, I agree with him."

*   *   *

Once again, I felt trapped into giving Robert medication. My gut told me not to do it, but Tina and two highly respected child psychiatrists said it needed to be done. I had to admit it made sense. I certainly didn't want Robert to suffer. We wanted him to be happy. We also wanted Robert to be mainstreamed sooner rather than later. Besides, he was already on Ritalin, and although far from perfect, it had helped Robert in several areas. Of course, I kept remembering my brother.

We set up an appointment with Dr. Schneider. Dr. Schneider was genuinely excited to see us. There would be no fighting today, no convincing, no cajoling, and no manipulation. He knew why we had come. We had finally come around to his point of view. He asked about our meeting with Dr. Parker without the least bit of defensiveness or anger. He just seemed curious, and I think, quite frankly, he was thankful for anything that convinced us to follow his instructions.

Interestingly, it turned out that the two psychiatrists knew each other. Dr. Schneider informed us that Dr. Parker had taken part in several of his training programs. He praised Dr. Parker, and then noted, I thought somewhat proudly, that Dr. Parker had, over the years, begun to accept the broader use of medication to treat children. We related what Dr. Parker had told us, which was the same thing Dr. Schneider had been saying for months now.

"So," he said, "are you ready to take the next step forward?"

"Yes," I said with a feeling of total resignation.

Obviously sensing my misgivings, he told us again that Prozac was perfectly safe, and that he'd give it to his own children without hesitation. He then assured us that we were doing the right thing. "Robert has been gone over with a fine-toothed comb," he said. "He has undergone far more evaluation than most children, and everyone has come to the same conclusion. Most parents don't go through this—they get an opinion and go with it. You've checked and double-checked and triple-checked. This is the right thing to do. Besides, we're not marrying Robert to this medication. He'll use it for a while, and hopefully, with the proper reinforcements and behavior modification, Robert will be able to control his behavior and anxiety on his own. Worst case scenario, it doesn't work and we take him off of it."

The last thing I wanted to hear was the idea of it not working. But we had been down this road before. Dr. Schneider wrote the prescription and explained its dosage and administration. As we left, he said one more thing. "I'd advise you not to tell your relatives about this. It took both of you—two well-educated, highly involved, and well-read people—months to get used to this idea. I'm not sure your relatives, especially your parents, would be able to accept your decision."

Sound advice, I thought.

*   *   *

I mixed Robert's Prozac in his chocolate milk, telling Robert we were giving him a "special syrup" that would make his "special vitamin" work better. He was happy and excited at the idea. He asked to see the bottle.

"What's it called?" he asked.

"Prozac," I said. "P-r-o-z-a-c."

"What's my special vitamin called?"

"Ritalin. R-i-t-a-l-i-n."

The whole thing was becoming surreal. I was putting a psychotropic drug in my little boy's chocolate milk to counteract anxiety brought about, in large part, by another psychotropic drug. I wasn't at all happy about this, and yet, here I was teaching him how to pronounce and spell the names of his medications.

What a disaster. The Prozac did exactly what it was supposed to do, and we couldn't stand it. On the positive side, Robert was noticeably happier and much more outgoing. The silly awkwardness stopped, and he was clearly less anxious in new or stressful situations. He was more tolerant of those around him, even his sister. He was even more articulate, expressing his thoughts and feelings more readily and using more complex vocabulary. Even coupled with the Ritalin, however, he was totally out of control. He didn't listen. He didn't pay attention. He was completely uninhibited and impulsive. He could not be quiet. Worst of all, he had grown nasty. He talked back all the time. He was increasingly rude. He did things solely to annoy those around him. In a word, he had become obnoxious.

His behavior reports at school took a sudden and absolute nosedive. He did not listen to anyone. He was disruptive. If he did not get his way, he'd have full-blown fits, screaming and kicking. His schoolwork suffered noticeably. He wasn't paying attention in class. His work was sloppy, incomplete, and often wrong. He rushed through everything. Robert's teachers complained he was regressing. They didn't know what to do. They called us frequently.

It was like the old days, before Ritalin, except worse. Robert didn't seem to care what anyone thought of him or his behavior. Even I couldn't get him to listen. And if he was regressing, so was I. I talked to him. I tried to reason with him. I screamed at him. I punished him again and again. No matter how many toys I took away, no matter how many privileges he was denied, no matter how many times he was sent to a corner, nothing changed. My bursts of anger, coming all the more frequently now, would go almost unnoticed. It was so much water off a duck's back. To Robert, no one else even seemed to exist. Tina and I were ready to kill him.

We called Robert's psychiatrist. He was ecstatic with our report.

"What on Earth is there to be happy about?" I asked incredulously. "Robert's behavior is atrocious, he's doing poorly in school, his teachers all think he's regressing, and we're about to strangle him."

"The Prozac is doing exactly what it's supposed to do," he replied. "It's gotten Robert over his anxiety and inhibitions. Now we just have to get the attention deficit back under control." He told us to increase the Ritalin dosage.

We didn't want to increase it. We didn't want to create a balancing act between two opposing medications. The way we figured it, if the Prozac was causing problems, then we should reduce the Prozac. But having already committed to the Prozac, we didn't argue with him. We did as we were told. Even with the increase in Ritalin, though, Robert continued to misbehave, especially as the Ritalin wore off. Prozac was in his system, and affected Robert all the time, while Ritalin had an effect for only a few short hours. Even grouping the administration times of the Ritalin more closely together made little difference. The Prozac was overpowering.

*　　*　　*

Worse than when we had first learned of Robert's problems, worse than when Robert had begun taking Ritalin, this time was, without a doubt, the most difficult I had ever experienced dealing with Robert's situation. It hurt me to see how the medications completely dominated my son. Instead of merely aiding his ability to control himself, the two medications battled for dominance over his being. He bounced back and forth like a yo-yo, experiencing mood swings ranging anywhere from giddiness to rage. His entire personality was dictated by his medications, and we didn't like it.

It got to the point where we could not remember what Robert was like without medication. We weren't even sure what Robert was supposed to be like while on medication. We had lost sight of the real Robert. Moreover, Robert's mood swings and apparent setbacks hurt and frustrated me more than I can describe. I lost all perspective. I came down hard on Robert—unbelievably hard. I wanted—no, demanded—perfect behavior reports from school. I expected him to listen without any argument whatsoever. Robert was punished for every little misstep. I had lost all patience. I began to wonder how Robert could stand being with me.

Maybe it was because I knew Robert could behave better. After all, he had received perfect behavior reports consistently at school before the Prozac. Even at home, he had, on more than one occasion, done everything I had asked of him. I had seen the best in him, and maybe I was wrongly expecting it from him all the time. Or maybe I was just desperate to get Robert on track. I wanted him to be better. I wanted him out of special education. I wanted him closer to home. I wanted him to have friends.

Most likely, it was the fact that we had done something I had wanted to avoid at all costs. We had given Robert Prozac, and now I was panicking over our decision. I also was angry. I felt we had taken a big risk and I wanted a big payoff.

Tina couldn't take it anymore. Our entire family was breaking down right before her eyes. All our hard work was going down the drain. No more quiet time, no more reading, no more fun, just fighting. She was angry and upset with Robert, and she was angry and upset with me.

*   *   *

What was wrong with Robert? Why was this happening? Why were we being forced to put him, and ourselves, through all this? I wanted to crawl inside his head and make him better. I could no longer bear the severity of the matter. I broke down and cried. Until then, on some level, I'd just ignored what his doctors had said about how much help Robert needed, how hard the situation would be on all of us, how hard we would all have to work to help Robert have a "normal" childhood, how long it would take to get the results we wanted. I had refused to believe it. I'd held fast to the idea that any day Robert would be all right, that something would do the trick. But it just wasn't true. We had gone so far, done so much, and the truth was that we were no closer to finding an answer than we had been before the treatments started.

We tinkered with Robert's medication (this time with Dr. Schneider's aid), seeking an acceptable mix of Ritalin and Prozac. Eventually we came upon a combination that was livable, but it was far, far from perfect.

10

Deeper and Deeper

No longer sure if Robert's medication would ever really work, Tina and I pushed for behavior modification. We enrolled Robert in a socialization group specifically designed for ADD children. While he seemed to interact well during sessions, very few of the social skills he learned were carried beyond the confines of the group. More consistent socialization training was necessary. We explored the possibility of placing Robert in a different school, hopefully providing him with more suitable role models. Because the public and parochial school programs averaged twenty-five to thirty-five students per class, a situation that would be intolerable for Robert, we turned our collective attention to private schools.

Of course, private schools were very expensive, and, quite frankly, I wasn't sure how we would manage financially, especially if we were to enroll both Robert and Kat. We were always fearful that Kat would grow up thinking we didn't care as much about her as we did Robert. Robert always needed more attention. God knows, we gave Kat a lot of attention, too. We played games and drew pictures with her, read to her, and did her nails and makeup. She just loved that stuff—although she hated when I brushed her long, beautiful hair. I just wasn't very good with the knots. We also signed her up for skating, gymnastics, and piano classes. The last thing we wanted to do was to send our son to a private school and deny our daughter the same opportunity. We began contacting schools only to be disappointed time and again. Many were inappropriate for Robert, with too many children per class or relatively unstructured learning environments. Others simply turned us away once they heard about Robert's problems.

There was no point in trying to hide Robert's background. First, we were proud of all that Robert had accomplished over the past two years. Second, we were sure the private schools would eventually request Robert's records, which, of course, they did (so much for confidentiality). Third, it's not in our nature to be secretive or dishonest. Finally, what was the point? We wanted—no, needed—the help of a private school. How could Robert benefit from enrollment if we weren't sure it was the right school for him and if the school didn't know of Robert's needs?

We were shocked and frustrated by the constant rejection. Here was an extremely bright child with proven academic skills and demonstrable learning strengths whose two involved and caring parents were willing to pay top dollar for his education, yet no one wanted him. It made no sense to us, and it seemed so brutally unfair. We had done everything expected of us.

Robert worked hard to improve his behavior and ability to stay on task. We worked hard with him. We brought him to the best doctors we could find. We worked closely with those doctors as well as Robert's teachers. He made tremendous progress. We sought no charity. We sought no favoritism. We did not hide anything. All we wanted was the educational experience that Robert so rightly deserved. It was time for the system to work for us. It was time for the schools to step forward and lend us the help and expertise we required. There was only so much we could do on our own. We were not teachers; we were not educators. We needed a school's help, and expected it. It's a school's job to see to the education of our children, isn't it? That means all our children.

We were eventually directed to a school that looked like the one for Robert. We were very impressed with the school's staff and facilities. We spoke at length with the head of admissions and the headmaster about Robert. We told them that Robert was in a special education program, had attention problems, and was lagging in his social development. We also told them how bright Robert was, how affectionate and caring he was, and how far he had progressed over the past two years. I bragged about Robert's high IQ. I made sure they knew that, despite his problems, Robert had attained an orange belt in karate (his success in extracurricular activities continued) and had been doing quite well in his various sports programs. I even managed to mention that Robert was now taking piano lessons.

We explained that Robert needed a school that was academically challenging, since he was already multiple grade levels ahead in his studies. It was important that his teachers had time to focus his attention and guide his development. He needed good role models and tight direction. While we felt that special education had done wonders for him in the past, it was time for Robert to move on. Nevertheless, Robert still needed a nurturing, caring environment in which to grow. After all we'd been through, after coming so far, we didn't want to lose Robert now. Robert would be a challenging student, but he would be worth it.

The admissions officer and headmaster listened intently. They thought they might be able to help. They told us of their resource rooms designed to provide students with extra help and attention if they needed it. They told us of their successes with other children that had special concerns similar to Robert's. They told us how much they cared. But they made no promises. Robert would have to spend the day there and be interviewed and tested before they could decide upon his acceptance. They would also have to review Robert's school records.

We made the appropriate arrangements. Although Robert's admission was in no way assured, I felt confident they would accept him. "Finally," I thought, "we've found some place for Robert. No more searching, no more interviews, no more worrying. Maybe he's finally on the right track." I felt as though a huge burden had been lifted.

*　　　*　　　*

Devastated does not even begin to describe how we felt when the school rejected Robert. While the administration recognized Robert's intellectual ability and were impressed with us as parents (apparently we were under scrutiny as well), it felt Robert would dominate class time, thereby depriving the other children of their due attention. If Robert required less attention in the future, the school would reconsider his application.

Bitterness and frustration soon replaced the devastation. We had worked hard with Robert. We had been so tough on him. We had worked closely with the experts and had done what we were told. We had allowed Robert to be labeled. We had separated him into special education. We had instituted behavior management. We had placed Robert in counseling. We had medicated him. And Robert had worked so hard. We had endured so much, and had put poor Robert through so much just to make him acceptable to mainstream schools. Now they didn't want him.

How could the people at this private school have done this to us? Why had they acted as though they cared? Why had they boasted of their special resources? Why had they told us of their successes with other children like Robert only to reject him? How could they have so completely overlooked everything Robert had done—everything Robert had to offer?

How could they turn us away when we needed them so badly?

*   *   *

We later found out that the private school had requested that Robert's teacher and the class psychologist complete a questionnaire regarding Robert. We had not been aware of this request, nor had we been given the opportunity to review the completed questionnaire prior to its submission to the school. As a matter of fact, we found out about the questionnaire by accident after Robert's application had been rejected.

I requested a copy. It wasn't particularly complimentary, and it didn't tell the whole story. While recognizing Robert as a "sweet boy" who was "unusually thoughtful" of others and "very capable academically," Robert's teacher and the class psychologist repeatedly noted that Robert "perseverate[d] in monotone," "call[ed] out constantly," and was "socially unrelated."

They had not bothered to explain that Robert's tendency to repeat things in a monotone voice and his propensity for calling out were very recent phenomena that seemed to be directly related to the Prozac, a medication with which we had just started to experiment. Nor had they explained the constant commotion in the classroom. Nor had they explained the fact that Robert was surrounded by what they themselves referred to as "angry" children who could not sit still, who called each other names, and who had to be physically removed from the classroom on many occasions. They claimed that Robert had a problem socializing with his classmates, but they never bothered to point out that most of his classmates were emotionally, socially, or developmentally delayed. Indeed, few of his classmates were capable of socializing.

This was one mistake that we vowed would never happen again. No one would ever communicate his or her observations or opinions of Robert without our prior knowledge and approval. We would not hide or distort the truth about Robert, but we would never allow misleading information to be disseminated again. This was a rule we would have to enforce many times.

*   *   *

We were back to square one. We wanted Robert in an environment where he could learn how to socialize and interact better. The class he was in at present was not appropriate, but where were we to place him? Quite a hole had been dug as far as Robert's education was concerned, and we were holding the shovel. By placing him in special education, we had allowed the school district to label Robert "disabled." Our continuing efforts to find answers and treatments had merely ended up in a string of diagnoses of one psychological disorder after another, each of which was added to Robert's permanent records. The treatments with which we experimented had only led to more and more inconsistent behavior.

Logic dictated that the longer Robert remained in special education, the more severe the problems of his classmates would be. Children capable of being mainstreamed are eventually integrated into mainstream schools. Thus, we couldn't imagine that the special education classroom makeup was going to improve.

Special education had no more to offer Robert. Everyone, including his psychiatrist and his special education teacher, agreed he needed a good, caring, private school with appropriate role models to improve his social and emotional behavior. If his school reports did not improve, however, no private school would accept him. It was a catch-22. How could Robert's reports improve in the very environment in which he was now struggling to develop?

Obviously, we worried that the longer we left Robert in special education, the harder it would be to mainstream him. He might become accustomed to the restrictive environment, making it difficult, if not impossible, for him to adjust to a less restrictive mainstream school. Moreover, the expectations and demands placed upon special education children were lower than those placed upon mainstream children. After reviewing Robert's schoolwork, Tina grew particularly concerned about its simplicity. Was Robert really learning what his mainstream counterparts were learning? We came to believe that the longer Robert remained in special education, the more his curriculum would diverge from the mainstream. The road chosen for him would be very different from his mainstream peers.

Through our own painful experience, we were learning firsthand about one of the major problems with special education. An expert with a doctorate in special education once lamented to me that special education was always meant to be an interconnected, integral part of the mainstream, but it took on a life of its own, developing into a creature unto itself. Special education often does not function in conjunction with the mainstream, as originally intended. Instead, special education stands separate and apart. While special education serves an important purpose, it does so at the cost of segregating our children, often with detrimental results.[1]

This same expert also told me that our fears regarding Robert's future were not unfounded. She declared it a fact that the longer a child remains in special education, the less likely it is that he will be mainstreamed.[2] And let us not forget the possible (and probable) ostracism by mainstream students, many of whom still feel special education students are different, odd, or dumb. How would Robert react knowing that this was what others thought of him? This was not what we had in mind for our son. Our expectations for him were high—and, I believe, justifiably so. We were desperately trying to create a normal life for Robert, only to discover our efforts had trapped him elsewhere.

I contacted the chairperson of the local CSE and explained our quandary. She promised that she would attempt to piece together a special education class of high-functioning, better-behaved children for Robert at the school he was presently attending. I appreciated her concern, and did not doubt that she would attempt to deliver, but knew that if there were children who were better behaved than Robert, they wouldn't be in special education. She was not going to be able to create a class that would be satisfactory.

We continued to canvass private schools, although I had long since given up hope of acceptance.

*   *   *

In regard to Robert's medical treatment, we were trapped in a downward spiral. Still not happy with Prozac's effect on Robert, we complained to Dr. Schneider. In class, Robert still acted impulsively, frequently yelled out uncontrollably, and was often disruptive. At home, he was completely impulsive and incapable of listening once the Ritalin wore off and the Prozac held sway. To no one's surprise, Robert's doctor repeated his suggestion that Robert needed clonidine—a third medication to be used in conjunction with Ritalin and Prozac. The doctor again explained that clonidine seemed to enhance Ritalin's performance. But before he could prescribe clonidine, he would require a cardiogram from Robert. We asked why. In a perfectly matter-of-fact tone, he explained that there had been some heart failure-related deaths in children who had been taking clonidine in conjunction with other medications.[3] He hastened to add that there was no statistical evidence linking clonidine to these deaths, and noted that all the children had already had heart problems before taking clonidine. *Oh yeah, giving your children psychotropic drugs is just like giving insulin to a diabetic,* I thought to myself.

"If you're uncomfortable with clonidine, there is a similar drug called Tenex. There have been no problems reported with that," the doctor said.

I couldn't take it anymore. None of these medications had ever worked as they were supposed to work for Robert. Worse, Robert seemed to be prone to every "rare" side effect associated with the use of these medications. Now we were discussing a third medication to take care of a side effect of a second medication given to Robert to take care of a side effect of the first medication given to Robert?

"No," we said. "No, no, no, no. Why are we discussing a third medication? If Prozac's the problem, why don't we just take Robert off Prozac?"

I had never in my life been yelled at by a doctor until that moment. "You cannot take Robert off this medicine," he shouted. "He needs it. Robert is very sick. He has a brain disorder—a neurological problem that goes far beyond ADD or hyperactivity! Why do you fight with me? Why do you come to see me at all? It's so frustrating. Robert is a challenge and needs treatment! Just look at him! He is not doing well. Look at his progress reports. Even that private school rejected him!"

(He just had to throw that in.)

"His reports won't get better and no other school will take him the way he is!" he said. "Why won't you let me treat him? Why won't you let me give him the medication he needs? Why do you object to these medications so much?"

"Because he's just a six-year-old boy," I replied.

"A very sick six-year-old boy." He emphasized the word "sick." "He has serious neurological problems. This situation is not his fault or yours. Robert is not this way because you are bad parents or because of his diet or because of the environment. He has a physical problem that requires medication to treat. Anyone who doesn't believe that is naive and foolish. Don't deny your son the medication he needs."

The "naive and foolish" part had, of course, been directed at me.

*   *   *

The doctor was right to ask why we continued to seek his expertise only to reject his advice. It must have been frustrating. Why wouldn't we let him do his job? Didn't we trust him? Yes, we did. Did we think we knew better than he? Of course not. Were we merely disappointed in his answers, ignoring his advice until he told us what we wanted to hear? Disappointed, yes, but we were not ignoring him—not at our son's expense.

What was the problem? Why were we so strongly opposed to this course of action? Why were we forcing the doctor to bully us into submission? I suppose part of my reluctance to the use of medication was the abdication of control over our son. We knew nothing about the medication. We didn't understand how it worked. We didn't know exactly what it was doing or what long-term effects it might have. Moreover, once Robert started down this road, his future would be dictated by the doctor, not by us. We would no longer be able to make crucial decisions—we would have to rely on the doctor's expertise. We would have to wholeheartedly trust his judgment and follow his directives.

I never wanted to relinquish that control. Robert was my son. And, of course, there was always the uncertainty. I never doubted that Robert's doctor truly believed multiple-drug therapy was best course of action for Robert. I never questioned his sincerity, motivation, or expertise. But how could he be so damn sure? *He's guessing, just like the rest of us,* I thought. I'm sure his guesses were highly informed and educated, but the bottom line was he was experimenting with different medications and dosages, and didn't know, and couldn't know, what would prove effective or what the long-term effects might be.

Dr. Schneider even admitted it wasn't an exact science; it would take experimentation to discover what would work. We had already tinkered with Ritalin, experimented with Prozac, tried Dexedrine (a one-week trial from Hell), and considered clonidine and Tenex. Despite his confidence and knowledge of what a particular drug was supposed to do, his theories and reality often diverged.

I could not ignore my gut. I truly felt as though I had hit a wall and could go no further down this path. Tina and I were clearly at a critical juncture in our relationship with Robert's doctor; one that I knew would define Robert's treatment from then on. It was much more difficult than I had imagined or care to admit, but we stood our ground. Despite this world-renowned expert's opinion, we could not allow Robert to take a third medication. But what were the alternatives? Ritalin by itself was not acceptable. Dexedrine produced more side effects than Ritalin, and Ritalin and Prozac together had proved intolerable. I timidly made a suggestion. "Instead of adding a third drug to the mix, why not change the medication that seems to be causing the problem?" I said. "Can't we give Robert something similar to Prozac that maybe won't have the undesirable side effects?"

"Well," said the psychiatrist, calming down, "there is a drug called Luvox that is used a lot in Europe and has proved effective in treating problems like Robert's. It's not nearly as widely used as Prozac, though—it doesn't have the same track record. Also, it does not come in liquid form, so it will be harder to measure exact dosages. You'll have to split pills."

I didn't care. We didn't like the Prozac. Luvox couldn't be any worse. And we had already been splitting Robert's Ritalin tablets to get the right dosage. Besides, in my mind, anything was better than giving Robert yet another medication.

Robert got a cardiogram, just to be on the safe side, and we switched to Luvox. I promised Robert's doctor that we'd keep the bottle of Prozac. ("Perhaps Tina and I will end up taking it," I joked.) We would also consider Tenex, if necessary.

* * *

Robert's behavior improved dramatically once he was taken off Prozac. He was not nearly as sensitive to the new medication, nor did he suffer from the impulsiveness he had experienced while taking Prozac. Nevertheless, while the results we obtained with Luvox were certainly better, they were far from perfect. We found ourselves constantly tinkering with the timing and dosages of Luvox and Ritalin in an attempt to find an acceptable mix.

The whole medication issue took an interesting twist when we "lost" Robert's psychiatrist. He wrote a book, got a new position, and left his local practice. He immediately referred us to another doctor in his office. I later found out that he had offered at least some of his patients the opportunity to continue with him. No such offer had been extended to us. We didn't even get a copy of his book. His last communication to us was a letter that accompanied Robert's latest prescription. He wrote, "Robert should be seen more regularly."

*   *   *

We tried our hardest but were unable to enroll Robert in private school. Although he interviewed and tested well, Robert's background and idiosyncrasies led school after school to reject his applications. Despite his gifts, despite his talents, no mainstream private school would admit our son. Thus, when Robert's CSE meeting eventually came, we knew we had little to choose from as far as placement was concerned.

Present at the meeting were the chairperson, the local school psychologist who had attended Robert's last CSE meeting (I don't mind saying that I was awfully glad she was there), a special education teacher from our district, and the parent member. Robert's teacher and the school psychologist would be included by telephone conferencing.

At first, the committee did not seem disposed to giving us a choice concerning Robert's placement. Based upon its site review of Robert (members of the committee had actually visited Robert in the classroom) and his teacher's and the school psychologist's reports (also prepared months before), the committee was going to recommend that Robert remain where he was—in the fully restrictive environment of the special education school outside our district. The committee members viewed Robert as a very bright boy with attention and impulse problems, social problems, and now an "aggressive" streak.

This time we were there to set the record straight. We admitted that Robert had experienced tantrums and impulse problems at the time they had seen him. But hadn't anyone at the school explained that it these behaviors were short-lived phenomena caused by Robert's adverse reaction to Prozac? Apparently not. In fact, the committee didn't even know that Robert had been placed on a second medication. We asked the committee to ask Robert's teacher about his recent behavior now that he was on Luvox. We also explained that Robert's lack of social interaction with his classmates was not surprising given his classmates' behavior. Moreover, Tina told the committee that Robert had been getting along unusually well with a new child in the class (the new child was clearly headed for mainstreaming and quite well behaved). As for the "aggressive" label, I noted that once, when Robert was first on Prozac and subject to tantrums, he had said something that would end up branding him with this completely unfair description. The night before it happened, Robert had been playing a video game with his older cousins. In this video game, one of the characters is told to kill his opponent by "ripping his heart out." Robert, angered by the behavior of one of his classmates, ended up uttering this line in class the next day. It was the first and last time he would ever say it. He had not touched or attempted to touch his classmate. It had been the first time this particular school psychologist was called upon to intervene with respect to Robert, and she had heard Robert say this phrase. The damage had been done.

Although Robert never acted in that manner or uttered those words again, or was asked to see this psychologist again, whenever this psychologist was asked to discuss Robert, this story was the first thing she mentioned. Thus, people got the impression that this was what Robert was like all the time.

I explained the whole story to the committee. I wasn't sure they believed me. Then the conference call began. The committee members asked if Robert had been on Prozac when they had visited.

"Yes, he had been," was the reply.

They asked if Robert's behavior had improved since the switch to Luvox.

"As a matter of fact, it has."

"Is Robert more social given the change in medication?"

"Now that you mention it, he is—especially with a new boy in the class. He gets along great with him."

The committee members gave us knowing nods. But the best was yet to come.

"What about the tantrums? Have they stopped?"

"Yes," said the psychologist. "But there was one episode where Robert was enraged completely out of proportion to the situation."

I looked around the table, put my hands in the air, and calmly announced, "Here it comes." And it did.

The committee members could not help but smile.

"Has Robert ever done anything like that again?"

"No. As a matter of fact, except for that incident, I have never been called upon in connection with him again."

Unbelievable, I thought to myself. *What makes these people say what they say? They're supposed to be helping, but their casual approach to the facts is killing us.*

What would the CSE have thought of our son had we not been able to attend the meeting? Well, we were there, and the CSE would learn how well Robert had been doing. The only question that would remain: What do we do with him?

The committee asked if the psychologist had been able to find more appropriate classmates for Robert at the school.

"No. Not really."

We were asked if we wanted to keep Robert there under the circumstances.

"No," we answered. "We want him closer to home. We want him to have friends in the neighborhood, and we can't stand the bus ride anymore. The longer he's in that school, the harder it's going to be to mainstream him. We just don't think the school has anymore to offer him."

The committee members nodded in agreement. The chairperson asked Robert's teacher and the school psychologist whether they thought Robert could return to district in an academically based special education class with an aide assigned solely to him.

"Yes."

The committee members thanked them and hung up the phone.

"What do you think?" they asked us.

We weren't thrilled with the idea of special education in district. We had seen the class, and Robert was well ahead of those students academically. On the other hand, they were good kids and quite well behaved. We were also concerned about the fact that it wasn't Robert's "home" school, although the school under discussion was in district. In a way, it seemed worse to us—Robert would now be only a few blocks away from the school to which the neighborhood kids went, including his sister. So close, yet so far.

We asked about the possibility of mainstreaming Robert at his home school with an aide assigned solely to him. The chairperson frowned.

"Robert's presently in a very restrictive environment. I'd be afraid to go from a class with one teacher, eight students, and two or three aides to a classroom with one teacher and twenty five or thirty mainstream students, whether or not Robert had an aide assigned solely to him."

We weren't convinced this proposal was best for Robert, but the psychologist on the committee put it in perspective for us. "Clearly, the school across town has nothing better to offer. And if Robert continues to excel academically, he'll continue to be taught at his own pace, just as he is now. It's a very academically based program. And the kids in his class are terrific. If that's what you want Robert to be around, it's right here. I know it's not perfect, but your son is unique. It's the best we have, and wouldn't it better than sending him back?"

We had to agree, it would be.

"Besides," added the chairperson, "if Robert keeps making progress and keeps learning at the same pace, he'll be out of special ed. As you know, we can offer special services only to children who have problems learning. It doesn't seem like Robert does—but I recognize that he is learning in a very restrictive environment. Let's see how he does outside it before we think about mainstreaming."

11

Enough Is Enough

Despite Robert's continued progress, we still weren't satisfied with his medications. Nothing really worked the way it was supposed to, Robert still suffered side effects, and quite frankly, we continued to be fearful of the long-term effects these medications might have on him. It was all so aggravating. Well, they say necessity is the mother of invention, and I, for one, felt it was time to be inventive. I began to consider alternative treatments.

I must admit, my sister, Chris, had urged us to explore alternative therapies well before this time, but we had been reluctant to do so. I was used to and comfortable with medical doctors—people who wore white lab coats and had degrees from prestigious institutions. More importantly, I wanted quick, predictable, reliable results. I did not want to stray from the beaten path. I did not want to experiment. But it was obvious that what I had considered standard, established courses of treatment were not working. Moreover, I knew that the doctors were, for all intents and purposes, experimenting on my son. In fact, it would be hard to characterize Robert's treatment to date as established, predictable, or reliable.

Other parents told me the wonderful results they experienced through alternative therapies. It seemed every time I turned on the radio or read a newspaper or magazine, nutrition, homeopathy, biofeedback, touch therapy, and other forms of healing were being discussed in connection with the treatment of hyperactivity, ADD, and autism. I was bombarded with descriptions of children who sounded like carbon copies of Robert, cured through special diets. I learned of radical improvement in the behavior of children through biofeedback monitoring and touch. I was growing acutely aware of a movement by doctors and parents who were rejecting the use of drugs to treat children like Robert.

Was someone trying to tell me something? I couldn't help but listen. I began my research, concentrating on homeopathy and nutritional guidance. I was particularly intrigued by a theory linking food aversions, allergies, and sensitivities to conditions such as hyperactivity and ADD. Tina was hesitant. She was not sure that such treatments would have any noticeable impact on Robert's condition, and she did not want to subject Robert to testing and treatments that offered little hope of success. I am also sure she thought this change in approach was a desperate act by a desperate parent. I wouldn't have disagreed with her.

There were many that sided with Tina. Several allergists I consulted thought it was a complete waste of time and money. "Surely, if your son was allergic to food, you'd know about it," they said. "Besides, all allergies have a definitive physical manifestation—sneezing, hives, that sort of thing. It doesn't sound like your son has any."

Other doctors, including pediatricians, psychiatrists, and psychologists, agreed. They were unaware of any studies that showed a definite link between nutrition and the behavioral problems Robert was experiencing. Placing Robert on a restrictive diet could do more harm than good, they warned me. On the other hand, there were those who thought we should try. Some allergists I spoke with were intrigued with the theory, and while they did not altogether ascribe to it, they were willing to run the necessary tests. I came across book after book that claimed to have documented links between certain types of food and resultant physical, emotional, and psychological ailments.

Clearly, there was a difference of opinion. I suppose it is more accurate to say there was a definitive clash of ideologies. "To whom should we turn?" we asked. The answer was obvious: to ourselves. Indeed, if I take nothing else away from this entire experience, it is the knowledge that Tina and I could and did make good decisions. At the very least, we knew we had never hurt our son's progress, and, in many ways, we had helped it along. Our confidence in ourselves was growing, just as our confidence in Robert was growing.

Off I went to the library and bookstore to read what I could about nutritional treatment and homeopathy. I also spoke with individuals who used such therapies. The more I learned, the more these practices made sense. Despite what Dr. Schneider had told us, how could there not be a link between diet and health? After all, we are what we eat. Everyone knows that certain foods can affect an individual's body in obvious and sometimes severe ways. Take the effects of caffeine, for example. And what about the effects of liquor? And what about the "energy" foods that runners and athletes consume?

Perhaps more to the point, no one would dispute the idea that people with high blood pressure or diabetes or high cholesterol must carefully monitor what they eat. So, too, must those who have allergic reactions to various foods. Thus, there can be no debate that what we eat most certainly has an impact on our bodies—at least from the neck down. But, isn't the brain part of our body as well?

What about the body's hormones and the glands that produce them? What about neurotransmitters, the chemical conductors in our brains? Why wouldn't each of our amazingly complex organs and systems be affected by what we eat? Indeed, how could they not be affected by what we eat? Haven't we all eaten stuff that just doesn't agree with us? Didn't we feel rotten afterwards?

Not even addressing the possibility of a food or substance directly interfering with or adversely modifying hormone levels or brain function, even something as seemingly minor as a subtle, undefined physical irritant might eventually have a detrimental effect on behavior. Imagine being a child and always feeling uncomfortable.

What did we have to lose? If we were not happy about medicating Robert, what other options were available? If there was a chance that a more natural form of healing could work, what could be the harm? Even Robert's new psychiatrist, whom we will call Dr. Lampman, agreed. He had heard that nutritional guidance had worked for some individuals. He thought it certainly was worth a try.

*　　　*　　　*

Through networking and referrals, we found a homeopathic doctor named Kamau Kokayi, MD, who worked closely with a nutritionist, Corinne Furnari. I spoke with Dr. Kokayi over the phone. Dr. Kokayi explained that homeopathy is based upon "remedies," medicines of a sort derived from natural sources, which stimulate the body's own healing processes. It sounded like allergy shots or inoculations designed to prepare the body's defenses against future attacks. Homeopathic doctors have a record of which remedies are effective with respect to given symptoms. The doctor told me he had had some success with children like Robert, although he obviously could not promise anything. In addition, he informed me that he obtained much better results when he worked in conjunction with the nutritionist in his office.

While the set-up sounded ideal, and the approach sounded logical, I still did not fully understand how or why homeopathy worked. When pressed, Dr. Kokayi could not really explain how or why it worked, either. But he assured me it did. This lack of explanation and assurance is no different from what we got from the medical doctors we had consulted, by the way. Regarding the treatment of psychiatric disorders with psychotropic medications, a psychiatrist once wrote, "[Doctors] don't know precisely why these medicines work. We just know that they do work. That's nothing new to medicine, of course."[1]

I decided to assume a pragmatic attitude and give alternative therapy a shot.

*   *   *

When my sister and I met with Dr. Kokayi (Tina refused to see him), he asked what Robert was like. He didn't want to examine Robert—instead, he wanted to know what our concerns were. Not interested in Robert's previous medical diagnoses, he was interested in hearing about Robert's sensitivity, his impulsiveness, his habit of making odd noises, and the self-generated sound effects that accompanied most of Robert's actions. He wanted to know about Robert's dreams, his restless sleep, and his disposition. He wanted to know how Robert interacted with those around him, his habits, and his hobbies.

We talked for the better part of an hour. At the end of the session, he told me he was having difficulty finding an established pattern of symptoms into which Robert truly fit. "Join the club," I said. "Robert is unique. Everyone who has treated him has said so."

He said he'd call me in a week with a recommended remedy. In the meantime, Robert was to continue on his prescribed medications.

We also met with Corinne that day. She, too, wanted to know about Robert. She was particularly interested in Robert's constant ear infections and the steady course of antibiotics he had been fed as an infant and as a toddler. Although it was too soon to come to any conclusions, she informed us that chronic infections are often associated with a food allergy or intolerance. In particular, ear infections are often associated with intolerance to dairy products. It seems that dairy products increase mucous production—even in people who do not have any particular sensitivity to dairy. For those who do have a problem with dairy, however, dairy triggers a sort of internal allergic reaction that, over time, weakens the immune system. Childhood ear infections could result.

This increased mucous production in the ears, coupled with a Eustachian tube that is not at the best angle to drain the fluids (small children's Eustachian tubes are angled out to the sides, not down, as they are in adults), creates a perfect breeding ground for bacteria. Combine this bacteria with a weakened immune system and voilà, you have an ear infection. It's an often overlooked cycle.

Corinne also noted that prolonged use of antibiotics could have long-term adverse effects upon the digestive system. Although such damage can be subtle in a physical sense, it can have dramatic consequences. In particular, she was concerned that certain "good" bacteria essential to vitamin production and effective digestion of food had been destroyed and displaced by "unproductive" bacteria, thus robbing Robert of nutrients necessary for proper neurological development. In the future, she told us, if Robert were to have any recurring infections of any type, we should carefully examine his diet to determine the cause. In addition, we should no longer give Robert antibiotics unless absolutely necessary. Corinne informed us that Dr. Kokayi could recommend highly effective herbal remedies instead.

Corinne ran a battery of tests on Robert. She took blood, urine, saliva, and hair samples. She explained that these would be tested for abnormalities, imbalances, and possible allergic reactions. She also explained that much of the testing would be focused on pinpointing certain nutritional deficiencies, which, when discovered in younger children, were indicative of future problems, including autism, developmental disorders, and attention problems. She had no doubt that antibiotics had somehow robbed Robert of the ability to digest certain foods properly, and that, as a result, Robert had problems producing the nutrients essential to his development. We were, unfortunately, only now seeing the impact of such problems.

Until the tests came back, Corinne could not be certain what sort of deficiencies Robert had, nor did she know exactly which foods were triggering the infections. Thus, for the time being, she wanted to employ a "shotgun" approach to treating Robert—she wanted to remove from Robert's diet anything to which he might be allergic. Foods that had a reputation for being allergens were to be eliminated, including all dairy products, all grains (except rice), preservatives, additives, and dyes. In addition, she wanted Robert to start eating organic food. She also told me that it would be best for Robert if the whole family followed this diet, since he would accept it much more readily if we did so. "Besides," she said, "it's actually an excellent diet for anyone to be on."

I began to wonder if this was such a good idea.

*   *   *

Despite Tina's misgivings, to her credit, she was willing to give this method a try. We began the new diet immediately. It was difficult, but not as difficult as one might imagine. Of course, we had to clean out the pantry. I got choked up as we threw away my chocolate chip cookies, but we were doing it for our son, after all.

There were many stores, including some national supermarket chains, which stocked organic food. Moreover, the food substitutes we found were adequate, although they would take some getting used to. We bought rice and soy milk instead of cow's milk. Instead of ice cream, we ate a product called "Rice Dream" (the chocolate flavor wasn't bad at all). We ate rice-based pastas, rice bread, and oat bread. The Italian in me didn't like the rice pasta too much, so we compromised; we found excellent pasta made from a mixture of wheat and artichoke. The bread was good, too.

Although they were slightly more expensive and less convenient to find, organic meats and produce (no hormones, additives, or preservatives) made their way to our dinner table without incident. In fact, the organic food seemed fresher and tasted better. Finally, cookies, candy, and junk food were discarded (whole boxes straight from the pantry to the trash—ugh) in favor of fruit, nuts, and rice cakes. I never got used to the rice cakes.

We were concerned whether Robert was getting enough calcium now that he was off dairy products. I had always been a big believer in lots of good, cold whole milk. Now we weren't allowed to have any. Corinne assured us that Robert would get more than enough calcium from eating dark, leafy vegetables. "Where do you think animals get calcium? Certainly not from cow's milk," she said. Moreover, Robert's vitamins would have calcium, and if we really wanted to be safe, we could purchase juice supplemented with calcium. (As it turned out, Corinne was right. When Robert was tested a few months later, his calcium levels were higher than average.)

Less than two weeks later, everyone in the family went through withdrawal and regression. No one felt "right," and we were all getting headaches (even my daughter) reminiscent of those I got when I stopped drinking caffeine. I began to wonder what was in the food we used to eat that would cause such a reaction.

Shortly thereafter, Robert went into total regression with respect to his behavior. He became moody, impulsive, and misbehaved constantly. Corinne had warned us this would happen. She said that Robert's body had gotten used to eating certain things. When deprived of those things, there would be a reaction. She said things would get worse before they got better.

They got worse. We took it as a good sign. Until then, we hadn't been sure that anything would happen. The fact that something was happening, even if it wasn't what we wanted, was reason to believe that nutrition might actually make a difference.

Another week or so passed, and we all started feeling better. Much better. Robert, in particular, began doing well in his summer program again. At home, his behavior was much more level. It was right around this time that we administered the homeopathic remedy. With all credit to Dr. Kokayi, he had delivered the remedy within a week as promised. Given Robert's reaction to the new diet, however, we decided to wait until things settled down before we introduced something new.

The remedy came in the form of tiny sugar capsules that contained the "molecular extract" of a plant of which we had never heard. More specifically, the remedy was the result of a succession of dilutions. The plant extract was diluted with "x" parts of water. Part of the subsequent solution was then diluted with "x" parts of water. This process of dilution was repeated until little, if any, of the original plant extract actually remained. Robert took ten of these tiny pills in the morning and ten at night. That was it.

We watched and waited. Again, after two to three weeks, Robert regressed, although it was much more subtle this time. The doctor had told us it would happen. Again, we took it as a good sign. Then Robert got better. Again, it was quite subtle, but encouraging nonetheless.

*   *   *

Robert's test results came back. Corinne noted significant vitamin and mineral deficiencies that, not surprisingly to her, were associated with the body's digestive system as well as a person's mental well-being. Specifically, she hypothesized that Robert's ability to properly digest food, and therefore to extract the nutrients he needed for proper neurological development, had been compromised by the extensive use of antibiotics. She theorized that antibiotics had destroyed much of Robert's "good" bacteria—bacteria that produce minute but essential amounts of nutrients vital to neurological development. As a result, we had to fix Robert's gut. He was to begin taking live bacteria (acidophilus—

designed to restore his digestive system) and digestive aids, including hydrochloric acid (HCL) and pancreatic enzymes.

Of course, we also had to address the discovered deficiencies. Robert's diet was to be supplemented with multivitamins and various supplements such as flax oil, essential fatty acids docosahezaenoic acid (DHA) and eicosapentaenoic acid (EPA), and a host of amino acids, including glutamine, tryptophan, and tyrosine.[2] This treatment was not easy initially. First, maintaining our restricted diet was difficult, especially given the constant suggestions for and easy availability of forbidden foods. Try explaining to your kids why Happy Meals are out of the question, pizza is off the menu, and a trip to the ice cream shop is nothing more than a pleasant memory.

Administering Robert's supplements was also a lot of trouble, as Robert had not yet learned how to swallow pills. Instead, we had to open capsules or crush tablets into juice and then blend a special concoction for him. Unlike the drugs Robert had taken, which had had demonstrable effects within minutes, homeopathy and nutrition would take weeks, if not months, before any truly noticeable results could be seen. We had to be patient.

Despite these problems, we felt good about what we were doing. In time, we grew to enjoy the new regimen. It was a worthy challenge. We even felt empowered by it. We had learned so much about these alternative treatments—far more than Robert's conventional doctors knew, and far more than Robert's teachers knew. In fact, Tina enjoyed a complete turnaround in attitude, becoming an expert on the nutritional front. She learned the general breakdown of foods, the vitamins and minerals contained therein, and the physical and psychological effects such foods are supposed to have. She educated herself on vitamins and supplements. She took the lead when we visited Corinne, and dictated what the rest of the family should take by way of vitamins and supplements.

Such knowledge gave us greater confidence to make decisions concerning our son's treatment. We had regained a large measure of control over our son's future. Our family grew closer together by taking part in the same program. The children even began to reject offers of foods that they knew they weren't supposed to eat. On several occasions, we received phone calls from Robert's teacher asking whether Robert could have a slice of pizza or a piece of candy at one of the children's birthday parties—the call being made at Robert's insistence. It all felt so right.

Imagine how great we felt when we realized the therapy was working. We began to notice that Robert's Ritalin and Luvox were having a much greater effect on him, although we had not altered any of the dosages. In particular, we observed that Robert was behaving as he had when he was taking Ritalin in far greater dosages. We reduced the dosage of Ritalin. We also noticed that Luvox was making him increasingly impulsive. Again, this was a side effect we had associated only with higher dosages. We reduced the dosage of Luvox to almost nothing. With Robert now taking much less Ritalin, even the minute amount of Luvox he was taking seemed too much. We wanted to take Robert off Luvox completely. We contacted Dr. Lampman. He was fascinated by what we told him and concurred with our decision.

We took Robert off Luvox completely, and reduced Robert's Ritalin dosage even more. Over a 70-percent reduction had taken place and he was doing great! Excited by these developments, we continued the nutrition and vitamin therapy, as well as the homeopathy. Further testing revealed that Robert was deficient in other vitamins, minerals, and amino acids reported to produce the same effects as the medications that had previously been prescribed for Robert. We further supplemented his diet with vitamins such as B_{12} and C, and minerals such as manganese, magnesium, and lithium. Robert's vitamin drink looked disgusting, but he drank it.

I drank it, too. Actually, I would make us each a "special drink." We'd clink our glasses together and gulp down every last drop. Each of us (including my daughter) took our prescribed vitamins. I've got to tell you, I felt better myself. After six months, Robert's activity levels had decreased dramatically and his anxiety had greatly lessened. Although focus and motivation remained problematic, even his skills in these areas improved a bit. In fact, we began letting Robert participate in his extracurricular activities without any medication whatsoever.

He participated—not as attentively as he had before—in these activities without disruption. At home, on vacation, at summer camp, in his extracurricular activities, Robert was never medicated anymore, and he did fine—not perfect (far from it) or nearly what we hoped for, but fine. It should also be noted that Robert did not have a single ear infection after quitting dairy products. That, in and of itself, was worth the price of admission.

Our family life improved. In fact, we began to enjoy what I imagined to be a more normal family environment. Properly motivated, Robert began to listen to us (as well as a little boy can listen, and certainly no less than his sister), his temperament became more even, and he interacted better with those around him. He even began to make some eye contact, and the self-generated sound effects that used to accompany his every action lessened and practically disappeared. We started to go out more, to restaurants, to museums, to the movies. And, except for the obligatory trip to the rest room, he was usually able to sit through dinner or a show.

*   *   *

Had Robert really improved so dramatically or were we just imaging things? No, too many people who had known Robert over the years noticed a definite, positive change in him. Corinne said she was treating a "completely different" child now. Our relatives raved about how well behaved Robert was and what a pleasure it was to take him for the day. Joanne, Robert's babysitter, called the change a "miracle."

Perhaps most telling was our visit with Dr. Lampman. He could not stop talking about how Robert had improved—how Robert stayed on subject longer, how Robert waited for the doctor to finish speaking, how Robert stayed with the conversation, listened, and responded appropriately to what the doctor had to say.

"Whatever you're doing," he said, "keep it up."

*   *   *

Robert was doing much better than he had ever done before, but issues still existed. Robert had difficulty adjusting to his new class, and despite some improvement, his ability to concentrate and remain on task was still relatively weak. Thus, we continued to give Robert small doses of Ritalin during school hours. We did try, though, on several different occasions, to send Robert to school without Ritalin. Although the majority of the bad side effects, including the facial tic and the hypersensitivity to noise, had disappeared, Robert still suffered from terrible rebounds when the Ritalin began to wear off. He would become very emotional, and the hyperactivity and jumpiness we had worked so hard to eliminate through diet would come back with a vengeance.

While his aide thought his behavior and concentration level were acceptable when Robert was off Ritalin, boy did we get an earful from the school psychologist, whom we will call Dr. Johnson, and, to a lesser extent, Robert's second-grade teacher. Apparently, Robert was much easier to handle when he was on Ritalin. And there is no doubt that his concentration and performance were enhanced by the medication. According to Dr. Johnson, Robert's behavior was also much more "appropriate" when he was medicated. Robert's teacher somewhat sheepishly agreed. Given the results she had observed, Dr. Johnson could not understand why we would even think twice about giving Robert Ritalin.

We tried to explain how far Robert had come. We told her about how bad the rebounds were. We tried to explain how great Robert was on the weekends, but I don't think she got it. While we were not exactly sure why Robert still had trouble in school, we suspected there was just too much stimulus in the classroom. So, again, we took the practical route. Although we were not happy medicating Robert, if it made things better for him, we would continue to use Ritalin. At least we knew we had managed to reduce the dosage dramatically, which lessened most of the side effects, and had removed Robert's need for additional medications.

Of course, we could not cease being vigilant where Robert's education was concerned. We were still anxious to see him mainstreamed. Although we suggested placing Robert in at least one academic mainstream class, the school officials and the CSE thought it was a bad idea. It was a new school and a new class. Let's not overload him, they argued. Besides, they explained that Robert would begin the mainstreaming process through nonacademic classes. Specifically, Robert would attend mainstream art, music, and physical education classes. Such classes were referred to by the school's administration as "specials."

We agreed with this approach. It made sense to ease Robert into it. Robert, however, soon began to act out in his "specials." He complained about attending them, but he never told us why. "I just don't like them," he would say.

We grew worried. Maybe, Robert wasn't ready for mainstreaming. We met with Robert's physical education teacher. How bad was it? Why was Robert misbehaving? Why was he complaining? What could we do? She told us that Robert was indeed having trouble; he could not keep up with the other children. She was surprised to hear that Robert did karate and hockey. She was even more surprised to hear that he was almost competent at both. Now, we knew Robert was not the best athlete, but was he really that bad in gym?

Apparently he was. At some point in our discussion, the physical education teacher asked Robert's age. We told her he was just seven. The shock on her face was evident. "He's so big!" she said. "I thought he was eight or nine! No wonder he's having so much trouble. You know, he's in with third- and fourth-graders."

No, we didn't know. No wonder he could not keep up with the other children. No wonder he was so miserable. You had a child who, chronologically, was a first or second grader (in other districts, Robert would have been in first grade; in our district, however, he was in second). Moreover, he was, by all accounts, immature socially and physically, even by second-grade standards. And despite our efforts, he was still fairly clumsy. Why, then, had he been placed in a mainstream class of twenty-five to thirty children who were in third and fourth grade—children with whom he had nothing in common—in classes in which he could not possibly keep up?

We immediately contacted the principal. He, in turn, spoke to Robert's classroom teacher and the "specials" teachers. Robert was transferred to the first- and second-grade "specials" the next day. Robert's behavior in his "specials" improved immediately.

Never a dull moment.

*　　　*　　　*

The following year, when Robert began third grade, we began the slow process of mainstreaming in earnest. It had been agreed upon that Robert should be mainstreamed into at least one academic class. If he did well, he would continue to be mainstreamed one class at a time. Reading was chosen. We would have picked math, but Robert was too advanced for the mainstream math class. Robert would continue to be taught math and spelling at his own pace by himself, while he would learn social studies and science in a group setting in his special education class.

This worked out fine for a while, and we would not have pushed for further mainstreaming but for the fact that Robert's homework in science and social studies was quite simplistic and repetitive. We had yet another meeting with his teacher and Dr. Johnson to discuss the matter. "Why isn't Robert being challenged in these areas?" we asked.

They explained that Robert was learning the same substantive areas in science and social studies as the mainstream students, but because the mainstream teaching materials were a bit too difficult for some of his classmates to comprehend and use effectively, his teacher chose to use the more simplistic handouts. Tina didn't take this well at all. "Why not teach him science and social studies individually—just like math and spelling?" she asked.

"Science and social studies are not really appropriate subjects for individual instruction," they replied.

"But Robert can understand the mainstream text, can't he?" Tina rightly asked.

"Without question," they answered.

"I'm sorry," Tina said, "but this is unacceptable." She explained that Robert was completely bored by the handouts. They were busy work—a waste of time. Besides, we didn't want Robert to fall behind the mainstream students.

There wasn't anything they could do, they said, unless we wanted to mainstream Robert in additional areas. There really wasn't much debate on this point. The latest series of events only reinforced our growing dissatisfaction with the special education system. More than ever, we wanted Robert mainstreamed as soon as possible. We were disappointed to discover that Robert was not using mainstream learning materials when it was readily obvious to all involved that he could and should be using them. Instead, he was being relegated to simplistic, repetitive materials that clearly failed to spark his interest. It was obvious to us that the special education class was no longer meeting Robert's individual needs; it was now holding him back.

We discussed the issue with the principal and made arrangements for further mainstreaming. Robert would be mainstreamed in science and writing composition in addition to reading. This meant Robert would be in the mainstream classroom for over half the day. Of course, his aide would accompany him.

We spoke to Robert about his new schedule. He was not happy. He did not want to go. His reaction only confirmed another of my fears. It seemed that Robert had grown used to his special education class. He was now afraid to be away from it. It was then that we had the discussion we had been avoiding. It was time to be frank with Robert. We had to explain to him that we really did not want him in special education. We would have to tell him why.

We stressed how very proud we were that he was doing so well in school. We told him it was a hard-earned honor to be moving into the mainstream class. We explained that we wanted him to be in the mainstream class, and more importantly, it was where he should want to be. We explained that the children in his special education class were in that class because they needed extra help with their studies. Some children needed extra help with their reading. Some children didn't add numbers very well or did not understand multiplication without extra help. "There is nothing wrong with being in special education," we explained. "It's just that some kids need extra help. That's just the way it is," we said. We then explained why he had been in special education.

"Even you needed some help," I said. "You sometimes have trouble concentrating and paying attention—that's why you take your special vitamin, right?"

"And sometimes I call out a lot, too, right?" he said to me.

"Yes," I smiled. "Sometimes you do. You've got so much going on in that head of yours, so many ideas, that sometimes you can't contain yourself. I love you for it, but sometimes you don't pay attention to what people are trying to teach you. But you've gotten much better. Now you don't need so much help. That's why everyone wants you to be in the other classroom more often."

"It'll be harder," he complained.

"Maybe," I said, "but I doubt it. Not for someone as smart as you. Besides, you'll see your friends a lot during the day. It will be great, Robert. I promise."

Robert didn't say much, and his protests died down pretty quickly. I had the distinct impression that he had already known everything we had just told him.

*   *   *

The push to place Robert in more mainstream classes could not have come too soon. Robert's writing skills (composition and handwriting) were woefully behind those of his peers. It was only after the transfer that we learned that the special education children were not being taught writing composition in second grade, while the mainstream children were. It was just another example of how Robert was falling behind. Further compounding this problem was Robert's apparent weakness in these areas when he finally was exposed to them. We later learned that poor handwriting and trouble with composition are fairly common problems associated with ADD children.[3] It took time for Robert to adjust to the increased workload and social demands. Had we waited longer to mainstream Robert, however, I believe the adjustment would have been far harder.

In the end, I am exceptionally proud to report that Robert did quite well in his mainstream classes. Indeed, when we asked Robert's teachers how Robert was adjusting, we were told he was doing just fine. Although he still had an attention problem, with the help of his aide and his small daily dose of Ritalin, he was getting his work done. In fact, he was doing so well that his mainstream teacher wrote us a letter at midterm expressing her opinion that it was time for Robert to be spending more time in her classroom. If it worked out, she felt Robert would be able to spend the entire day in the mainstream within weeks.

*   *   *

A few weeks came, a few weeks went, and Robert's special education class threw him a congratulatory party—he was out of special education for good. Robert had been mainstreamed for the entire day (accompanied by his aide). Robert had beaten the odds. Although he missed his friends from the special education class, and certainly missed the security he had found there, Robert was responding well. Academics continued to be easy for him. In fact, some of what he was learning was actually old hat to him. Socially, the teacher reported that he had made several new friends. The children liked him and he fit in well.

When we asked whether Robert appeared awkward, anxious, or odd, his teacher shook her head emphatically. "Absolutely not," she said. I couldn't help but smile.

Robert also continued to have a very active extracurricular schedule. He received his green belt in karate and was invited to join the "Black Belt Club." This was a serious class that demanded serious attention. It was the class in which students began to train with weapons. Sensei Mike and Senpai David absolutely loved Robert and were thrilled with his progress. The invitation had been their idea. And did Robert ever respond! Once he received his green belt, he became more attentive, more serious, and a harder worker. I would even catch him practicing at home sometimes. We also kept Robert in baseball, tennis, and skating. Was he graceful? Was he the best? Well, let's put it this way: No one ever called him a natural athlete, but he was out there, and he was trying.

12

Another Therapy, Another Breakthrough

A s a family, we continued to maintain a fairly strict diet, although we had allowed wheat to creep back in, and we had also been permitting the occasional slice of pizza or scoop of ice cream, but only about once a month. Corinne said doing so was fine, as long as we kept an eye out for any adverse reactions. We eventually discovered that Robert needed to avoid corn, popcorn, drinks containing corn syrup, and anything artificially sweetened with aspartame ("Equal" or "NutraSweet"), which contains phenylalanine. Phenylalanine is an essential amino acid found in high-protein foods, such as eggs and meat. It is involved in normal neurotransmitter production and function, but can be harmful to those with certain mental health conditions, including anxiety disorders, when consumed in large amounts.

Everyone in the family still took vitamins and supplements. Robert was now able to swallow pills, so this part of the routine was easier.

We were growing more concerned about Robert's use of Ritalin. As we saw greater and greater improvement outside the classroom, we wondered more and more why Robert needed to use Ritalin inside the classroom. Was it merely a matter of motivation or was it something else? We continued our efforts to find a more natural attention enhancer for Robert to take instead of, or at least in conjunction with, Ritalin. Based on Corinne's recommendations, as well as our own independent research, we increased Robert's intake of fish oil supplements, which contained high concentrations of DHA and EPA, the omega-3 fatty acids important to neurological, brain, and eye development. We further supplemented his diet with phosphatidylserine, a critical component of the cell membrane that plays a major role in cellular function, particularly in the brain; gamma-aminobutyric acid, or GABA, an amino acid known to help ease anxiety; and dimethylaminoethanol, or DMAE, a substance naturally produced in the brain and thought to improve mood and memory. This aspect of nutrition therapy was a bit disappointing. Clearly, none of these supplements were anywhere near as potent as Ritalin, as Robert's attention span was not dramatically affected.

*　　*　　*

In addition to my research on childhood psychological disorders, nutrition, medication, and learning disabilities, I had also been intently studying educational theories and school systems. This research, as well as my and Tina's experience, led us to the sad but undeniable conclusion that the ideal school for children like Robert simply did not exist. So, I did what anyone else would do: I complained bitterly to my friends for months and months. I must have complained a lot because one day one of my friends, Philippa, looked me square in the eye and said, "If you know there are a lot of children like Robert, and there's no school for them, why don't you start one yourself?"

What a ridiculous, intriguing, wonderful idea! Philippa was serious and offered to help.

*　　*　　*

A year and a half into the project of creating a school, I began to think we were wasting our time. Don't get me wrong, we sincerely believed in the idea, and had already sunk an enormous amount of time, effort, and money into the project to prove it. Indeed, Philippa and I had accomplished a great deal. We had hired an impressive staff of consultants and had put together an incredible set of descriptive papers (the philosophy of the school, a "day in the life of" statement, etc.). We had found a location, prepared a curriculum, and prepared a budget. We were getting set to do our state filings and begin fund raising when everything crashed.

People we had hired and paid were now not returning our phone calls. Our attorney was delinquent in the requisition of our filing papers. (Yes, I know I'm an attorney, but I had no experience in this field. I thought it better to hire someone who "knew what he was doing." Ah, famous last words.) People who had promised financial support pulled out. Getting through the red tape just got worse and worse. I was getting very frustrated. Robert wasn't getting any younger. Then something rather remarkable happened. After a particularly disappointing day— numerous unreturned phone calls from various officials at the state board of education and potential donors, the discovery that we had missed a critical filing deadline because our attorney had sent us the wrong forms, and learning that our hired educational consultant had apparently disappeared with all our budgetary information—I stopped by a local church, said a prayer, asked for guidance, and returned to my office. Within an hour, I received a phone call from the state department of education. I released upon this poor woman a torrent of disappointment. Merely returning a phone call, she got an unedited earful about what we had gone through with Robert, what we had gone through with his education, and what we were trying to do with respect to the proposed school. I told her how much time and effort and money had been poured into this project. I told her how many people were involved, how many people were counting on me. I made no effort to hide my frustration. When I had finished (and apologized), she very sympathetically and politely informed me that I was talking to the wrong person. She told me I needed to speak to Mr. Hogan in another department.

I responded with the fact that Mr. Hogan accounted for two of the five remaining unreturned phone calls about which I'd just told her. She said he was hard to reach. I sighed and thanked her for her time and patience. I figured I would simply have to try again. As I was about to hang up the phone, and clearly as an afterthought, she said, "You know, there's one other person who you ought to talk to." She explained there was a gentleman, Mr. Anderson, who worked in the same department as Mr. Hogan.

"Why do I need to talk to him?" I asked.

She replied that he was very knowledgeable in the education field, and that he might be able to give me some good advice as to how to proceed. I thanked her again, hung up the phone, and called Mr. Hogan. He was, of course, not there. Disappointed yet again, I was going to hang up when I remembered Mr. Anderson. Yes, he was in. Yes, I could speak with him.

Once again, I poured my heart out. From diagnosis, to medications, to special education, to the school project, I told this poor man everything, ending with the fact that one of his colleagues had referred me to him. I said she was only trying to help, and that he should not hold the referral against her.

Mr. Anderson loved the idea behind the project and congratulated me on all we had accomplished so far. No, there wasn't anything to add; we were doing the right things. Yes, Mr. Hogan was the person to talk to at this point. No, he wasn't around, but he'd be sure to pass on my messages. (I don't recall Mr. Hogan ever calling me back.) Then he said, "By the way, that's a very impressive list of consultants you have, but there's one place that you absolutely must call."

Mr. Anderson told me about a learning center that had "done miracles" (his exact words) with the type of children I was hoping to serve in my school. While the learning center was not a clinic designed to treat children with psychological disorders, Mr. Anderson told me that a great number of the children who availed themselves of the learning center's services had been diagnosed with disorders such as ADD, dyslexia, and even autism.

I was soon on the phone speaking with the center owner about sensory integration. It was his opinion that, absent the "exceedingly rare neurological issue" of an actual brain injury, disorders such as ADD and ODD did not truly exist. (This was not the first time I had heard this theory,[1] and, as I admitted before, I once had a hard time believing in the existence of these disorders. My disbelief has since been tempered, though, by among other things, witnessing episodes where Robert was completely unreachable. I may not have agreed with the medical profession's defined cause of the issue, but it was clear that the issue did exist— something was very wrong.) Instead, he stood by the theory that most children diagnosed with such problems had sensory integration issues that interfered with their abilities to attend and learn.

As he would explain, sensory integration is related to the manner in which a person's senses take in and respond to (or fail to respond to) external stimuli. (I would later discover that "sensory integration" is subject to different definitions, with each definition seemingly dependent upon the speaker's occupation and interests.) Tasks that most of us take for granted, such as reading text, keeping an "eye on the ball," or maintaining a musical beat, might be extremely difficult, if not physically impossible, for some children.

Specifically, he talked about such things as a child's ability to cross his imaginary midline. He explained how integration of the left and right hemispheres of the brain affected not only a person's ability to tell left from right but also the ability to read. Individuals could experience erratic eye movements, problems focusing on a written page of text, or even an inability to maintain eye contact when the brain is not properly integrated. Auditory issues could manifest as sound sensitivities, trouble hearing a human voice over background noise, or even difficulty in distinguishing sounds. Any of these possibilities could account for learning difficulties. Moreover, such integration problems could lead to behavior and attention problems, he suggested. When placed in the classroom, children with sensory integration issues are asked and expected to complete tasks of which they might be physically incapable. Inevitably, these are the children with short attention spans, poor hand-eye coordination, and reading comprehension problems. They have trouble in gym, they have trouble in class, and they have trouble with homework. The difficulty of the tasks coupled with pressure from parents, teachers, and coaches, could result in frustration, which, in turn, could lead to negative behavior, including acting anxiously and being easily distractible. If a person cannot do what he is asked, or if a task takes too much effort, why bother trying in the first place? He'll just do something else, like doodle, stare out the window, or talk to his friends.

My curiosity was piqued. If a child could be physically hampered in his ability to take in information, surely this would adversely impact his ability to focus. We had always known Robert was hypersensitive to both his environment and other people. I remembered Robert's aversion to loud noises and how he would pull away from unexpected touch. We didn't need any further proof of Robert's hypersensitivity.

We had always known that Robert was clumsy. He had difficulty in sports, and still could not hit or catch a baseball, despite my best efforts to teach him how to do so. One of my "How Not to Parent" moments took place while I was again trying to teach Robert how to catch.

We had been going at it for close to an hour, and Robert had failed to catch a single ball thrown gently to him from ten feet away. He would shut his eyes and duck or jump away with practically every throw, even though we were using a soft tennis ball. At this point, I stood in front of him and said, "Listen, I don't care if you're ever good at this game. You don't have to be the best, but you do have to try and, Robert, you have to learn to catch a ball." And I meant it. I really didn't care if Robert played baseball, let alone was good at it. But I knew the other kids made fun of the fact that he couldn't throw or catch. He just had to learn.

Robert's constant and, in my mind, completely unwarranted fear of the ball actually made me angry. I stood there and bounced the tennis ball off my head. Then I bounced it off Robert's head. He laughed.

"See, it can't hurt you," I said. "Now just hold your mitt open and I'll throw the ball into it. Don't blink, don't move, and don't duck. Okay?"

"Okay," he replied with a very nervous giggle.

I was two arms' length away from him. I gently threw the ball towards his open mitt, and . . . he ducked. I threw it again, and . . . he ducked again. Over and over and over. Finally, I lost all patience.

"Robert, keep your mitt open!" I wasn't even trying to hide my anger. "Don't you dare move your feet. Don't you dare duck. I am going to throw this ball into your mitt. If you move, you're punished!"

He was terrified, but to his credit, he stood his ground, and other than a shudder as I threw the ball into his mitt, he did not move. I sent him inside, much to his relief. This is what I put my baby through so that he could play baseball with the other kids.

We also knew that Robert had trouble maintaining eye contact. He didn't like reading, he often got headaches, and he definitely did not know his left from his right. Could there be something wrong about which we didn't know? I arranged a meeting with the center director. I was interested in this program for our school. He asked me to bring Robert along so that his sensory integration skills could be assessed.

*   *   *

We arrived at the learning center. Robert was experiencing a full-blown rebound as his afternoon dose of Ritalin wore off. He was literally bouncing off the walls—nothing like a good first impression. The screening consisted of nothing more than asking Robert to perform what appeared to be very simple physical tasks: moving his left and right hands in a specific order, walking a straight line, touching his nose, tracking objects with his eyes. I was reminded of Robert's examination by the neurologist that first prescribed him Ritalin, although the learning center's screening was more extensive.

Much to our considerable surprise, Robert had a terrible time completing every one of the requested tasks. Robert had displayed difficulty with his midline. It was obvious that he didn't know his left from his right. His balance was off as well. His visual processing was even worse. While Robert had perfect 20/20 vision, the tests uncovered the fact that Robert had a terrible time adjusting his focus from near objects to far objects. This, we were told, would account for the problems Robert encountered when copying from the board in school. Robert also exhibited very serious problems visually tracking objects. An object was moved slowly from side to side in front of Robert's eyes. Robert was asked merely to look at it. Despite our encouragement and Robert's complete attention to the task, Robert's eyes looked everywhere except at the object! I had never seen anything like it. I couldn't believe it. How could someone not be able to track with his eyes?

The test was repeated. Robert concentrated, he squinted, he contorted his face, and he turned his head from side to side—all to no avail. Try as he might, he simply could not follow the object as it moved slowly right before his eyes. (I later learned of a theory that states some ADHD children apparently see better using peripheral vision. This might have been the reason why Robert had turned his head from side to side. Is it possible the object had been easier to see peripherally rather than straight on?) I immediately thought back to Robert's participation in sports programs and a light went on in my head. No wonder he skated off by himself in hockey. No wonder he never tried for the puck. No wonder he couldn't catch a baseball. No wonder he couldn't hit. He actually lacked the physical abilities necessary to see the puck or the ball the way most people do. He couldn't follow the movements of these objects, and he couldn't focus on these objects as they approached, so he couldn't know when they would arrive![4] It wasn't that he hadn't been trying; he couldn't physically do it.

I felt absolutely sick about the way I had treated him when I was trying to teach him to catch. Of course he was afraid of the ball. He could not see it coming! We even realized why Robert would become so easily distracted in a group but had no trouble interacting one-on-one. Not being able to process movement properly, the coming and going of people must have been erratic and unpredictable to him. If he couldn't really make sense out of what was around him, maybe he went into his own world and just did something else. Or maybe the unanticipated, poorly processed motions startled him. Taken by surprise, of course he would be completely distracted. One-on-one, there was no movement to follow, no surprises, no distractions.

And what torture hockey and baseball must have been for him! He couldn't physically do what was asked of him, but he had been forced to participate. How much worse was it that other kids, parents, and coaches watched him struggle, watched him fail—and fail for no reason he was capable of explaining.

It was obvious at the completion of the screening that Robert's sensory skills were severely underdeveloped. In fact, Robert's visual processing skills were so problematic that it was recommended that we take him to a developmental, or behavioral, optometrist before we considered enrolling him in the learning center.

Our research began.

*   *   *

There are numerous books that address developmental optometry[2] and sensory integration dysfunction,[3] as well as many relevant items on the Internet. We contacted optometric organizations and individual optometrists seeking their research. I spoke with one doctor who described his successful work with individuals diagnosed with schizophrenia and autism. He informed me that those diagnosed with such disorders had significantly different visual perception than other people, even if their eyesight was 20/20. Through the use of special lenses, prisms, and visual exercises, many of these people showed improved behavior.

I read about professional athletes who had used developmental optometry to improve performance. We contacted other parents who had enrolled their children in vision therapy. We heard nothing but good news. Every parent with whom we spoke told us their children had experienced significant results through the therapy, both in terms of behavior as well as academic and athletic achievement. They urged us to try it.

We discovered a prominent developmental optometrist who just happened to be located in our neighborhood, Dr. Martin H. Birnbaum. While the initial examination would be covered by our medical insurance, we did need a referral from Robert's pediatrician.

And here we went again. The pediatrician refused to give us the referral. He said he didn't believe in vision therapy. If we thought Robert had a vision problem, he told us we should take Robert to an ophthalmologist. This was the same doctor who had said there was nothing wrong with giving Robert milk. The same one who had declared that Robert's constant ear infections were not related to diet. The same one who had poured a steady course of antibiotics into our little boy.

Tina spoke to the pediatrician at length, and in the end, it was agreed that we would bring Robert to the ophthalmologist first to ensure there was nothing physically wrong with Robert's eyes. Then, regardless of the results of that examination, Robert would see Dr. Birnbaum.

*　　　*　　　*

The ophthalmologist's exam was somewhat uneventful, although two noteworthy events did take place. First, when I explained why we were there, we were handed a bunch of pamphlets written by ophthalmologic groups that attacked the practice of developmental optometry. Basically, these writings claimed that the visual dysfunctions developmental optometrists sought to address were caused by untreatable neurological problems and that vision therapy was a waste of time. While there was no question that such problems existed, there was nothing that could be done to correct them. We found that very hard to believe, and I didn't really appreciate receiving such materials in this unsolicited manner.

Second, while Robert's examination revealed he had healthy eyes and 20/20 vision, when asked by the ophthalmologist to do so, Robert could not follow an object with his eyes. The doctor took out a penlight and instructed Robert to follow the light. When the light went one way, Robert's eyes went another.

The doctor snapped at him, "Pay attention!"

"I'm trying," Robert said meekly. "My eyes need help focusing," he explained to the doctor. We felt so bad for Robert. He was trying—you could see it in his face—he just couldn't do it. The doctor only made him feel worse. He continued without acknowledging what Robert had said. He didn't pause for a second or bother to respond. He moved the light to another location. Robert's eyes moved the other way.

"Pay attention," the doctor snapped again. There was no understanding. No sympathy. Tina and I shook our heads. The doctor started talking into a tape recorder. Pausing momentarily to ask us a question or two, the doctor quickly recorded the results of the examination. He turned to us and gestured towards Robert. "His eyes are fine," he said. That was it. The exam was over.

Tina was furious with me. "Why didn't you say something? Why didn't you question him?"

"For what?" I asked wearily. "We knew before we even walked in what was going to happen. The only reason we agreed to this was to make sure that Robert's eyes were physically okay. And they are. Now we go to the doctor we wanted to see in the first place."

*   *   *

150

Robert underwent yet another assessment with Dr. Birnbaum. Robert was examined over a two-day period, and, as expected, the optometrist found that Robert had a severe tracking problem.

"On a scale of 1 to 100, 1 being the worst and 100 the best," he said, "Robert's ability to track is about a 1."

Robert began therapy the following week. It consisted of two forty-five-minute sessions in the doctor's office every week and a ten-minute set of practice exercises at home every day. It was expected that the therapy would be completed in four to six months.

Therapy consisted of eye-movement and focusing exercises, for the most part. Some of the exercises involved finding and tracking colored dots across a video screen. Robert also had to track a ball suspended from the ceiling as it spun and twirled across the room. There were many other exercises, to be sure, but we were never witness to them. Since therapy was done behind closed doors and other children would be treated at the same time, we were not permitted to watch the sessions. Thus, our knowledge of what went on at the office was limited.

At home, we did exercises that challenged Robert's ability to follow objects in motion. For example, he had a flashlight with a green filter. Tina had a flashlight with a red filter. It was Tina's job to move the red circle of light across the ceiling; Robert's job was to keep the green circle of light on top of the red circle. We also had Robert "spot" the corners of a wall, follow his thumb as he moved it from one side of his body to the other, and read from charts he held and those we had hung on the wall. And we had staring contests. In the beginning, Robert couldn't last longer than a few seconds.

The weeks went by. Robert seemed to be doing well in therapy. We noticed some definite improvement in Robert's ability to perform his at-home exercises. We were anxious, however, for proof that some aspect of Robert's life was actually improving. We found it on the diamond.

Robert played his first baseball game of the season about two months after therapy had begun. He went four for four against the pitching machine—good, hard shots, including a line drive that made it to the outfield. This performance came from a boy who went six for forty—and that's being generous—against the same pitching machine on the same field the season before, with more awkward strikeouts than we care to remember. Luck?

Robert went four for four the next game. During warm-ups, he caught the ball when I threw it to him. Coincidence?

Robert went three for four the following game (he popped out to third base for his only out). He also fielded a fast ground ball at shortstop and completed the play by tagging the advancing runner. Three times is skill. But even more amazing than the remarkable leap in athletic ability was Robert's seemingly abrupt change in behavior and attitude. Robert was actually growing serious about the game. He wasn't fooling around as much. He didn't stand on the plate when he came to bat anymore. He didn't hold the bat upside down as a joke anymore. He stopped playing in the dirt when he was in the field. Other parents asked us what we had done.

Now, I wasn't sure what to think. Here was a kid that had just doubled the number of hits he had accumulated over the entire previous season—and doubled that number in only three games. Here was a kid that had dropped dozens of balls thrown gently to him from no more than ten feet away a season ago, now able to catch and make fielding plays. Here was a kid who had seemed completely uninterested and inattentive, now far more focused on the field. Was it just that he was a year older? Was it all the practice? Or was it the fact that now he could "see" the ball and play the game thanks to the vision therapy?

13

The Right School

We decided to take Robert off Ritalin—again. We were encouraged by Robert's success with vision therapy. He was doing much better in sports and his self-esteem was growing. His behavior and attitude steadily improved. Even though we had drastically reduced Robert's Ritalin intake, and thus had vastly diminished the associated side effects, Robert still suffered from very nasty rebound effects when the afternoon dose wore off.

Knowing that Robert was okay without Ritalin on weekends; knowing that he was able to function in baseball, karate, piano, and skating without Ritalin; and knowing that his disturbing daily regressions were a result of Ritalin, we were torn up inside. The daily rebounds were even interfering with Robert's vision therapy. Dr. Birnbaum told us that Robert's behavior often disrupted sessions (Robert's sessions were scheduled after school, when his rebounds usually started). We, too, weren't happy with Robert's behavior while he was rebounding. He couldn't do his homework, and he couldn't listen to us.

The worse part, though, was that Robert had been complaining about the Ritalin again. He really didn't want to take it anymore. He said he didn't feel "right" when he took it. It bothered him in ways he was unable to express. We were growing weary of forcing Robert to take something we hadn't wanted him to take in the first place.

Ritalin might have made life easier for Robert's teacher, but it was making life miserable for us. Yes, we were told to give Robert a little more Ritalin when he got home to reduce the rebound effect, but we couldn't

bring ourselves to do it. We had successfully reduced his need for medication and were hoping to get him off Ritalin completely. Moreover, the
logic of this proposed course of action escaped us. Why give more of the
very thing that was causing the problem? Besides, the school year was
just about over. In two more months the staff wouldn't have to deal with
a Ritalin-free Robert for a whole summer.

We told Robert's teacher, Robert's aide, and the school psychologist,
Dr. Johnson, our plan. Dr. Johnson, to no one's surprise, didn't think it was
a good idea. I again tried to explain the rebound effect and how difficult it
was to deal with Robert when he regressed. I told her how much it hurt us
to see him like that. I also told her that we had become completely disenchanted with medicating Robert. The more we read about the medications,
the less we were willing to tolerate them.[1] I had even begun to refer to
Robert's Ritalin as the "evil stuff." I told her how my research revealed
that there were no studies that proved Ritalin had any long-term benefits.
I told her of the results we were obtaining through alternative methods
such as nutrition and vision therapy. I told her how far Robert had come. I
told her to sit through one of Robert's rebounds and then ask why we
wanted him off the stuff so badly. The continued use of Ritalin merely to
make Robert compliant simply wasn't worth it anymore.

I never did convince her, but Robert was our child. We took him off
the "evil stuff." We didn't know it then, but it would be the last time
Robert ever saw a Ritalin tablet again. We would also no longer have any
contact with Robert's psychiatrist, Dr. Lampman. Off Ritalin and without
need of psychotherapy, Robert stopped seeing this doctor.

*   *   *

Robert made it to the end of the year in one piece, and it was time to
revisit the issue of his school placement. We were presented with three
choices. We could leave Robert where he was, mainstreamed in district
(although not at his home school) with an aide; we could transfer Robert
to his home school with an aide; or we could transfer Robert to a private
school with or without an aide—if we could find a private school that
would accept him.

The first choice had little appeal to us. We were still upset that Robert had fallen behind his peers academically despite the school's assurances to the contrary. We felt that the expectations maintained by the school with respect to the abilities of special education students simply were not the same as the expectations they maintained for their mainstream students. We wanted Robert removed from special ed, and we wanted him removed yesterday. Thus, we really only considered placing Robert in his home school or a private school.

We met with the principal of Robert's home school. With a strong background in special education and experience with very bright and "different" children, he understood our concerns. We discussed the various options, Robert's potential placement, teachers, and class composition. He encouraged us to move Robert to his home school. He promised to place Robert with appropriate classmates in a classroom taught by one of his best teachers. There were only two drawbacks. First, the class would number in the midtwenties. While not huge by most standards, it would be a far larger class than anything to which Robert had been exposed. Second—and more problematic—the principal pretty much insisted that Robert continue to have a one-to-one aide. Robert, however, had grown to hate having an aide. He complained about it constantly. He said he didn't like or need someone always telling him what to do.

Now, there was no doubt in our minds that Robert needed constant reminders to stay on task and complete his work. But I guess Robert felt like his aide was just nagging him. He wanted a divorce. Moreover, while aides were commonplace in Robert's present school, they were unusual in his home school. I could hear the kids making fun of Robert already. Where did that leave us? Private school. As Shakespeare once wrote, "Once more unto the breach, dear friends, once more. . . ."

*   *   *

When we mentioned the possibility of transferring Robert to a private school, the chairperson of the CSE told us that the district would absolutely not pay Robert's tuition (not that we had even asked), as she felt the school district could provide an "appropriate" education. "Appropriate," she reminded me, did not necessarily mean "best."

While Tina and I disagreed, and we knew it was perfectly within our rights to ask the school district to pay for Robert's private school education if we thought the public school was inappropriate, we never thought we would want to go through the bother of a lawsuit in order to enforce that right. We had no problems with the CSE. In fact, it had always been exceptionally accommodating, and we never doubted they had Robert's best interests at heart. I didn't want to spoil that relationship, even if it cost us a few bucks.

Logistically speaking, the search for a private school this time around would be easier. First, we already knew which schools to cross off the list. Second, it was so late in the year that most of the handful of possibilities had closed out registration. Thus, we were presented opportunities at only a few schools. After speaking with the directors of the various school programs and explaining Robert's history—not in as much detail as before and with a far better spin to the tale (I had learned my lesson)—we set our sights on two schools. The first was Portledge, a prestigious (and expensive) private school that prided itself on its high academic standards. The second was Westbury Friends, which was smaller, less expensive (but expensive, nonetheless), and boasted an environment of community and acceptance. Robert was to attend each school for a day, after which time each school would decide if it would accept Robert. If Robert "checked out," then we would enroll our daughter as well.

Tina and I explained the situation to Robert. We told him we were looking at some schools for him and his sister. We said we hadn't picked one yet, and that we might not pick one; it all depended upon whether he and his sister liked the school and whether we thought it was best for them. We also told him that the school had to like him, too. It was very, very important that he behaved and listened as well as he could during his visits. He said he understood. We brought him to Portledge. No medications, no aide, no support system. We gave him a kiss, said goodbye, and held our breath.

How did he do? Not bad, but not well enough that the school greeted us with open arms. Robert, the school said, was very fidgety. He was

good-natured, well behaved, polite, and very smart, but easily distracted—and he had a difficult time sitting still. "We think," the director,
Ms. Mooney, said, "that Robert's main problem is that he's too intelligent. We think he gets bored and that's why he gets distracted." We
couldn't argue with her assessment. In fact, it was rather flattering.

It seems the school had had a child like Robert before (another little
boy, in fact), and the situation hadn't worked as well as everyone had
hoped. If teachers taught that child at his own speed, the rest of the class
was lost. The lost children would inevitably become disinterested and
behavior would deteriorate. On the other hand, if teachers taught to the
class, the opposite would happen. The class would behave and pay attention, but the little boy would not. It was obvious Ms. Mooney really
hadn't been happy with the situation or the way it had turned out. It was
equally clear she didn't want to go through it again. She all but said so.

Still, we had to ask, "Would you accept Robert?"

"Well," she started with that telltale awkward look, "Robert certainly
doesn't belong in a public school." A pause. "You're checking other
schools, right?"

We told her we were. She gave us a whole list of schools to try (most
had already closed registration) and told us to see if any of them would
accept Robert. If none would, she would reconsider Robert's application.
I think the school genuinely liked Robert. We thanked her for her time
and help, and left feeling a strange mix of vindication, discouragement,
and hope. Our sense of vindication arose from the fact that a private
school finally recognized both Robert's intelligence and the fact that he
would be better served in private school. And although we were discouraged that Robert hadn't been accepted outright, Ms. Mooney had
given us hope that this school might still accept him.

Would that do? Would we want to send Robert to a place that
accepted him reluctantly? Best not to think about it, I thought. There was
still Westbury Friends. We'd have to keep our fingers crossed. We had
the same talk with Robert, gave him the same kiss goodbye, and felt the
same breathless anticipation.

How'd he do? Déjà vu. Not bad, but not well enough that this school
rolled out the red carpet. What was the problem this time? "Robert," said

Ms. Edelman, the director, "was too innocent." She explained that Robert had a certain naïveté that was both charming and sweet. The classroom that Robert would enter, however, was composed of a group of kids who had all formed cliques—and each clique wasn't particularly nice to members of other cliques. And the poor children not in a clique fared even worse. Well, Ms. Edelman didn't think Robert was ready for this type of social scenario. (I recalled that Dr. Parker had made nearly identical observations about Robert.)

Of course, no one was happy about the cliques. Ms. Edelman and the school teachers had spoken with the children and parents and were determined to fix the situation, but . . .

"You don't think you can do anything for Robert right now," I finished the director's thought.

Ms. Edelman had Robert's best interests at heart. Concerned about Robert's welfare, she felt that the children with whom Robert would attend class could hurt him emotionally. Robert just wasn't ready. But again, like Ms. Mooney, the director of Portledge, she sympathized with us and agreed Robert would be better served in a private school. The bottom line: Westbury Friends, too, would consider taking Robert if we couldn't find anywhere else for him.

Oh, the irony. Robert was apparently too intelligent for the school that boasted high academics, and too nice for the school that stressed community and acceptance. We were upset and confused, to say the least. We sorely wanted to look on the bright side. No one had said anything about "trouble with transition" or "bad behavior" or "inattentiveness." But how could they basically deny him because he was too smart or too innocent?

I was also, very, very angry—a fact made clear to me a few weeks later. Robert was attempting to do his homework, but it involved writing, and he was fighting me every step of the way. After about an hour of nothing but aggravation and stress, an inexplicable rage swept over me. I left Robert at the kitchen table and started punching a door again and again and again. I wanted it to break, to shatter under my fists. I felt so helpless. I dimly heard Robert sobbing in the kitchen, trying to get his writing done between the tears.

I sat down on the floor, my anger spent. I wondered why I had become so angry. Robert had refused to do his work before and it had never upset me this much. Then I realized what was truly bothering me. I had taken the directors' opinions of Robert to heart. I was angry at Robert and his "failure."

But what was Robert's crime? He was too smart? He was too nice? It was then I realized how much of my feelings about Robert had been shaped by the opinions of others, even when those opinions had no valid basis or were simply wrong. Why did such things matter so much to me? My fundamental problem in dealing with Robert all along was that I was beginning to believe everyone else's view of Robert. I couldn't let that happen. Robert was my son, and I loved him, and I believed in him.

Like it or not, however, we had to deal with the reality of other people's perceptions. What were we to do? Enroll Robert in our home school, where he would continue to receive support he didn't want? Or force him (if we could) on a private school that really didn't want him?

*   *   *

Summer had come, and the chairperson of the CSE contacted us. She needed a decision. We had decided that if the private schools were at all reluctant about accepting Robert, we would enroll him in his home school. We would not force our son on anyone. They should want to have him. I picked up the phone one last time to consult with the directors of the two private schools.

Nothing had changed at Portledge. I called Westbury Friends. Ms. Edelman was happy to hear from me. It seemed that some of the children who were more problematic would not be attending come September. Moreover, there had been a relatively large influx of new students. She felt she could put together a nice class of children—one that would include Robert. Had I heard her correctly? Had she actually said they would accept Robert? Yes, she had. What could I say? I asked her to enroll both my children.

Finally, after all this time, Robert had been accepted to a private school. No more special education, no more tortuous bus rides. With a limited number of children in the class, Robert would get the kind of attention he needed and deserved, all in a mainstream setting. His intellect would be challenged and his differences respected. It was cause for celebration, and we should have been thrilled, but it had come so late, and after so much pain. There was no sense of triumph. There was no sense of joy, only a strange sense of relief. I couldn't describe it. I turned to Tina. "The beatings have finally stopped," I said.

We placed Robert in a grade-three-four class. He would be with eleven other students. Officially, Robert would be a third-grader, even though the public school system would have placed him in fourth grade. We held Robert back for several reasons, not the least of which was the fact that we had wanted to do so for a long time, but our public school district wouldn't allow it. Robert's maturity level was still well behind his chronological age, and we wanted him to be with children with whom he could socialize more easily. Moreover, the cut-off date for enrollment in the private school was even earlier than the one used in our school district. By placing Robert in third grade, we insured that he would be with children who were actually his age.

The academic and social expectations were much higher in the private school. While some people thought that Robert might get bored academically if we held him back, the fact of the matter was that the private school was teaching approximately one grade level ahead of the public school system anyway. Besides, Robert needed remedial work with respect to his writing skills, which were still exceptionally weak. Couple all this with the fact that it was a new school, with new kids, and, other than a writing tutor, absolutely no supports whatsoever (no medications, no aide, no lowered expectations), and there was no question in our minds. We were doing the right thing.

*   *   *

Robert's first year in private school was pretty rough. Things started out well enough, and then about a month into the new year, we began to hear about how fidgety Robert was, how difficult it was to keep him on task, how he constantly interrupted and called out. We were pretty sure that his teacher, Mrs. Boyle, didn't know the full extent of Robert's background—we certainly never discussed it with her—and we are not sure she knew how to handle the situation.

We met with Mrs. Boyle several times. We asked her to try some behavior modification and give Robert just a little more attention. Most times, when Robert interrupted, as impolite as that was, he was merely trying to express a thought that had popped into his head. Yes, we knew he had to learn to contain himself, but if you would take a second to hear his thought and gently remind him not to interrupt, he would quiet down. Ignoring him only made it worse. We also explained that the transition to a new school was difficult for him. In time, he would adjust to the new demands. It would probably take months, we told her, but he would adjust.

Academically, there were few complaints, although writing was incredibly hard for him, both at home and in class. Also, his inability to focus for more than twenty minutes was taking its toll with respect to his special classes, like physical education and music. In fact, although all third-graders were expected to take an instrument, Robert was forced to stop his lessons. Given a choice of violin or recorder, Robert chose violin. He had played the recorder in public school. He rarely practiced and was such a distraction during music lessons that the music teacher asked that we stop his lessons and try to resume them when Robert gained more self-control.

We ran into the same problem in the language arts program, although the exclusion this time was not so much related to behavior, but rather an inability to master the subject matter. Instead, Robert was to take supplemental English instead of a Spanish class, in an attempt to improve his composition skills.

Then there was the homework. Robert had far more assigned to him in the private school than had been given in the public school, and the homework involved far more writing. It was torture for all of us to get it done. Hours and hours of torture. Worst of all was the fact that Ms. Edelman's warning about Robert's naïveté proved true. Robert's interactions with one particular child were causing serious problems. This very intelligent little boy would alternate between playing the role of Robert's best friend and that of his tormentor. One day, everything was fine and the two would play nicely together. The next day, the boy would tease Robert incessantly. Robert had never been exposed to this type of behavior before and didn't know how to handle it. He would become extremely agitated and upset, and then clumsily attempt to strike back—never physically, mind you. Instead, Robert would yell at the boy or tease him back. But Robert was not at all subtle, and invariably he would get in trouble.

The school understood that both children were involved. They spoke to both boys about how they should treat each other and what were appropriate responses to inappropriate behavior. Things would be okay for a while. Robert would forgive the boy, and then bam! It would start all over again. Pretty soon, we were called to discuss the situation. The school wanted to separate the boys. We felt terrible. The two had started out the year together so well. It seemed like Robert really had a friend, and despite it all, Robert was always asking to play with this child. Why did this have to happen?

We had several meetings with Mrs. Boyle to discuss these issues. She was very concerned about Robert and thought Robert needed to be evaluated. My heart sank. I thought we had moved past all this, but I suppose that was wishful thinking. I could just hear Robert's ex-psychiatrist, Dr. Schneider, snickering at us and our "naïve" and "foolish" belief in our son's abilities and our chosen courses of treatment. But we had come too far. We steadfastly refused to discuss those old times, and would not do anything that would take us back in that direction. We told Mrs. Boyle that we understood what she was going through, and that we would work extra hard with Robert. We'd work on his fidgeting and calling out, and we'd talk to him about how he should behave with the boy in his class. In time—and we stressed the "time" part of the equation—we were sure that Robert would adjust.

We also met with Ms. Edelman. She seemed to take all this in stride. I think she knew it was going to happen. She said Robert was making progress on all fronts, and that we had to be patient. All this was new to him. It would take time and work, and she was monitoring the situation very closely. I am sure she knew Robert would have problems adjusting, and her matter-of-fact approach was at once welcome and a little disconcerting. I kept waiting for the phone call to come–the one where they would ask us to take Robert out of the school.

Now, of course, it wasn't all bad news. Robert's intelligence came shining through. He got along fairly well with the other kids in his class, and we even think the girls liked him, too. (We found a "love" note one day. Tina and I were so excited! A little girl liked Robert! I hope my son will forgive me, but I must quote part of the letter. The little girl said she really liked Robert, and wrote that even though he could "act like a jerk sometimes," he was the nicest boy she knew. What a perfect description of our son.)

Even though we had made the move to private school because of Robert, it was by far the best thing we could have done for our daughter, Kat, too. How she thrived in the new environment. She went from a quiet wallflower in a kindergarten class of twenty-five to an enthusiastic, story-writing, problem-solving machine of a first-grader with an ability to learn that would blow your doors off! She adored her teacher, who readily became quite an inspiration to her, and she loved school.

*   *   *

By the time Robert and Kat had enrolled in their new school, I had taken a new job. I had decided to join the learning center whose program had been recommended to me by Mr. Anderson at the department of education—the same center that first discovered Robert's severely underdeveloped sensory skills. I had kept in close contact with the people there during my son's treatment with the developmental optometrist, Dr. Birnbaum. We had developed a mutual respect for each other, and they had expressed their belief that I might be able to help them grow the business.

There was a tremendous amount of risk involved in such a move, but quite frankly, I was ready to go. I was extremely excited about the progress our son was making. I had thoroughly researched the philosophical and technical aspects of the learning center's approach, and I liked what I'd learned.

It wasn't easy leaving my law practice, but it wasn't as hard as one might imagine. As I mentioned before, my part-time status had hurt me on a professional level. Despite excellent performance reviews, I was having a hard time getting assignments from senior attorneys, and I was not receiving any promotions. I'm sure many viewed me as not being committed to my profession. And perhaps they were right, although one might reply that the practice's expectations were unreasonable. I was reluctant to sacrifice my time with my family to travel and socialize—necessary commitments if I wished to build name recognition and generate sales. Instead, I focused on getting my job done and done right. Apparently, that wasn't enough. No matter how hard I worked, no matter how many late nights I still managed to put in, no matter how well I did my job, I just wasn't "with the program."

On a certain level, the senior partners at the firm undoubtedly realized I had already left the practice. I wasn't very happy, and the fact that I was having trouble hiding that unhappiness no doubt contributed to my diminished status at the firm. I was completely caught up in Robert's plight, both emotionally and intellectually. Everything we were learning was fascinating. I couldn't read enough about it or talk to too many experts or overly debate the merits of differing theories and methodologies. I had found something of worth, something to which I could easily dedicate my life. How could this even begin to compare to sitting in an office all day long, reviewing documents, writing briefs about the meaning of a word in a contract, or fighting with people whose only goal seemed to be to make my life miserable? No, I knew if I left I wouldn't miss the work. I had already tried to start a school of my own, after all.

The folks at the learning center presented me with an amazing opportunity. Certainly, their approach was no more risky than starting a school. And although I still had hopes for a school, that project was at best a year and a lot of backtracking away. Here was something I could jump into immediately. In addition, the learning center offered me a chance to help far more children than I could in a school setting, and in a lot less time. I couldn't let this chance slip away.

Yes, I would miss the money, but there are far more important things in life than money. I left my law practice with no regrets and threw myself headfirst into my new career.

* * *

Tina and I enrolled both our children at the learning center. Robert was still having difficulty maintaining focus. His coordination, although somewhat improved, was still weak. His handwriting was miserable, confirming the need for further development of his sensory integration skills, since "[w]riting is dependent upon visual-motor integration."[2] My daughter also seemed like she could benefit from the program. Although not nearly as problematic as Robert, she did not like to read either.

We understood that it would be several months before we would notice any change in either child. The official explanation was that students like my son, held back by underdeveloped sensory or cognitive skills, usually would not experience any increase in learning ability for anywhere from a few months in the program to completion of the program, since the program was developmental in nature. While the majority of children finished the program within six to nine months, the actual duration of any individual student's program was dependent upon the amount of remediation necessary to develop and strengthen his skills, and Robert had a lot of remediation to get through. Well, we knew this wasn't magic. We would get through this just like we got through everything else.

* * *

At about seven or eight months into the school year, things got noticeably better, both at the center and at school. Robert had adjusted fairly well to the demands and expectations placed upon him. His schoolwork was coming more easily, and his reading had improved tremendously. In fact, I can recall the day all the work Robert had been doing at the learning center finally kicked in.

I always insisted that Robert bring a book and read whenever I needed to take him to the center. On one particular trip, he sat in his back seat, and I did not hear a peep from him during the entire forty-five-minute ride. Naturally, I assumed he was sleeping. Robert was never that quiet for that long when awake. When we got to the center, I discovered that he had been reading. I asked how far he had gotten in the book. He told me he had read five chapters. I didn't believe him. He'd never read for that long or that fast. I took the book, thumbed through the chapters he'd supposedly read, and asked him questions from them. He answered every single question correctly. It was simply amazing.

Our daughter also showed signs that the program was working for her, at least athletically. She had been enrolled in a gymnastics class. Clearly not clumsy, she was, nevertheless, not quite at the same level as the majority of the girls in her class, and she knew it. We encouraged her as best we could. Then came the day that her gymnastics teacher pulled us aside to comment on how much better she was suddenly doing. You could see it. The only thing we could attribute the improvement to was the work she had been doing in the gym at the learning center.

I was very proud of my kids and often pointed them out to other parents at the center who were experiencing difficulties similar to those we already had gone through. Yet, while I knew Robert had made substantial progress, I didn't recognize the full extent of it until it was pointed out to me. Remarking to one of the other parents at the center that Robert had come a long way, I turned to one of my coworkers and asked if she remembered the first day Robert had come in. She rolled her eyes, nodded her head, and in a particularly exasperated voice said, "Yeah, I remember."

I was somewhat taken aback by the extremity her response. I asked, "What's that face for?"

"The truth is, we worried about him entering the program," she said sheepishly.

"Was he that bad?" I asked, genuinely surprised.

"Yes, yes he was. Don't you remember?" she asked.

I shook my head no.

"He was bouncing off the walls and wouldn't listen to anyone. It was scary."

"And now?" I asked.

She turned to the parent with whom I was speaking and said, "He's great now. Who knew?"

Of course, things got better for Robert at school as well. While we attribute much of the improvement to the work Robert did at the center, an even bigger factor may have been the fact that the boy with whom Robert had encountered so many difficulties transferred to a different school. While Mrs. Boyle still had some complaints about Robert's behavior, they did not approach the level of anything we had dealt with before. Our final parent-teacher conference with her even made me smile. She was in a very serious mood, and we weren't sure what to expect. We had heard from the school director that Robert had been doing much better. Why was his teacher pursing her lips at us?

"Robert still has an annoying habit of tapping his pencil in class," she began. (By the way, please imagine this being said in Mrs. Boyle's Irish brogue.)

Okay. At least he's not shaking his desk or standing up or walking around the classroom like he used to do.

"He still calls out a lot," she said.

We knew that continued to be a problem. I asked if it was still nonsense or had he at least learned that the calls must be related to the subject matter.

"It's always on point," she said.

All right, that's a start.

"And, one more thing," she said as she looked me square in the eye. I braced myself. (I'd have ducked under the desk if I could have.) She shook her head and said that Robert had started "teasing the girls."

It was my turn to shake my head. "Is that it?" I asked.

She looked at us very seriously and said, "Yes; it is quite a problem!"

I almost laughed out loud. We were thrilled! Robert was finally interacting with other children like a regular nine-year-old boy. If Mrs. Boyle only knew! There was no denying that Robert was well on his way to where he needed to be.

*   *   *

The next two years were blissfully uneventful. Robert continued his piano lessons and ice hockey, and eventually he was able to resume violin lessons. Robert was now a sweet, well-adjusted student, no longer dependent on special education, drugs, or special therapy. Was he a perfectly complaisant, quiet little boy who always did what was expected of him without a fuss? No. Is any little boy?

Robert still got nervous when presented with uncertainty. He still interrupted. His handwriting still needed work (although it had improved dramatically), and he still needed a lot of coaxing before he would deliver his best effort. Robert still had bad days, too. Days when he couldn't sit still or stay focused. Days when he acted very silly and could not seem to stop doing so. But those days were few and far between, and most times, we were able to trace the behavior to some upcoming event about which he was nervous, or to something that we shouldn't have let him eat.

*   *   *

In a beautiful ceremony that brought tears to my eyes, Robert graduated from his private school. The school served students only until sixth grade, so it was time for Robert to move on. The director, his teachers, and everyone that knew Robert told us how far he had come, how wonderful he was, and what a pleasure it was to have him in class.

He was accepted with open arms and a generous financial aid package (we can't thank you enough, Ms. Mooney and Mr. Gregory!) to Portledge—the school that had been worried initially about Robert's intelligence—for middle school. I am proud to say that Robert made Dean's List or Honor Roll nearly every semester. He also played on several of the school sports teams, excelling in cross country running and fencing. He joined the choir, took up the viola with surprising ease, and made many new friends.

This was not the end of Robert's story, of course, but rather the very beginning. Of course, we knew Robert would always walk to the beat of his own drummer. But we also knew that despite all the problems, treatments, and dire forecasts, we had helped ensure Robert would have a happy and successful life. And isn't that what being a parent is really all about?

14

What We Learned

As I mentioned at the outset, I never intended to write a "how to" book. Every child is different. Every situation is different. Every manifestation of these disorders is different. Like Robert, every child is unique, as is every family, as is every parent. I can't give you a specific course of action that's guaranteed to "cure" your child. I would not dare to be so presumptuous. Although I firmly believe that what Robert attained can certainly be attained by others, and that the therapies we employed could surely help any child lead a more healthy life, I can't promise that anything we did with Robert would have the same profound effects on a different child in a different setting. What I can say is that the information contained in the appendix to this book is a good place to start. I can say that different approaches and different methodologies have proven very effective in helping many children. I can say there is hope. Robert is living proof.

What I offer here is some advice based upon our hard-learned experiences. It is advice that, I think, applies universally—advice that, I hope, will help you and your child.

■ TRUST YOUR HEART

No one knows your child better than you do, so never go along with a decision made for your child if you do not agree with it. Doctors and other experts see your child for mere minutes—an examination here, a test there. Only you see your child twenty-four hours a day. Your observations and opinions are paramount. People will have opinions on everything—what the problem is, what caused it, how it should be treated, and who should be doing the treatment. But this is your child. You are ultimately responsible for what happens. Let your heart be your guide and you'll sleep better at night.

While it is easy for me to offer this sage piece of advice, I also know it is very, very difficult to follow—especially when you are dealing with your child's doctors. The same holds true for the other professionals with whom you will deal, including teachers. I have no doubt that doctors and teachers have the best interests of our children in mind, and I have never told parents to disregard what their child's doctors or teachers have said, but the fact remains that sometimes doctors and teachers are uninformed. Sometimes they make bad decisions. Sometimes they are wrong. Sometimes you need to speak up.

Why was it so hard for us to question Robert's doctors and teachers? We've been socialized—that is, trained—to accept doctors' statements as pronouncements of law. We've been raised to trust that doctors know best. We've been told to trust our teachers to properly educate and, in a sense, raise our children. When they state what is best for your child as fact, when you look at their degrees, offices, and white coats, and when you have all those years of expertise and experience bearing down on you, how could you possibly disagree with these people?

Robert's doctors were professionals. They were supposed to know, to have all the answers, not us. We weren't formally trained in medicine, psychology, or education. But sometimes you just have to have the courage to say no. At a bare minimum, you have to have the courage to question, to push for answers, to make those working with your child aware of your concerns. We have spoken to several parents whose children were on some pretty serious medications. Unfortunately, sometimes the symptoms for which these children were being treated got worse, not better. As a result, doctors told the parents to increase the dosages. Noting that a worsening of certain conditions was a documented side effect of these drugs, I told the parents that they should really ask their doctors whether the condition being treated was, in fact, worsening of its own accord, or if their children were experiencing side effects from the medications.

One parent was told in no uncertain terms that his child's condition was worsening and the increase in meds was absolutely necessary, so the increased course of meds continued. But so did the severity of the symptoms. The child eventually became physically ill and was hospitalized. It was only then discovered that the level of medication in the child had reached a toxic level. The parent switched doctors, and the child was weaned off the medications. The parent then started all over again.

Another parent, a mom with whom we worked, was told that her child's medication was absolutely necessary, but she wasn't convinced of this idea. Moreover, she thought her child was exhibiting side effects of the medication. Specifically, her child suffered mood swings and often became defiant and angry. While the doctor said this was just the way her child was, she did not agree with him. She sought a second opinion. This second doctor agreed with the mother. With this doctor's help, the child was weaned off the medication. At that point, the child's behavior improved tremendously. While it turned out that the child still required a reduced dosage of the medication, this event alerted everyone to the child's sensitivity to that particular drug—invaluable information for the child's future treatment.

The simple fact is that no one has any definite answers when it comes to treating your child. That's why you have to ask for information from numerous sources. You have to push. You have to insist. We know for a fact that a whole lot of doctors were very wrong about Robert. We know for a fact that much of what was suggested for Robert at school was not best for him. We know for a fact that Robert would not be the person he is today had we continued to follow directions blindly. So, at the risk of repeating myself, if you truly feel that the course being laid out before you and your child is not best, do your research, learn your alternatives, find other competent and knowledgeable practitioners that can guide you, and find the strength to do what you think is right.

■ FIGHT

You are your child's best advocate. Sure, there are lots of people who care about your child, but who cares most, really? Remember, teachers, committee members, and doctors all have other children with whom to con-cern themselves in addition to yours. Who really has the time and energy to fight for your child, to learn all the options, to stand up for your child's best interests? Only you do.

There were battles Tina and I fought and those we chose not to fight. In retrospect, I don't think we should have yielded an inch at any time. I especially regret having not held Robert back in preschool. We knew holding him back would only help him, and that any advantage we could give him, no matter how seemingly insignificant, was an advan-tage he deserved. If you think something will help, insist on it. And don't forget: The squeaky wheel gets the grease. The more concern you show for your child, the more involved you are in helping your child, the more concern and help he will receive from others.

Finally, remember there are people out there who can help you. You can hire an advocate (usually not a legal representative, but rather some-one who knows the system and jargon, and what your rights are) to accompany or help you deal with the bureaucracy. Did you know there are lawyers that specialize in representing parents and children in con-flict with school districts? Don't be afraid to consult these specialists if you feel you and your child are not receiving what you need and deserve, or if your situation is more than you can handle on your own. See the Resources section on page 221 to learn how to connect with these helpful individuals.

■ LEARN

You can have an informed opinion only if you are informed. You can be an effective advocate only if you know all your options. Read about your child's issues. Read about proposed treatments. Read about schools. There's a lot of information to be found—more than just what your doc-tors may know or offer to share. The Resources section of this book (see page 221) lists many great books on alternative therapies and treatments.

Another way to learn is to talk to other similarly situated parents. They know schools. They know doctors. They know therapies and good practitioners. They have hard-earned experience from which you can benefit. Start in your local school district. Check with your local parent-teacher association, or PTA. Even better, if available, contact your local special education PTA, called SEPTA. Get in touch with the chairperson, ask if there are parent members with whom you might speak, and attend SEPTA presentations. We met many parents like us at our local SEPTA. Attendees can offer a wealth of information on many different subjects, as well as provide solid references for services. We were privy to many informative presentations and seminars. In fact, SEPTA afforded Tina and me the refreshing opportunity to speak about our experiences with Robert. If your local school's SEPTA or PTA is not helpful, try neighboring school districts.

I also would suggest parent support groups, but be careful where you go. Early on in our experience, Tina attended a support group for parents of children with ADD. Unfortunately, most of the night consisted of parents complaining about all the problems they had with their children, all the different medications their children took, and the side effects their children were suffering from these medications. There was precious little discussion of how best to deal with these problems. Indeed, most parents in attendance did not believe there was anything they could do other than administer the drugs and hope for the best. In the vein of "misery loves company," many of these parents wore their hearts on their sleeves and their children's problems became their identities.

It turned out that the group Tina had attended was sponsored in part by the company that manufactures Ritalin. All in all, it had turned out to be a thoroughly depressing event. Years later, I went to one of this group's meetings myself and found that little had changed. The litany of complaints about comorbid conditions and medication side effects still ran strongly. Moreover, the mere mention that maybe there wasn't anything about these children that actually demanded medication made some parents downright angry. Sadly, when I mentioned our own experiences with alternative therapies, and talked about Robert's amazing success with drug-free treatments, I was met with only skepticism. No one wanted to hear it. Indeed, a family therapist with a master of science degree told me flat out that Robert's story was impossible. "No one gets 'cured' of ADD or PDD," she said. "Your son must have been misdiagnosed." When I assured her that Robert had received these very diagnoses by no less than three psychiatrists and four psychologists, she just shook her head and walked away. I never heard from her again.

Now, I do not mean to suggest that support groups should be avoided. Nor is it even fair to say that this particular support group was truly problematic. I have to believe it was simply unfortunate that we happened to attend these two particular meetings. Hopefully, other meetings proved more fruitful for others. If you decide to seek support groups, look for those that are well organized and caring. Find groups that invite guest speakers who specialize in treating psychological disorders and are well versed in behavioral management, diet control, and different therapies. Many groups conduct seminars and workshops on various topics including discipline, home schooling, and special education. With the proper effort, helpful support groups can be found. It's up to the parent to be a demanding and discriminating consumer. The benefits of such groups are often worth the effort spent searching for the right ones. The Internet, of course, is a good place to get started. The Resources section (see page 221) contains a number of helpful websites.

Don't be afraid to ask questions. Take the doctor's time and don't be brushed off. Ask committees what your rights are, and don't back off until you fully understand them. Visit your child's classroom. Question the teachers. Ask for specifics. People love to talk "fluff," but you need to know exactly what people are going to do and why.

Ultimately, if you really want to learn, observe your child. Observe your child in class. Observe your child with other children. Observe your child around the house. Observe those who work with your child. Find out what's going on. Sit in the classroom. Visit the playground. Watch your child at practice and on the field. Knowledge really is power.

■ RESEARCH MEDICATION

I'm sure you've noticed that I have not yet addressed the use of medication. No doubt, you have realized that Tina and I are not big fans. We firmly believe it is the very last thing you should try, not the first. While there is no doubt many children benefit from medication, why not try more natural, safer approaches initially? After all, the meds will always be there.

Why do we believe meds should be a last resort? Well, in addition to what you've read about our experience with Robert, the fact of the matter is that meds are not nearly as safe and effective as most are led to believe. Perhaps even more alarming is the rapidly increasing use of psychotropic drugs by young children. For example, the use of drugs such as methylphenidate (Ritalin), fluoxetine (Prozac), and clonidine (Catapres) by children between the ages two and four doubled, if not tripled, between the years 1991 and 1995.[1] In 2009, reporting on a study that found a possible link between ADHD medications and sudden childhood deaths, the *Washington Post* stated that some 2.5 million children in the United States were taking such medications at that time.[2]

The use of such drugs continues to surge. In 2014, it was reported that the number of Americans taking ADHD medications had leaped some 36 percent between the years 2008 and 2012, with 9.3 percent of boys ages twelve to eighteen on these drugs. In fact, in 2012, almost 4.8 million privately insured people took ADHD medications.[3]

Worse still, the use of antipsychotic medications, including risperidone (Risperdal), aripiprazole (Abilify), quetiapine (Seroquel), and olanzapine (Zyprexa), to treat ADHD and other behavior problems in children and teens has "skyrocketed in recent years."[4] It may come as a surprise to learn that some of these antipsychotic drugs are being prescribed "off label," that is, they have been neither tested nor approved by the Food and Drug Administration (FDA) for such use. Of course, these drugs come with their own set of side effects.

On the topic of off-label prescriptions, I can't help but note a bit of hypocrisy on the part of the medical profession. Alternative therapies often are criticized for a lack of scientific support. While anecdotal evidence and case studies abound, if there hasn't been a full-blown double-blind published piece of research on a particular therapy, the medical industry often times dismisses it and dissuades patients from trying it.

This is not the case, however, when it comes to prescribing powerful psychotropic drugs in an off-label fashion. Then, based solely upon the doctor's experience or expertise with the drug, it can be prescribed in an untested and unapproved manner. It doesn't seem right, does it?

A particularly alarming fact is that none of the most commonly prescribed drugs have been approved for use in connection with children under the age of six, and little has been done to study the long-term effects such drugs may have on children this young,[5] and due to a "fundamental lack of knowledge," no one knows "whether there is a danger point below [a certain age] which [doctors] should not be prescribing."[6] The increased use of psychotropic drugs in children is startling "in light of the limited knowledge base that underlies psychotropic medication use in very young children."[7] Indeed, "controlled clinical studies to evaluate the efficacy and safety of psychotropic medication for preschoolers are rare," and the use of clonidine "is particularly notable because its increased prescribing is occurring without the benefit of rigorous data to support it as a safe and effective treatment for attentional disorders."[8]

Serious problems are being discovered more and more in connection with the use of many of these psychotropic drugs, as well as with the use of antidepressants, prescriptions of which are also on the rise. Researchers are now warning that these drugs may carry severe side effects ranging from depression and suicidal thoughts to stroke, cancer, and death. In fact, the *Washington Post* has reported that at least one study found a possible link between sudden death and ADHD medications. "[A]ccording to a study . . . funded by the Food and Drug Administration and the National Institute of Mental Health . . . [c]hildren taking stimulant drugs such as Ritalin to treat attention-deficit hyperactivity disorder are several times as likely to suffer sudden, unexplained death as children who are not taking such drugs."[9]

Of course, the FDA was quick to respond in a perfectly predictable manner: "In a press briefing called on short notice . . . FDA officials said that given the seriousness of ADHD and the rarity of sudden death—which strikes fewer than 1 in 10,000 children—the benefits of the drugs outweigh their risks."[10]

The psychotropic drug Adderall XR was pulled off the market in Canada after reports linked its use to a dozen strokes and twenty sudden deaths.[11] Fourteen of these sudden deaths and two of the strokes were suffered by children.[12]

Researchers at the University of Texas and the M.D. Anderson Cancer Center found chromosomal damage in twelve children that used Ritalin for three months. The chromosomal damage was similar to that caused by known cancer-causing drugs.[13]

The FDA now warns of suicidal thinking and behavior in children who have taken the ADHD medication Strattera[14] and antidepressants.[15] The FDA has also asked that the makers of antidepressants Prozac, Zoloft, Paxil, Luvox, Celexa, Lexapro, Wellbutrin, Effexor, Serzone, and Remeron add warnings to their labels regarding risk of suicide.[16] This same concern, as well as risks of hallucinations and violent behavior, was expressed in connection with the psychostimulant drug Concerta.[17] After reviewing relevant scientific studies, Britain's Medicines and Healthcare Products Regulatory Agency concluded there was "no solid evidence that the benefits outweigh the possible side effects" of antidepressant use by individuals under the age of eighteen. American researchers, however, were quick to fire back with a study of their own that concluded the risks associated with depression outweighed any potential harm caused by antidepressants.[18]

At the end of the day, you have to ask: Are these drugs as safe, effective, and well researched as we parents have been led to believe?

■ FIND THE RIGHT SCHOOL

Although I have only the utmost respect for the special education teachers that worked with my son, I cannot advocate special education placement other than as an absolute last resort. No matter what people claim, special education carries a stigma—a stigma many individuals cannot see past. People talk, mistakes happen, and confidential records don't always remain confidential, especially when you try to move out the special education system. The obviously lowered expectations associated with special education had a direct and detrimental impact on my son. Lowering expectations does not help anyone.

Had we the chance to do it over again, we would have done everything possible to keep Robert out of special education. His record followed him wherever he went, and if not for those individuals willing to trust us as parents and give Robert a chance to prove himself, those records would have prevented him from ever truly leaving special education behind.

One particular incident drove this point home. Robert interviewed and tested especially well at a school to which we considered sending him after he was to graduate from Westbury Friends. The director of the school told me how well Robert had done, and that it was just a matter of reviewing his teacher recommendations and school records. So, imagine the shock I got when this woman called me at work and treated me like a used car salesman trying to sell her a car without a motor. "You never told us Robert was an 'at risk' child! He has an IEP. He's been classified." She was absolutely indignant. (Recall that "IEP" refers to an "individualized education program." Classified children, like Robert, receive an education program designed specifically to meet their particular educational needs, including, among other things, a report of current performance, annual goals, and any accommodations given.)

When I explained that that was all old news, that Robert wasn't going by an IEP anymore, that he hadn't received any special services for two years, and that we had never bothered to have him declassified because it was all moot at this point, she turned a deaf ear. I told her to talk to the director of Westbury Friends, read the teacher recommendations, and remember how well Robert tested and interviewed. She would hear none of it. She told me Robert's application would no longer be considered. I called the director of Westbury Friends. She was as upset by this turn of events as we were. We pulled all Robert's special education files, and Tina and I made arrangements to have Robert formally declassified as soon as possible. We had to make sure those papers never resurfaced.

Finding a school that will willingly work with your child without branding him is absolutely critical. Your child spends an enormous amount of time in school, and learns much more than just "the three Rs" from teachers and students. Look for an understanding staff and diverse student body. Visit the school. Talk to the principal or director. Talk to the teachers that will actually work with your child. Visit the classroom into which your child will be placed. The teachers should be patient, understanding, and flexible. Moreover, the classrooms should not be overwhelmingly large in number. Small classes are a must if the teacher is going to have the time and resources necessary to address your child's particular needs.

The teachers also should be willing to make reasonable accommodations. Robert was allowed to doodle while he was in class. His teacher let him do this because it kept him from fidgeting and because she knew he was actually concentrating. In addition, doodling helped him develop his fine motor skills. By allowing a tactile learner like Robert to draw, the teacher was, in fact, helping Robert concentrate. Other accommodations? Using laptops, giving extra time, special seating arrangements, periodic breaks, or even just a quiet corner. The list goes on and on.

You, the teachers, and the school's administration should have frequent and open communication about your child's progress. Raising children, with or without special needs, is a team effort. Only through open communication can those who work with your children work effectively together. Above all, everyone who works with your child must have the highest expectations. Children live up to (or, unfortunately, down to) expectations.

■ FOSTER YOUR CHILD'S SELF-ESTEEM

The term self-esteem refers to how you feel about yourself. It is not about how others perceive you (although how you think others perceive you often impacts your self-esteem) or even what objective observation reveals. What you believe becomes reality. How you feel about yourself governs your attitude, behavior, and actions. Children with high self-esteem are happier, have more friends, and are more accepted by others than those with poor self-esteem. They do better in school, accept challenges better, and are even healthier.

Parents have the most influence in shaping a child's sense of self-worth. What can you do to ensure your children have high self-esteem?

You can respect your children, communicate with them, provide them with guidance, be involved in their lives, encourage and nurture them, and love them unconditionally.

Children are people, too. They are not objects to be ordered about or ignored. They have feelings, need love, and seek approval and acceptance. Don't label your child, and don't allow others to do so. Don't call your child "stupid" or "dumb" when something goes wrong or your child performs a task poorly. And while some schools require that a child be classified in order to receive special services, don't call a child with special needs "handicapped," "learning disabled," "dyslexic," or any one of the other labels that exist. If you do, your child will learn to become the label.

Children should not be told that they "always" do something wrong, that they "never" listen, or that they will "never" make the team or get the grade. Avoid absolutes! Things change; a situation can improve. It often does if the child believes it can. When you say "never," your child believes it.

Give your children the same attention you'd expect other people to give you. In other words, give them your undivided attention. Look at them directly. Listen—really listen—to what they have to say. Scrunch down to their level. Get close. Let them talk without interruption, even if you think you know what they are trying to say or you think you have the answer. If you interrupt, they will feel you are rushing them or not listening. If you give them the answer, you may have missed the point of why they were talking to you. Maybe they just needed to talk. Maybe they just needed to hear a comforting voice.

Of course, you must still set behavior standards and moral guidelines. You must also share your values with your children. Guidelines give children a sense of purpose and order. They are a source of comfort. When children know how they should behave and what is expected, they are far more confident in the moment. They feel better about themselves.

Make sure your child is aware of your standards, guidelines, and values, and make sure your child sticks to them. How? First and foremost, be a role model. Parents are a child's first and most important teachers. How you act is the model upon which your children will shape their own behavior. Respect each other. Treat each other well. Treat other people well. Treat your children well. Second, discipline the right way. I know this is tough, but try not to only say no. Instead, explain the factors that led to your decision, express your understanding of how your child may feel (hurt, unfairly treated, angry, etc.), give your decision, and allow questions, but do not debate. Once you have laid down the law in detail, the discussion should be over.

I cannot tell you how many times I came home to find Tina arguing with my then three-year-old daughter. It was a very amusing sight, at least for me, to see both of them standing with their hands on their hips, squared off against each other, Tina glaring down at Kat, Kat defiantly returning her stare. Of course, Mom wasn't winning. Hardly ever able to hide my smile, I would ask what was going on. Tina's glare would then be turned upon me, and I would get an earful about how my daughter was refusing to clean up her toys. I would ask Tina why she was arguing with a three-year-old (always a big mistake–both my asking her and her arguing with a three-year-old), and after I got yelled at, I would simply pick my daughter up, deposit her with her toys, and explain that she had to clean up because it was dangerous. She had to do it now, and she would not be allowed to leave until it was done.

Yes, I understood she wanted to go out and play. The toys got picked up first.

"But," she would begin.

"No 'buts,' and no more discussion. You may go out when you are finished and not before."

"But, Mommy said . . ."

"Ahem. The toys. Now."

And, believe it or not, that's usually when she would pick up her toys. I refused to get pulled into an argument.

The point of the story? Tina allowed herself to get roped in by this child, and this child took advantage of that fact.

You should also maintain rules and guidelines. It is important to explain your expectations. When you do so, remember to speak positively. Tell your children what you want them to do, not what you don't want them to do. For example, the best way to ensure your child spills his drink is to say, "Don't spill your drink." The better way to instruct your child would be to say, "Please be careful with your drink." Equally important is to make sure your children know beforehand the consequences of your expectations not being met. Of course, make sure these consequences are appropriate, and be firm and consistent. Attack the behavior, not the child, and try to discipline without anger. It should seem as though the consequences are the natural result of the misbehavior. Try not to yell. It is unbelievably hard not to get angry and yell sometimes, but the more you practice, the easier it gets. Besides, anger is rarely productive and only brings tension to the situation. Instead, tell your child how you feel about the behavior in question, and express the fact that you understand the child will behave in the proper way next time.

I know this is easier said than done. It is almost impossible to know where to draw the line and how to keep from losing your temper. Knowing what your child truly can do and cannot do is probably the most important factor in determining how you react to your child's behavior, yet it is the most difficult factor to determine. For example, if you know your child simply cannot deal with transition, you make arrangements. It is a given, and therefore more acceptable. True, it may be maddening, but with understanding and acceptance comes a bit more patience. When you know something is going to happen and realize there is nothing you can do about it, you adapt and accept it.

If you believe your child should and could deal with transition better, then your expectations color your reaction. Not dealing well with transition may be viewed as a deliberate act undertaken by the child, something controllable, and something that, through proper discipline and training, could be corrected. In this view, the behavior will no longer seem acceptable or even be understood. It will be seen as a problem that must be fixed. When it does not get fixed, that's when the anger and frustration boil over.

Finally, tell your children you love them. A hug, a kiss, or a simple "I love you" will do wonders for a child's self-esteem, especially after that child has been disciplined. This affection lets children know you still love and care for them, even though you do not approve of certain behavior and cannot condone it. You can never tell a child "I love you" enough. Doing so is good for both parent and child.

■ GET INVOLVED

Show an interest in your children's interests. It means a lot to them. Go to their baseball games. Go to their recitals. Go to school ceremonies and events. Talk to your child's teachers. Talk to your child's coaches. Find out how your child is doing. Discuss your child's progress, feelings, and the best approaches to issues that might arise. Get involved. If you show other people that you are interested in your child, those people will be far more likely to show an interest in your child, too.

Encourage and nurture your child, and maintain high expectations. Do not set preconceived limits on your child's abilities or what your child may hope to accomplish. When you believe in children, they believe in themselves. Applaud success and remember that children are successful when they have done the very best they can, even if the best they can do is less than you'd like it to be. For example, if getting half the answers on a test correct is the best your child can do at the moment, then a 50-percent grade is a success, even if a 65-percent mark is the passing grade. Now, this does not mean that you should celebrate mediocrity; neither you nor your child should be satisfied with a 50-percent mark if your child is truly capable of more. And remember that things change. Just because your child is capable of only a 50-percent grade today, this doesn't mean you won't see a 65-percent grade or better tomorrow.

Don't belabor failure. Let little imperfections go. Let your children overhear you complimenting them to others. Conversely, never let your children overhear you criticize or complaining about them. When you speak directly to your child, about good or bad, the information gets filtered through defense mechanisms and its full impact is not realized. When the information is overheard, however, there are no defense mechanisms in place. Overheard compliments are a joy; overheard criticisms can be devastating.

Don't forget to love your child unconditionally. We all love our children no matter what, but do our children believe that? Remember, what they believe becomes reality. Do you compliment only when your child performs to your expectations? Are hugs and kisses doled out only as rewards when your child behaves? Do you listen better only when your child talks about something of interest to you? Do your actions belie your words?

You cannot show or tell your children enough that you love them. Hug them, kiss them, and hold them—all the time and for no reason other than the fact that they are there.

■ DARE TO TRY SOMETHING DIFFERENT

If you are not happy with your situation, try something different. There is an old saying that goes something like this: If you don't change the path you're on, chances are you will end up where you are going. In other words, if you are not getting the results you desire, try something different, otherwise you'll end up exactly where you are heading already—an unhappy ending. I was very guilty of this. It began when I would not admit Robert had an issue. It progressed when I continued to trust the mainstream medical system, even though I was very unhappy with the results it was producing. It took years for me to see our situation as it truly was and change directions.

The trick is to examine your particular situation from the perspective of an objective third party. Do not let your preconceived notions and prejudices color your observations. And do not get caught up doing something that is not producing the results you want just because it is what you think you are supposed to do.

Live in the moment. What is happening now? It is counterproductive to feel guilty about the past or to worry incessantly about what might be. What is the situation today? What can be done today to start you on the path that will lead you to the result you really want?

Do not become so emotionally tied to the situation that you cannot even begin to examine alternatives or admit things could be better. You are not your child, and more importantly, your child is not the disorder. There are lots of ways to do things. Obviously, some may work better than others, some may work only for some people, and some may be more difficult to institute, but you'll never know until you try.

In light of this last point, I'd like to mention a "systematic review" of "novel and emerging treatments for autism spectrum disorders" published in *Annals of Clinical Psychiatry* in 2009. Addressing many of the therapies we had used in connection with Robert, the article reviewed the available literature for any studies that would document the effectiveness of "alternative" or "complimentary" therapies, both biologically and non-biologically based, ranging from dietary changes and supplementation, to chelation therapy, music therapy, acupuncture, auditory integration, and neurofeedback.[19] Not surprisingly, many of these therapies did, in fact, have studies supporting their use. Indeed, the Autism Research Institute (ARI) published a comprehensive set of parental ratings comparing the observed effects on behavior of a vast host of biomedical interventions, including drugs such as Ritalin, Prozac, and clonidine, as well as dietary interventions and supplementation.[20] Based upon data collected from more than 27,000 parents who completed the ARI's questionnaires on the perceived effectiveness of such varied interventions, the results should be considered nothing short of remarkable and should not be ignored.

Of some forty-five different medications listed, only seventeen were reported to have improved the child's behavior at least 33 percent of the time. In other words, the vast majority of drugs prescribed to our children for "behavioral issues" are perceived by parents to work less than one-third of the time. On the other hand, only four of the twenty-eight "non-drug supplements" surveyed had shown an effectiveness of less than 33 percent. In addition, a staggering 100 percent of the eleven special diets listed were effective at least 45 percent of the time.[21]

▦ GIVE YOURSELF A BREAK

Parents are not superhuman. We can do only so much in a day. We can take only so much. There is a limit to selflessness, and sometimes you need a break. Give yourself one. Leaving your child with family members, neighbors, or babysitters from time to time is okay. Parents need time for themselves, and for each other. The kids will be okay if you're away from them for a little while. In fact, they'll be better for it, and so will you. You won't resent the time they take from you if you regularly get some time to yourself.

Go out to dinner (it doesn't need to be expensive or fancy) or a movie with your spouse—just the two of you. Get yourself to the gym. Go for a walk or ride a bike. Enjoy your favorite hobby. Read a book. Take care of yourself. Even children without special concerns place a tremendous strain on parents and their relationship with each other. Don't play the martyr. It's not good for you, your spouse, or your child.

While this last bit of advice may be the shortest, it may well be the most important. I've seen too many parents drift apart, due, in part, to the issues presented by their special needs children. But it doesn't have to be that way. Our children are our gifts. If anything, they should bring us together.

As Neil Postman states, "Children are the living messages we send to a time we will never see." They are our legacy. Being a good parent requires a tremendous investment—of time, of energy, and of unconditional love. Be willing to give what it takes. You will reap the benefits of your effort many times over.

■ CONCLUSION

In dealing with Robert's situation, and in connection with our many years of working with children with attention, learning, and behavioral issues, we have uncovered a tremendous amount of research that supports our beliefs and actions. Much of that research may be found in this book's appendix (see page 191). While the information contained in the appendix is in no way complete (indeed, I believe I have only been able to scratch the surface of what is available, and, in any event, more and more information about children on the spectrum is being discovered all the time), we believe it is a good place to start (or continue) your own search for knowledge and answers. It is my and Tina's sincerest wish that our story has helped you in some way. We hope it has provided you with useful information, hope for you and your child, and comfort in the recognition that you are not alone.

Afterword

Robert has taken Tina and me on an emotional roller coaster of happiness, frustration, hope, and despair. While being Robert's parents has been more enriching than we ever could have imagined, it has also taken its toll—one we were willing to pay, of course, but a toll nonetheless. I am not ashamed to admit that Robert has personally driven me into fits of rage that reduced me to tears. At this point, I wish I had something truly profound to say about our experience, but nothing really comes to mind. In the end, we did what we had to do. I have learned that the one constant in life is that it is never constant. Things change. Surprises, both good and bad, occur. You can try to force events and people and things to be just the way you want them to be—just as you imagined they should be—but that hardly ever works. When you really think about it, our lives are nothing more than one occurrence after another, and those who adapt and make the best out of whatever situation presents itself, those who live in the moment, are the ones who are happy. I have worked with parents whose children faced greater challenges than Robert, and who were able to make remarkable improvements to their children's lives through pure belief and effort. I look at such ingenuity, determination, commitment, and resourcefulness with respect, admiration, and awe. How were they able to handle their circumstances? Time and again, they simply did what needed to be done.

I have seen parents and children do some amazing things. I believe we are all capable of similar achievements once we acknowledge the truth of a situation, commit to what needs to be done, and manage to get out of the way of our own doubts and insecurities. Tina and I learned that our instincts can be trusted. We learned that we are capable. We needed only to believe in ourselves.

There were many people who did not believe in us, though. We encountered many who had different views of our son and his future. Everyone had an opinion. Sometimes they screamed so loudly that I could not hear my own heart. It was during those times that I was misled. But despite the wrong turns, setbacks, and disappointments, in the end, our journey was worth it. Although it was not the journey I had envisioned, it was mine to take. Strange that while I toiled under the illusion that I was molding my children's lives, they were, in fact, molding mine. Hopefully, I have learned how to be a better father, husband, and person from them. I certainly know they have taught me what is truly important in life. My family has inspired me. They have given me purpose. They have freed me. They have made me stronger. I am lucky to have them.

As I mentioned earlier, I left my law practice to start working with children like Robert as part of a small start-up company. That was back in 1998. It offered a wonderful, effective program and a chance for a fresh start doing something I loved, and it was an opportunity too good to pass up. While I did not have a formal education in this area, between my experiences trying to start a school for high-functioning children with learning disabilities and my and Tina's personal research concerning Robert's situation, I walked in the door with a substantial amount of knowledge. It also didn't hurt that I was a quick and very motivated learner. As time went on, I continued to research, learn, and train, and soon earned advanced certifications in several developmental programs. Thankfully, I was able to network with other experts in various related fields, and, best of all, I got to work directly with and help hundreds of families. I was able to see firsthand what worked, what did not, and what required improvement.

With the help of a network of developmental experts, I found myself revising and refining our programs, broadening them in both scope and effectiveness. In time, Tina and I established a small center of our own: Spark Development. With our own center, I was afforded the opportunity to lecture, present seminars, conduct workshops, and write. (In addition to this book, I have, over the years, maintained a blog and written articles for a local parenting magazine.) I have had the luxury of developing, testing, and adding several new components to our programs, including auditory training, internal rhythm training, physical fitness, coordination, and most importantly, clinical nutrition. That's where Tina comes in.

Astonished by the change that diet had on Robert's behavior, Tina began researching nutrition interventions on her own—a task made easier by her background in the sciences. Highly motivated (Tina was also pregnant with our third child, Matthew), she returned to school to earn her master's degree in clinical nutrition from New York Institute of Technology. In addition to her work as a cardiovascular technologist, she provides clinical nutrition services to families enrolled in our center.

Working with the children at our center to strengthen their cognitive skills, sensory integration, and diet—just as we did with Robert—we can honestly (and proudly) say we have seen improvement in nearly all our children. I must admit, though, like all things Robert-related, this experience has been difficult. While remarkably rewarding, our learning center endeavor has had its share of ups and downs. I am continually reminded that we are just a bit ahead of our time.

One time, a parent whose child had gone through our program with tremendous results asked if I would do a presentation for the Special Education Parent Teacher Association of her child's school. I was soon told, however, that some board members were opposed to my speaking. "He's just here to sell his program," they said. The parent, of course, knew that my presentations were not about the program. I would generally start my talks with a brief history of Robert, explaining why we did our work. That, in turn, would lead to a discussion of various theories regarding ASD and its possible causes, different approaches to treatment, and the problems associated with the use of medication in the treatment of special needs kids. She insisted that I speak, and after I promised not to "sell," the board capitulated. I wish it hadn't.

The minute I opened my mouth, one woman in the audience went on the attack. Deeply committed to her doctors and obviously vested in the medical model, she really didn't want to hear about Robert. "What you did with him may have worked, but that doesn't mean it has any application when it comes to our kids!" she said. Flabbergasted, I continued, but I had been truly thrown off by her open hostility. From then on, it was just one interruption after another, as she questioned the legitimacy of my research, all of which is documented in this book, the efficacy of the treatments we had tried, and my motivation for appearing there in the first place. It served as a stark reminder of just how far we still had to go to be heard and believed. Yet, despite the ups and downs, we know what we do is valid and important, and our work will continue as long as there are parents who honor us by putting their children in our care. As Tina has reminded me over and over, we have a message to deliver.

As for Robert, he is fine. If you met him today and were not aware of his history, you would not be able to tell that there was once something "wrong" with him. A confident (perhaps overly confident) twenty-four-year-old, he stands over six feet four inches tall and is as handsome and bright as ever. A gifted artist, he plays the guitar and bass, writes music for several bands, and has a great circle of friends and a very sweet girlfriend. He got into his first choice of college and received his degree in a highly competitive design program.

Robert also volunteers at my learning center. He pushes the kids hard and is surprisingly tough, but he is also exceptionally patient and fair. The kids love him (well, most of them, anyway) and so do the parents. Even my senior instructors agree he is great with the kids—a chip off the old block.

There is one last thing I'd like to tell you about Robert. Before this book was ever considered for publication, I asked Robert for permission to tell his story. I asked if hearing about the "before times" would bother him, and I certainly did not want to embarrass him or make him feel uncomfortable in any way. He looked me square in the eye and said, "It's fine with me. This story has a happy ending."

Appendix A

What You Should Know

Back in 1996, when Tina and I were in the middle of wrestling with Robert's issues, a published psychiatrist postulated that childhood psychiatric disorders such as ADHD were "nobody's fault."[1] He argued that such disorders were the result of genetics and brain chemistry imbalances over which no one had any control. Clearly defined and diagnosable, these disorders had accepted medical treatments. At that time, and in our ignorance, we accepted such assertions without question. Surely Robert's doctors knew what they were talking about. Also, on some level, statements like these made Robert's situation more palatable. It wasn't our fault. We weren't bad parents, we didn't do this to him, and we couldn't have prevented it. But now, after our experience treating Robert, after watching the number of children diagnosed with these disorders skyrocket, and after our discovery of so much new research, we think differently. While there is no doubt that some children suffer from neurological problems resulting from "DNA roulette"—a term coined by the previously mentioned psychiatrist—we believe environmental elements play a significant role in a great number of the attention, learning, and behavioral disorders being diagnosed.

In the year 2000, it was conservatively estimated that anywhere between 3 and 5 percent of children in the United States had ADHD.[2] By 2003, that number had risen to 7.8 percent. In 2007, it was 9.5 percent. In the mid-1980s, it was estimated that 1 person in 2500 was autistic. In the year 2000, the Centers for Disease Control and Prevention (CDC) estimated that as many as 1 child in 500 was autistic.[3] In 2003, a study of metropolitan Atlanta kids between the ages of three and ten years old found that some form of autism affected roughly 1 child in 295.[4] In 2004, the autism rate was 1 in 166 children, and 1 out of every 6 children was diagnosed with a developmental or behavioral disorder. [5] In 2009, it was generally accepted that 1 in 100 children had autism spectrum disorder.[6] In 2012, the CDC announced a staggering rate of 1 in 88.[7] Even worse, in 2011, a comprehensive study done in South Korea found the autism rate to be an unbelievable 1 in 38.[8] In May of 2014, the CDC stated that the prevalence of ASD was 1 in 68, with 1 out of every 42 cases being a boy.[9]

If these statistics are anywhere near accurate, they reflect a crisis of "epidemic proportions."[10] While genetics must play a part in this matter, we believe that environment and lifestyle may well play an even bigger one. Moreover, even if a link exists between certain genes and the incidence of these disorders,[11] it does not negate the fact that harmful environmental factors, poor nutrition, and certain childrearing practices may contribute to, if not trigger, the behaviors and symptoms that define these issues. And if such environmental factors, nutrition, and childrearing practices can contribute to these problems, it is reasonable to assume that these disorders might be alleviated by making changes in these areas.

Now, on some level, most of us would be relieved to find out that these disorders are nothing more than genetic accidents, that we cannot prevent them, and that they cannot be treated by changing our lifestyles. I want to watch too much TV. I want to eat fast food. I want to believe that pharmaceuticals are perfectly safe. But Tina and I have seen the benefits that can accompany certain shifts in habits such as a change in diet, and these benefits have forced us to question what else might be having a negative effect on children.

■ GENETICS AND ENVIRONMENT

Genetics surely play a role in the occurrence of ASD, but they are likely not the sole determining factor. In June of 2011, researchers at Cold Spring Harbor Genetics Lab indicated that they had found an association between certain genetic mutations and ASD. Specifically, researchers had seen "gene copy number variations (CNV)," which are duplicated or deleted genome segments that result in extra or missing copies of one or more genes, at 250 to 300 locations in the human genome of autistic individuals.[12] This was not the first discovery of a particular genetic aspect to autism, but it received a large amount of press. Unfortunately, many claim this study demonstrates that autism is a genetic disorder in which environment plays a limited role. Tina and I disagree.

While these genetic findings are interesting and potentially helpful, they do not rule out environmental causation. First, this study's results are severely limited, indicating that these purported gene mutations are connected to only two to three percent of all autism cases. Second, correlation is not the same as causation. In other words, an association between a pattern of gene mutations and ASD does not mean such mutations cause autism. Moreover, we cannot assume that these genetic changes occur without any external catalyst. The fact is that we don't know what causes these mutations and can only speculate. Are such mutations spontaneous events, or did some outside factor cause them? Moreover, even if this genetic pattern is linked to ASD, does its mere presence inexorably lead to autism, or must there be some external trigger involved? Perhaps these mutations merely make a child susceptible to autism. "To have the full autistic syndrome we might need the genetic predisposition as well as some other event or exposure. . . ."[13]

Environment simply cannot be dismissed. Indeed, through the use of concrete examples of how environmental factors negatively affect pregnancy outcomes, such as the consumption of alcohol during pregnancy or exposure to Rubella during pregnancy, it is evident that outside elements can be extremely powerful causative forces. It is reasonable to assume that environmental factors may play a large role in autism even where genetics are involved. In fact, on the heels of the Cold Spring Harbor research came two other studies and a review article written by a former pharmaceutical drug company scientist[14] that demonstrate that ASD is likely linked to environmental factors.

One study examined the incidence of both strict autism and ASD in identical and fraternal twins. The researchers discovered that neither strict autism nor ASD occurred as frequently in both of the identical twin boys and girls—that is, boys and girls who shared the same genetic material—nearly as often as it should if autism is caused primarily by genet-ics. Conversely, with respect to fraternal twins—that is, boys and girls whose genetic material is not identical—concordance rates for both strict autism and ASD were much higher than should be expected if genetics are to blame. This led the researchers to conclude that "[s]usceptibility to ASD has moderate genetic heritability and a substantial shared twin environmental component." Even more specifically, the researchers determined that "[f]or strict autism . . . [t]he best-fitting model had a genetic heritability of 37% . . . and a shared environmental variance com-ponent of 55%. For the broader ASD . . . [h]eritability was estimated to be 38% and the shared environmental component to be 58%. The shared environment component was estimated to be larger than the genetic her-itability component."[15]

In other words, according to this research, genes account for 37 per-cent of the risk of strict autism and 38 percent of the risk of autism spec-trum disorder. Environmental factors, on the other hand, account for 55 percent of the risk of autism and 58 percent of the risk of autism spectrum disorder.

Further proof of the adverse effects of negative environmental expo-sure and specifically its link to ASD may be found in a study that sought to determine whether exposure to antidepressants during pregnancy has any connection to the incidence of autism. Unfortunately, such exposure does seem to increase the risk of ASD, especially if it takes place during the first trimester.[16]

■ TREATMENT AND PREVENTION

Whatever the specific causes of learning disorders, it seems that some-thing has changed over the last few decades, and changed enough to impact our children's development in very negative ways. While it might seem impossible to pinpoint the reason, or reasons, behind the increase in ASD, we must nevertheless start somewhere. Tina and I believe we must look at the environment to which we and our children are exposed, what we feed our children, and how we raise our children. Specifically, we believe the following factors, most likely in combination, contribute to learning and behavioral disorders: severely compromised immune systems; exposure to damaging environmental factors such as toxins and chemicals; and insufficiently developed sensory integration skills. We also believe that, with a little effort, we can control these factors and, in doing so, mitigate these disorders. We may be able to lower the incidence of these problems, or at least reduce the severity of the symptoms that define these disorders, by making changes to our lifestyles and adopting helpful habits.

One reason to believe that such disorders are preventable or at least improvable is the fact that diagnosing these learning disorders—from ADD through full-blown autism—is dependent upon the subjective observation of symptoms. Essentially, a child is diagnosed with one or more of these disorders if it is determined that the child displays signs and symptoms associated with such developmental difficulties. In other words, the symptoms define the disorder. If there is evidence that we can improve or eliminate the symptoms of a particular disorder, it means that we can improve or eliminate that disorder.

To explain further, when Robert was first diagnosed, the criteria for diagnosing ADHD, as set forth in the fourth edition of the American Psychiatric Association's *Diagnostic and Statistical Manual of Mental Disorders*, or *DSM-IV*, were based upon the presence of "symptoms of inattention." Such symptoms included making "careless" mistakes, having "trouble" keeping attention, and "not following through" on chores, and pointed to a child who "avoids, dislikes, doesn't want to do things," is "easily" distracted, "butts into" conversations, and "excessively" runs about or talks. These symptoms were furthered defined as being criteria for an ADHD diagnosis when they are often present.[17]

The use of such words as "often" to define frequency, "excessively" to define quantity, "impairment" to define affect, and "blurts," "dislikes," and "butts into" to define diagnostic behaviors does not provide any true objective basis upon which to anchor a diagnosis. It is important to note that there is no biological marker of any sort given to define these disorders. The *DSM-IV* diagnostic criteria for Asperger syndrome, PDD, and autism are equally subjective.[18] In fact, well after Robert's diagnoses, the literature began to refer to an "autistic spectrum." I have no doubt that this was in response to the sheer number of diagnoses being made, as well as the difficultly in clearly defining the vast variation and severity of symptoms. (When we first began networking with other parents, nearly everyone with whom we spoke told us of their children's simultaneously occurring disorders. More likely than not, these children had been diagnosed with more than one disorder, with many of these disorders having been qualified as "severe," "borderline," or "unique" in combination.)

We have always believed that these disorders are simply different manifestations of the same issue, and we have always firmly believed that ADHD should be on the autism spectrum. Indeed, recognizing that "[d]oubt remains about the boundaries between" such learning disorders, as well as "the degree to which [the separate diagnoses] signify entirely distinct entities, disorders that have overlapping foundations, or different variants of one underlying disease," one study found that autism spectrum disorder, attention deficit-hyperactivity disorder, bipolar disorder, major depressive disorder, and schizophrenia all share genetic links.[19] Further proof of the association between ADHD and the spectrum can be gleaned from a recent study that found ADHD was linked to language difficulties[20]—a problem also associated with, among other things, dyslexia and ASD.

On May 18, 2013, the American Psychiatric Association released a new version of the *Diagnostic and Statistical Manual of Mental Disorders,* or *DSM-5*. Among other things, the revised manual includes diagnostic criteria for the now formally recognized autism spectrum disorder. ASD has subsumed a range of related disorders, including Asperger syndrome and PDD, which are no longer considered separate disorders. Of note to this discussion is the fact that these new definitions still rely upon the subjective observance of symptoms for diagnosis. I was disappointed to discover that ASD had not been defined to include ADHD, which still retains its independent status.[21]

It is important to understand that diagnosis of these developmental disorders is not dependent upon cause. If it is the observer's opinion that a child often does not give close attention to details, has trouble maintaining attention, does not seem to listen when spoken to directly, has trouble organizing activities, doesn't want to do things that take a lot of mental effort for a long period of time, and is easily distracted; that such symptoms were present in the child before the age of seven; that there is clear evidence of clinically significant impairment; that some impairment from the symptoms is present in two or more settings (for example, at school and at home); and that these difficulties cannot be attributed to another disorder; then the child will be diagnosed with ADHD. It does not matter why this child displays such symptoms; it does not matter what caused the existence of such symptoms; it does not matter that there is no objective measure of such symptoms; it only matters that the individual making the diagnosis believes the symptoms exist. And based upon such diagnostic criteria, the medical profession will then prescribe powerful, psychotropic drugs to the child, sometimes even if that child is only two years of age.[22]

If these disorders are defined by their symptoms, then pragmatically speaking, improvement and prevention must focus upon the factors that affect these symptoms. In this, we may find hope. Research has demonstrated that many of the most prevalent symptoms associated with numerous learning disorders may be affected by non-genetic factors that are within our control. It is not a coincidence that the very environmental and social factors suspected to play causative roles in developmental problems have, in fact, been associated with the incidence of these disorders. I have no doubt that if we are careful and pay attention to the available research, we can reduce the incidence and severity of these disorders. We need only look at what may be done.

In regard to the following information, we are not suggesting any particular course of treatment and cannot offer medically qualified guidance, and therefore we cannot make any specific recommendations. We strongly urge anyone interested in pursuing any of these ideas to consult with qualified and experienced practitioners.

▓ Diet

It is important for a child to eat healthfully. That's pretty standard advice, but it is incomplete. Specifically, it is important for a child to eat healthfully even when still in the womb. A child should be appropriately nourished during pregnancy, as a newborn, as a toddler, and beyond. Indeed, it is a good idea for an expectant mother to start eating healthfully well before she becomes pregnant to ensure she has a strong immune system and is not lacking in any essential nutrients—nutrients her baby will need from her in order to develop properly. In July of 2011, it was reported that mothers who took prenatal vitamins three months prior to conception or during the first month of pregnancy were statistically less likely to have a child diagnosed with autism.[23] Likewise, in February of 2013, published research found that "[u]se of prenatal folic acid supplements around the time of conception was associated with a lower risk of autistic disorder. . . ."[24]

In addition, women who are breastfeeding should be sure to maintain an adequate intake of essential fatty acids (EFAs) in their diets. These fats play critical roles in the development and maintenance of a newborn's neurological system, immune system, and overall physiology.[25] Of particular importance are long-chain polyunsaturated fatty acids (LCPUFAs) known as omega-3 fatty acids—specifically, eicosapentaenoic acid (EPA) and docosahexaenoic acid (DHA). Studies have shown that LCPUFAs are critical to the proper development of the brain and eyes,[26] and there is no question that LCPUFAs are vital to the brain and nerve development of fetuses and newborns.[27] In animal studies, rhesus monkeys deprived of proper amounts of LCPUFAs had abnormal retinal functioning and reduced visual acuity.[28] Moreover, it has been demonstrated that LCPUFA deficiency may impair the learning ability in the offspring of animals,[29] and may contribute to "aberrations in [animal] cognitive development."[30] LCPUFAs affect both neurotransmitter composition[31] and function.[32] (Recall that drugs like Ritalin are designed to affect the transmission and reception of neurotransmitters at brain synapses.)

The positive impact of LCPUFAs has been scientifically proven time and again. For example, preterm infants who received DHA supplementation had improved visual development and visual processing skills.[33] Ten-month-old infants whose formula was supplemented with LCPUFAs from birth to four months showed significantly greater problem-solving skill than those whose formula was not supplemented.[34] Finally, preterm infants whose diets were supplemented with DHA enjoyed a ten-point advantage in IQ over their non-supplemented peers.[35]

Similarly, LCPUFA deficiency has been observed in children diagnosed with ADHD, and not surprisingly, physical manifestations of LCPUFA deficiency are often seen in ADHD children. The profile of a LCPUFA-deficient child fit Robert to a tee. For example, a telltale sign of LCPUFA deficiency is increased thirst and urination. Coincidentally, studies have observed increased thirst in hyperactive children.[36] Eczema and dry skin are symptoms observed in test subjects that lack essential fatty acids,[37] and many children with ADHD experience these same conditions.[38] Robert himself had excessive thirst and urination, as well as the dry skin condition known as cradle cap.

Thankfully, adequate EFA levels can be attained through nutrition and, if necessary, supplementation. The first way to provide your child with EFAs is through breastfeeding. Assuming mom is not deficient, human breast milk is an excellent source of LCPUFAs.[39] In fact, breastfeeding has been shown to benefit the overall development of children. It has been reported that breastfed children suffer fewer allergies and ear infections, display higher cognitive skill, have fewer behavioral problems, and have a lower incidence of ADHD.[40]

As the American Academy of Pediatrics (AAP) reports, "Extensive research . . . documents diverse and compelling advantages to infants, mothers, families, and society from breastfeeding and the use of human milk for infant feeding."[41] The AAP also notes that "[h]uman milk is uniquely superior for infant feeding," and that "breastfeeding of infants provides advantages with regard to general health, growth, and development, while significantly decreasing risk for a large number of acute and chronic diseases," including ear infections.[42]

Obviously, breastfeeding is not a viable option for everyone. Economic concerns, time constraints, and even physical obstacles can make breastfeeding difficult, if not impossible. Does this mean that your child will necessarily be negatively impacted as a result of not being breastfed? No. In addition, breastfeeding your child is no guarantee of perfect development. Nevertheless, as the relevant research continues to favor breastfeeding over bottle-feeding, breastfeeding should be pursued whenever possible.

Essential fatty acids are found predominately in plant-based oils and fish.[43] Fish is the major source of long-chain essential fatty acids EPA and DHA (especially fatty fish like mackerel, herring, and salmon), while the major sources of short-chain essential fatty acids, including alpha-linolenic acid (ALA), are oils such as soybean, canola, and especially flaxseed.[44] Other sources of essential fats include nuts, seeds, egg yolk, poultry, and meat.[45]

Long-chain EFAs and short-chain EFAs are different in that short-chain EFAs must be converted by the body into long-chain EFAs before they can be utilized. Unfortunately, some people are unable to accomplish this conversion effectively. There are researchers who believe that problems converting short-chain EFAs into long-chain EFAs may explain the LCPUFA deficiency found in many children diagnosed with ADHD. If a person cannot properly convert short-chain EFAs to long-chain EFAs, then that person will need to ingest long-chain EFAs directly. In addition, certain foods may actually interfere with the ability to obtain optimum levels of LCPUFAs. Fried foods, processed foods, and snack foods—in fact, anything containing hydrogenated or partially hydrogenated oils—block the production of DHA in the body.[46]

In terms of getting essential fatty acids from fish, the Environmental Protection Agency (EPA) and the FDA advise pregnant women, women who are breastfeeding, and children to avoid eating fish species that are high in mercury content, as mercury causes brain and development problems in children.[47] These governmental bodies warn that "methylmercury is a potent toxin" and that "babies of women who consume large amounts of fish when pregnant are at a greater risk for changes in their nervous system that can affect their ability to learn."[48] Because fish is still a good source of essential fatty acids, the FDA recommends eating eight to twelve ounces of fish a week, but suggests choosing fish lower in mercury, including salmon, pollock, and cod. It specifically warns against consuming tilefish from the Gulf of Mexico, swordfish, king mackerel, and shark, as these fish are likely to contain substantial amounts of mercury, which is detrimental to the developing nervous systems of unborn children.[49]

Perhaps the most convenient source of LCPUFAs is the over-the-counter supplement. Readily available, potent amounts of LCPUFAs are contained in supplements derived from fish and krill oils as well as algae.[50] Studies demonstrate that LCPUFA supplementation can provide significant improvement with respect to some disorders, including dyslexia, dyspraxia,[51] and bipolar disorder.[52] A 2012 University of Oxford study shows that daily supplements of omega-3 fatty acids can improve the reading skills and behavior of underperforming children in mainstream private schools. As the study notes, "Previous studies have shown benefits from dietary supplementation with omega-3 in children with conditions such as ADHD, dyslexia and developmental coordination disorder, but this is the first study to show such positive results in children from the general school population."[53]

The authors also state that their study "provides the first evidence that dietary supplementation with omega-3 DHA might improve both the behavior and the learning of healthy children from the general school population." Indeed, while supplementation helped only the lowest achieving 20 percent of children with respect to reading skill, the study's authors also found that "reductions in parents' ratings of ADHD-type symptoms were evident across the entire sample studied here." The study concludes that its "results thus extend the previous findings in this area from clinically-defined groups to healthy but underperforming children from the general school population, and suggest that dietary deficiencies of DHA might have subtle behavioral effects on children in general, as has been shown for some combinations of artificial food additives."[54]

Building on their previous work, the researchers conducted a second study and found a correlation between omega-3 blood levels and learning ability and behavior. As the paper notes, "From a sample of nearly 500 school children, we found that levels of Omega-3 fatty acids in the blood significantly predicted a child's behaviour and ability to learn. Higher levels of Omega-3 in the blood, and DHA in particular, were associated with better reading and memory, as well as with fewer behavior problems as rated by parents and teachers."[55]

Please note that while it may be advantageous to use essential fatty acid supplements, I am not recommending blindly adding supplements to a child's diet. Maintaining a proper balance of essential fatty acids is important for proper health and development. Not long ago there was a raging debate among scientists and researchers regarding whether infant formula in the United States should be supplemented with LCPUFAs, although infant formulas overseas have been supplemented with LCPU-FAs for a number of years. In 2002, taking steps to address this issue, at least one company began offering a new formula supplemented with a blend of omega-3 and omega-6 fatty acids. The bottom line is that LCP-UFAs are powerful and best obtained through a balanced diet. If you are considering supplementation for yourself or your child, consult a qualified professional before doing so.

Another exceptionally important, and often overlooked, nutrition-related element is gut flora—the microorganisms that live in the digestive system, or gut. Obviously, the gut is responsible for, among other things, digesting food. If there is a problem with your gut, it will impact your ability to properly "feed" your body and your brain. In addition, the gut acts as a protective barrier. If your gut is not functioning correctly, substances that ordinarily should not get into your bloodstream often will. Another interesting fact is that the immune system resides primarily in your gut. Again, if there is an issue with your gut, it could affect your body's ability to fight infection or deal effectively with environmental toxins. Lastly, did you know that the greatest concentration of serotonin—a neurotransmitter involved in mood control, depression, and aggression—is found in your intestines, not your brain?

Studies confirm that the gut affects not only physical health but also mood and behavior. For example, in one study, mice that lacked gut bacteria behaved differently from mice with normal gut bacteria. Specifically, bacteria-lacking mice engaged in what the researchers referred to as "high-risk behavior." Moreover, these bacteria-lacking mice displayed neurochemical changes in their brains. As a result, the researchers now believe gut flora impacts brain development.[56] These researchers also discovered that the absence or presence of gut microorganisms during infancy permanently alters gene expression. Specifically, gut bacteria affects genes and signaling pathways involved in learning, memory, and motor control, closely tying gut bacteria to early brain development and subsequent behavior.

As one would suspect, given the importance of proper gut flora and its connection to the immune system, behavior, gene expression and general health, a number of theories have emerged suggesting a connection between human gut flora and ASD. Noting an association between autistic children and a high prevalence of recurrent medical problems, including ear infections, sinus problems, and upper respiratory illnesses, some researchers theorize that these children suffer from "immune abnormalities," which may have predisposed them to adversely react to a variety of environmental factors, with autism being a possible result.[57]

According to researchers, there are certain types of gut flora associated with the incidence of ASD as well as other learning and behavioral problems. One is *Candida*. *Candida* is a fungus that normally constitutes a very small proportion of human gut flora. It is kept in check through competitive inhibition by other gut flora and certain immune functions.[58] When it thrives, however, it can easily over populate a person's system and bring with it some well-documented side effects, including vitamin and fatty-acid deficiencies. In addition, some species of *Candida* are known to produce a range of toxins when they die off in great numbers. This is known as the "Jarisch-Herxheimer reaction," and is especially acute when an individual takes an oral antifungal or antibiotic. Symptoms vary widely but may include fatigue, moodiness, depression, inability to concentrate, headaches, loss of energy, food cravings, mold sensitivity, multiple food and chemical intolerances, and nerve problems.[59] Tina and I once saw this reaction happen in a student. One day, I received a phone call from this boy's mother, who was very upset by her son's recent behavior at school. The boy was not himself, often in a foul mood, and getting into trouble. I asked if anything had changed recently, and she replied that he had just started taking an antifungal for a skin issue. Tina suspected a *Candida*-related issue. Once off the antifungal, the boy quickly reverted to his former self.

Another relevant type of intestinal flora is called *Clostridia*. I believe I have witnessed the improvements that can follow the elimination of

Clostridia. I once saw a noticeable change for the better in the behavior of a student on the spectrum over a very short period of time. When I mentioned this improvement to the boy's mother, she replied that he "always got better" when he was ill and on antibiotics. This sounded absolutely wrong to me. Don't kids behave worse when they are not feeling well? A bit of research revealed that this apparently is not unusual for children on the spectrum. It could be that once the antibiotics have destroyed the unwanted gut bacteria, improved behavior results.

In one study, autistic children were found to have eight species of *Clostridia* not present in non-autistic children. In another study, reminiscent of my own experience, a group of autistic children were treated with oral vancomycin, a powerful antibiotic. Improvements were noted in both social interactions and intellectual function. Unfortunately, the children regressed within two weeks of discontinuing therapy.[60]

Proper nutrition should help deter the growth of "bad" bacteria, while supplementation with probiotics, which contain "good" bacteria, should help restore proper balance, and may even result in improved behavior. For infants, human breast milk helps establish gut flora properly. Clearly, there exists a connection between the mind and the gut, and more specifically, there exists a connection between a child's mind and a child's gut flora. If there is a problem with a child's gut flora, that child will almost certainly suffer negative mental consequences, possibly even ASD. Ensuring a properly balanced gut is essential to treating and maybe even preventing ASD. Reestablishing normal gut flora and treating the digestive system of the child should be the number one treatment for learning disorders, and it should be considered before any other treatments with drugs.[61]

The maintenance of proper gut flora is another reason to be wary of overusing antibiotics. Tina and I often worried that the continuous course of antibiotics prescribed for Robert may have had negative impacts on his ability to digest and process foods properly. As Corrine, our nutritionist, warned us, you can permanently damage your child's digestive system (not to mention the fact that overuse of antibiotics lessens their effectiveness), which may in turn, adversely affect neurological development. We believe Corrine was right.

Researchers at the Stanford University School of Medicine found that repeated use of antibiotics "induces cumulative and persistent changes in the composition of the beneficial microbial species inhabiting the human gut."[62] Studying the antibiotic ciprofloxacin (Cipro), these researchers raised questions about possible long-term effects of antibiotic administration. In addition to the concerns of creating drug-resistant disease, the study demonstrates that we must also worry about gut flora that has been lost or diminished by antibiotics, as well as any impairment to the beneficial functions performed by a patient's gut microbial community as a whole, "such as signaling cells of the intestinal lining, which are constantly turning over, to maintain an appropriate barrier against ingested toxic compounds, or secreting anti-inflammatory substances that may prevent allergic or autoimmune diseases."[63]

In terms of diet, some foods or food additives may cause behavioral issues, hyperactivity, allergies, or even chronic infections.[64] As mentioned earlier, before we "cleaned up" Robert's gut, his behavior would deteriorate rapidly after eating corn products or anything that contained artificial sweeteners. Also, Robert's ear infections seemed tied to his ingestion of dairy products. As our nutritionist informed us, there may be a connection between chronic ear infections and dairy products.[65] Robert has not suffered a single ear infection since he stopped eating dairy. We received further proof of the connection between food aversions and chronic infections when Robert suddenly began experiencing recurring sinus infections. Convinced that Robert was again suffering from a type of allergic reaction, our homeopathic doctor, Dr. Kokayi, urged us to examine Robert's diet. "What has changed?" he asked. We discovered that many children who have aversions to dairy products often react adversely to eggs. Shortly after Robert became inordinately fond of eggs for breakfast (people tend to crave what is bad for them), the sinus infections began. Robert was right in the middle of a full-blown, ENT-diagnosed sinus infection when we came upon this information. We immediately stopped feeding him eggs. The sinus infection cleared up within days without us having to resort to antibiotics.

Finally, in 2007, a British study published in the *Lancet* found that "[a]rtificial colours or a sodium benzoate preservative (or both) in the diet result in increased hyperactivity in 3-year-old and 8/9-year-old children in the general population." [66] As a result, the European Parliament now requires that foods containing those chemicals bear a label warning that the dyes "may have an adverse effect on activity and attention in children." In response, the FDA decided to look into the matter. While it has thus far refused to require similar labels, it now takes the position that there may be a connection between artificial dyes and behavior and attention problems in some children.[67]

There seems to be no question that diet should be considered when treating children diagnosed with an attention, learning, or behavioral disorder. This is certainly the case in regard to ADHD. As one study notes, "Attention-deficit hyperactivity disorder (ADHD) is multi-determined and complex, requiring a multifaceted treatment approach. Nutritional management is one aspect. . . . Nutritional factors such as food additives, refined sugars, food sensitivities/allergies, and fatty acid deficiencies have all been linked to ADHD. There is increasing evidence that many children with behavioral problems are sensitive to one or more food components that can negatively impact their behavior. . . . In general, diet modification plays a major role in the management of ADHD and should be considered as part of the treatment protocol."[68]

■ Play and Exercise

Many children on the spectrum are not able to process sensory input properly. Some are understimulated (hyposensitive) and some are over-stimulated (hypersensitive) by light, sound, and touch. Moreover, many of these children have weak muscle tone and appear clumsy or uncoordinated. As a result, they often don't enjoy sports or get enough exercise. Robert certainly had severely underdeveloped sensory skills and sensory sensitivities. He could not make eye contact. He would cover his ears when there were loud noises. He didn't like to be touched. He seemed overwhelmed by his environment. Until he received therapy, he could not really function in any sports activities. Is it any wonder he had so many difficulties participating and paying attention?

In the book *The Reason I Jump*, a thirteen-year-old autistic boy named

Higashida describes how eye contact makes him feel "creepy," noise can sometimes make him feel "lost," and light can "needle" its way into his eyeballs, all of which forces him to shut out the world in order to escape feeling overwhelmed, confused, and in pain. He tells how repetitive stories and repetitive actions bring comfort and relief. Similarly, as described in the book *Son Rise,* repetitive activities, such as rocking and spinning, were thought to be used by an autistic boy to block out an overwhelming and confusing world of external stimuli. Rituals, it seems, might be akin to meditation. I am reminded of how Robert would line up his toys and repeat himself over and over. Doing so might well have been the only way for him to achieve a real sense of comfort.

Underdeveloped sensory skills impact attention, learning, and behavior, and this fact has not been lost on those who work with children. For example, visual processing issues have been associated with reading problems, learning issues, and ADHD. As a result, according to a law that went into effect in July 2000, all children in Kentucky are required to undergo a comprehensive vision exam—one that examines not only visual acuity but also whether the eyes focus and shift properly between distances, as well as if the eyes work together—before they are allowed to enter school.[69] Similar legislation has been considered in several other states, including New York, Arkansas, Georgia, Nebraska, and New Hampshire.[70] Additionally, the National Parents Teacher Association has recognized the link between visual processing problems and learning problems.[71]

Researchers have also found an association between sensory issues and attention, learning, and behavioral disorders. A study on dyslexia found that dyslexic students had difficulty discriminating letters against visual background "noise."[72] Specifically, the dyslexics had difficulty seeing letters that were printed in front of certain visual backgrounds. They could not see the letters for the noise. In correspondence, Anne Sperling, one of the researchers, indicated that she believes dyslexia is a problem that "affect[s] all the senses." Concerning ADHD, another study found that there may be a connection between the incidence of ADHD diagnosis and vision-related problems.[73]

Another fascinating sensory condition is called synesthesia, which is characterized by the stimulation of one sense triggering a response in a completely different sense. For example, someone with synesthesia might see a color after hearing a particular sound. A recent study found that the rate of occurrence of this condition is almost three times greater in autistic individuals.[74] Interestingly, when I mentioned this condition to my son, he told me he gets very strong "impressions" of color when he hears music, and often associates particular colors to particular songs.

A recent study published in the *Journal of Neuroscience* states that "individuals with ASD have difficulty perceiving the temporal relationship between cross-modal inputs. Such impairments in multisensory processing may cascade into higher-level deficits . . . such as speech perception."[75] In other words, research shows that some ASD children have trouble integrating what they hear with what they see. As the study explains, "There is a huge amount of effort and energy going into the treatment of children with autism, virtually none of it is based on a strong empirical foundation tied to sensory function. If we can fix this deficit in early sensory function them maybe we can see benefits in language and communication and social interactions."[76]

The fact is that children diagnosed with disorders such as autism, PDD, and ADHD have had their underdeveloped sensory skills treated successfully through sensory integration therapy for over fifty years.[77] Dyslexic issues, for example, have been helped through visual processing training. In one study, scientists observed that "[p]atching one eye can improve eye control and reading in dyslexic children with poor eye control."[78] At the end of a nine-month period, severely dyslexic children with unstable eye control who used specially designed glasses that covered one eye were reading at a level eight months ahead of those who had not used the glasses.[79] The results were explained by a researcher: "[I]f the two eyes do not point steadily at print, letters can seem to dance around and change order, so the child becomes very confused."[80]

In 2008, the National Eye Institute (NEI), a division of the National Institutes of Health (NIH) of the United States Department of Health and Human Services (HHS), funded a study on a condition known as convergence insufficiency (CI), which is a problem that occurs when the eyes do not work together when attempting to focus on a nearby target, such as a book. In these cases, the reader can experience symptoms such as double vision, "moving" words, headaches, fatigue, and inattention. This double-blind study involved both optometrists and ophthalmologists working together at nine sites throughout the United States, including such prestigious clinics as the Mayo Clinic, Bascom Palmer Eye Institute, and The Ratner Children's Eye Center. The researchers found that in as little as twelve weeks, CI issues could be effectively treated through vision therapy.[81]

Yet another study relating to reading-disabled and dyslexic students found that students who received visual therapy not only improved their reading skills, but also experienced a decrease in their headache symptoms—an improvement not experienced by the study's trial group, which received only reading tutoring.[82]

In *Reversing Dyslexia*, Phyllis Books describes how dyslexia can be treated by "rewiring" the brain—a theory known as neuroplasticity. She suggests several non-drug treatments, including sensory integration, nutrition, and even simple play.

In our experience, taking care of physical issues seems to have a tremendous impact when treating learning disorders. Everything is connected. By affecting one system, you will affect them all. For example, do some push-ups. Think you're working only on your arms and chest? Think again. You are also strengthening your core, legs, back, and shoulders. Work hard enough and your heart will get stronger, your metabolism will get a boost, your stress levels will go down, and you will feel better, have more energy, and increase your mental abilities. Physical therapies can have a positive effect on a child with sensory problems, problems that can cause life to feel utterly overwhelming. If a child is overwhelmed by the world outside, how can that child ever hope to learn properly or behave appropriately?

The best way to ensure proper sensory development and avoid any need for later sensory integration therapy is to play with your children. It's that simple. Take them out of their cribs, playpens, and swings and get them down on all fours, crawling and rolling on the ground. Crawl and roll around with them. Be part of their world. Play games that will exercise their eye-tracking and depth perception. Roll a ball to them, do puzzles with them, play blocks with them. Involve your children in what you do at home. Have your children watch as you cook. Let them help you wash and cut fresh vegetables, measure and mix ingredients, and set the table. Let them help fix the loose drawer, plant seeds in the garden, or clean up the house and yard. Not only will they be learning valuable life skills and interacting with you on a meaningful basis, they will be developing and enhancing their sensory skills.

Make sure your children exercise. In his book *Spark,* Dr. John J. Ratey explains how exercise coupled with complex movement and balance components (karate, yoga, gymnastics, tennis, etc.) can have a positive, profound impact on mood, attention, and learning. He cites extensive research demonstrating the connection between exercise and measurable changes in the brain that directly impact the ability to learn. Moreover, he also points to research showing that exercise can be more effective than medication in treating learning, behavioral, and mood-related disorders, and it does not have any dangerous side effects.[83]

In regard to infants and sensory processing, I would advise against rushing a child into walking. Children need the visual and kinesthetic stimulation of crawling during the early stages of development. (I was so proud that Robert had skipped the crawling stage and had begun walking at ten months old. Now I wish he had learned to crawl properly, no matter how long it might have taken.) I would also advise against using a walker. Walkers prevent children from seeing their legs and feet move, and deny children access to objects they would ordinarily be able to reach, pick up, and touch. Developmental studies on infants suggest that visual feedback and hands-on stimulation are critical to sensory and cognitive development, and that walkers might disrupt proper sensory integration and slow cognitive growth.[84]

■ Screen Time

Televisions, computers, video games, cell phones, and electronic devices of all kinds are part of life. But there are serious documented problems experienced by those who get too much screen time. Television viewing by young children has been linked to reading problems, attention issues, developmental issues, obesity, and even violence later in life. In fact, the AAP recommends that television viewing and similar activities be avoided entirely by children under the age of two (the critical period of a child's brain development), and that total television time for older children be limited to one to two hours per day.[85] Citing the fact that "research on early brain development shows that babies and toddlers have a critical need for direct interactions with parents and other significant care givers . . . for healthy brain growth and the development of appropriate social, emotional, and cognitive skills," the AAP states that exposure to television should be avoided by such young children.[86] And don't be fooled into thinking educational television and video games are exceptions to the rule. Too much screen time interferes with language development even if your kids watch programs that are supposed to enhance language and development.

It has been reported that "[t]elevision reduces verbal interaction between parents and infants, which could delay children's language development." In one study, researchers found that "for each additional hour of television exposure, there was a decrease of 770 words (7 percent) heard from an adult by a child. This study also found that the more hours spent watching television, the fewer vocalizations infants made when adults talked to them, adding that these results may help explain previous findings of a link between television viewing and delayed language development."[87] In addition, increased daily television viewing and increased television viewing at bedtime negatively impacts a child's sleep habits, leading to resistance to bedtime, delays in falling asleep, anxiety concerning sleep, and shortened sleep duration.[88] It should come as no surprise that sleep problems are associated with behavioral issues,[89] ADHD,[90] and autism.[91]

Additionally, television and computer screens can be detrimental to visual processing and may adversely affect attention. With respect to vision, these screens train the eyes to fixate on a stationary point at a fixed distance for long periods of time. They are two-dimensional stationary devices that "fix [the] eyeball in one place," "do not offer the eyes different points of convergence," and "cause tremendous eye strain."[92] Of course, prolonged screen time also takes away from other forms of play that develop a child's depth perception, and focusing ability. It can even distort the growth of the eye and cause a myriad of other health problems, ranging from blurred vision to muscle and nerve injury.[93] Television and computer screens may also be responsible for improperly wiring the brain's visual attention system. A baby's eyes will instinctively lock on rapidly changing screen images.[94] Known as the "orienting response," it is a human's natural and instinctive response to any sudden or novel stimulus.[95] Thus, these ever changing images demand the child's constant attention on a biological level.[96] If a child gets used to viewing an ever-changing panorama of images, that child may attempt to recreate the flow of rapid-fire images by moving his eyes and head around![97] Television may be wiring children's brains to seek out quickly varying images all the time. But images don't change that rapidly in real life. A person's face doesn't change every five seconds, books don't change every five seconds, and classrooms don't change every five seconds. If the brain has come to expect such variation, problems arise.

It is no wonder that early television exposure reduces reading by children at later ages[98] and is associated with attention problems by the age of seven. Noting that "the types and intensity of visual and auditory experiences that children have early in life . . . may have profound influences on brain development," the authors of a study published in *Pediatrics* found that "television hours watched per day at both age 1 and age 3 was associated with having attentional problems at age 7," and suggest that "[l]imiting young children's exposure to television . . . during formative years of brain development . . . may reduce children's subsequent risk of developing ADHD." [99]

Restrict the overall time you permit your children to stare at screens each day. Moreover, limit the amount of time spent by your children during each viewing session. For older children, if you allow an hour's worth of television, break it into two half-hour sessions.

■ Chemicals and Pollutants

Unfortunately, there has been a radical increase in the use of industrial chemicals since World War II. These chemicals can collect in our tissues—even in breast milk. The dangers and risks posed by exposure to these products increases when such exposure is in combination rather than isolated to any particular chemical. While a 2006 article in the *Lancet* states that the causes of "[n]eurodevelopmental disorders such as autism, attention deficit disorder, mental retardation, and cerebral palsy" are "mostly unknown," it also notes that certain industrial chemicals, including lead, methylmercury, polychlorinated biphenyls (PCBs), arsenic, and toluene, "are recognized causes of neurodevelopmental disorders and subclinical brain dysfunction" and suggests the need for control of such chemicals.[100] The authors of this article followed up with further research, identifying another six developmental neurotoxicants: manganese, fluoride, chlorpyrifos, dichlorodiphenyltrichloroethane (DDT), tetrachloroethylene, and polybrominated diphenyl ethers (a type of flame retardant). In this research, the authors also note that "[i]ndustrial chemicals that injure the developing brain are among the known causes for th[e] rise in prevalence" of "[n]eurodevelopmental disabilities, including autism, attention-deficit hyperactivity disorder, [and] dyslexia."[101]

Exposure to these chemicals and others, including pesticides, dioxin, bisphenol A (BPA), should be avoided whenever possible. Such chemicals have been linked to cancer, reproductive problems, birth defects, mental handicaps, and learning issues, including ADHD.[102] More specifically, a study was conducted to examine whether there was any association between ADHD and phthalate exposure. "Phthalates, called 'plasticizers,' are a group of industrial chemicals used to make plastics like polyvinyl chloride (PVC) more flexible or resilient, and are also used as solvents. Phthalates are nearly ubiquitous in modern society, found in, among other things, toys, food packaging, hoses, raincoats, shower curtains, vinyl flooring, wall coverings, lubricants, adhesives, detergents, nail polish, hair spray and shampoo."[103] The research "showed a strong positive association between phthalate metabolites in urine and symptoms of ADHD among school-age children."[104]

In addition, researchers at the University of Montreal and Harvard University examined the relationship between ADHD and exposure to certain pesticides called organophosphates. Analyzing pesticide residue levels in more than 1,100 children, they found those with the highest levels of dialkyl phosphates (the breakdown products of organophosphate pesticides) had the highest incidence of ADHD. Overall, they found a 35-percent increase in the odds of developing ADHD with every tenfold increase in the concentration of pesticide residue. "The effect was seen even at the low end of exposure. Kids who had any detectable above-average level of the most common pesticide metabolite in their urine were twice as likely as those with undetectable levels to record symptoms of the learning disorder."[105]

Exposure to cigarette smoke or lead also may lead to an ADHD diagnosis. One study found that children exposed prenatally to tobacco smoke had an over twofold increase in their likelihood of being diagnosed with ADHD.[106] Those whose blood showed what researchers categorized as "high lead levels" were over two times more likely to have ADHD. Exposure to both lead and prenatal tobacco triggered an alarming "synergistic effect"—children in this category were eight times more likely to have ADHD.

Smog has been linked to the incidence of ASD. A case study from California found that "[c]hildren with autism were more likely to live at residences that had the highest quartile of exposure to traffic-related air pollution, during gestation . . . and during the first year of life."[107] More recently, a study out of Harvard University linked high air pollution to an increase in the incidence of ASD.[108] This finding apparently did not surprise the researchers, who note in their research, "[O]ur study adds to existing evidence that maternal exposure to air pollution in the perinatal period may increase risk for ASD in children. We observed significant positive linear trends between pollutant concentration and ASD for diesel particulate matter, lead, manganese, methylene chloride, mercury, and nickel."[109]

Coincidentally, it has been found that many autistic children are significantly deficient in substances known as metallothionein and glutathione.[110] These substances are known as natural chelators, which help clear the body of heavy metals, including mercury.[111] If heavy metal toxins prove to be linked to ASD, this finding could offer a plausible explanation for why certain children seem to be genetically predisposed to the disorder. It is also interesting to note that testosterone tends to inhibit the effectiveness of these natural chelators, while estrogen enhances it. These facts might provide a possible explanation for why ASD tends to appear more in boys than in girls.[112]

Adding to the problem of potentially injurious environmental substances, certain prescription medicines may also increase the incidence of impaired cognitive function and autism. Studies have found that expectant mothers' exposure to antiseizure medications—in particular, valproate (Depakote)—may impair cognitive function in their unborn children. A 2013 paper published by the *Lancet Neurology* found that "[m]ultivariate analysis of all children showed that age-6 IQ was lower after exposure to valproate. . . . Children exposed to valproate did poorly on measures of verbal and memory abilities compared with those exposed to the other antiepileptic drugs and on non-verbal and executive functions. . . ." In fact, high doses of the drug were associated with lower IQ, verbal ability, nonverbal ability, memory, and executive function scores. The study concludes that "[f]etal valproate [Depakote] exposure has dose-dependent associations with reduced cognitive abilities across a range of domains at 6 years of age." In other words, the more valproate taken by a mother, the greater the chance is of her child suffering cognitive impairment.[113] Even more recently, the *Journal of the American Medical Association* reported that "[m]aternal use of valproate during pregnancy was associated with a significantly increased risk of autism spectrum disorder and childhood autism in the offspring. . . ."[114] Indeed, Abbott Laboratories, the makers of Depakote, warns that "[t]here have been reports of developmental delay, autism and/or autism spectrum disorder in some children of women who took this medicine while pregnant."[115]

Even over-the-counter medications may be harmful. While it does not prove a causal relationship, a 2014 study found an association between the use of the common pain reliever acetaminophen (Tylenol) during pregnancy and the incidence of ADHD in children.[116]

Finally, at least two studies have found that cell phone radiation may have a causal link to ADHD. The first is an epidemiological study that found "[e]xposure to cell phones prenatally—and, to a lesser degree, postnatally—was associated with behavioral difficulties such as emotional and hyperactivity problems around the age of school entry."[117] The second study found that prenatal exposure to cell phone radiation in mice has multiple negative effects on development, including impaired memory, hyperactivity, and other "neurophysiological alterations that persist into adulthood."[118]

While nothing short of moving away to an unspoiled, utopian wilderness far removed from civilization will prevent all exposure to these chemicals and other problematic substances (and even then, some exposure is probable), there are steps that can be taken to lessen such exposure. If you are pregnant or nursing, don't use pesticides around the house. Let the bugs live. Don't use pesticides or herbicides on your lawn or in your garden. Eat organic foods whenever possible, and if eating organic foods is not an option, wash your produce with a natural cleaner designed to remove pesticides. Have your water tested for contaminants—perhaps a good water filter is in order. No dying your hair, no painting, and no refinishing furniture. You may even consider using household and garden products that are toxin-free. Such products are available over the internet and in health food stores. There also exist natural substitutes devoid of toxic chemicals for many household and garden items. While these substitutes may be purchased, oftentimes you can make them on your own.[119]

I am not suggesting you totally avoid exposure to every little troublesome substance out there. Indeed, it is hard to imagine how to accomplish such a feat. But if you are pregnant, you should be far more vigilant. And if you notice your child behaving differently in different environments or displaying any of the physical manifestations previously noted, it is worth finding out whether your child is being exposed to harmful levels of particular substances or is overly sensitive to certain materials. Remove these materials or remove your child from the area in which these materials are situated and see if there is a change in your child's physical appearance or behavior. Reintroduce these questionable materials and see if the symptoms return. The increasing number of chemicals and environmental pollutants coupled with the weakening of immune systems due to poor nutrition or exposure to such chemicals and pollutants should raise a giant red flag in the minds of all parents. If your child has behavioral, learning, or attention issues, these substances may be contributing factors.

■ CONCLUSION

If well-nourished, television-deprived, physically active, and toxin-free, is a child guaranteed to develop properly and avoid an autism spectrum disorder? No. There are surely children who suffer from genetic anomalies completely unrelated to environmental exposure that play a role in the diagnosis of autistic spectrum disorder. By the same token, I do not believe that every junk food-eating, television-addicted couch potato will manifest a learning, attention, or behavioral problem. But these factors can certainly impact a child's ability to pay attention, learn, and behave, and they are factors over which we have some control. Are they the reason behind the recent surge in ASD diagnoses, or is the true cause simply a difference in brain development? Still, if a difference in brain development is to blame, the question then becomes: What caused this difference? Might not such a manifestation be the result of nutritional deficiencies or exposure to one or more environmental pollutants? Might not it be the result of a lack of normal sensory development? Might not it be the result of some compensatory adjustment made by the brain? The question of whether there is a genetic link or a physical distinction in the brain that accompanies ASD is not the only issue. Such a link or manifestation, without definitive proof of its cause, does not prove that these disorders are beyond our control or influence.

Tina and I firmly believe in the theory that many of the symptoms associated with these disorders are nothing more than the unfortunate result of failure to ensure proper neurological development before conception, during pregnancy, and after birth in children predisposed to such symptoms. "It is not just the genes that control how our body chemistry works; sometimes environmental factors interact with our genetic predisposition."[120] As a Harvard neurologist once said, "[A]utism is not simply a genetics problem. . . . Autism involves the whole body."[121]

Saying that these disorders are "no one's fault" is a seductive choice. It relieves the parent and child of the burdens of undertaking time-consuming, sometimes difficult, and sometimes expensive child-rearing practices and treatment therapies. It limits responsibility, and it certainly eases a lot of guilt. Unfortunately, believing that these conditions are nobody's fault also ensures that they will continue to be diagnosed at an ever-increasing rate, and that mind-altering drugs will be prescribed in ever-increasing numbers to children of ever-decreasing ages.

Perhaps the worst part of the "no-fault" attitude is the fact that it fosters a sense of "learned helplessness."[122] Neither the child nor the parent need take responsibility for the poor behavior. Because it's nobody's fault, there is no need to examine or change lifestyle or child-rearing choices, since the disorder was unavoidable and such changes won't make any difference. Instead, everyone, including the child, assumes the child's poor behavior is caused by the disorder, and that there is nothing that can be done except to employ medications designed to suppress the behavior. Thus, when the child misbehaves, it's the disorder's fault; when the child behaves, it's because the medications are working.[123] But what happens if the medications lose their effectiveness?[124] This issue is never more apparent than when a child's body changes, perhaps at puberty, and the medications don't work the way they once had. I have spoken with parents who experienced this exact scenario. Their children never learned any coping skills, consistently blamed their inability to learn and behave on their disorders, and were forced to rely on their medications to perform. When the meds failed, they were utterly lost.

Ultimately, it comes to this: The therapies mentioned in this book can do nothing but help a child's development. The many and varied benefits of following these suggestions have been scientifically validated. If following these routes turns out to be an effective preventive measure when it comes to childhood psychological disorders—even if only some of the time—aren't they worth following all the time? I believe Tina and I could have prevented many of the symptoms Robert displayed, symptoms which were taken by his doctors as proof of his ADHD, PDD, and

ODD. At the very least, I think we could have lessened the severity and impact of Robert's symptoms if we had taken some of these preventative measures. My advice to you is to consider these outside factors if you are investigating alternative treatments for your child's attention, learning, or behavioral disorder or simply trying to prevent these disorders from occurring in the first place.

APPENDIX B

Resources

The following organizations can provide you with the information and support you need as a parent or guardian of a child with a developmental, learning, or behavioral disorder.

■ ALTERNATIVE HEALTH

International Guide to the World of Alternative Mental Health
www.alternativementalhealth.com
This website provides information on drug-free approaches to mental health. It includes resource listings, doctor and practitioner references, and general information with the understanding that many people can eliminate or significantly reduce their dependency on psychiatric medication by addressing underlying medical problems, allergies, toxic exposure, nutritional or diet-related problems, lack of exercise, or other treatable physical conditions.

Kirkman
www.kirkmanlabs.com
Founded in 1949, Kirkman is the oldest and one of the largest manufacturers of nutritional supplements for individuals with food allergies, special dietary requirements, and environmental sensitivities.

Suzy Cohen, RPh
www.suzycohen.com
Suzy Cohen, RPh, is a licensed pharmacist and functional medicine

practitioner. This website contains a great deal of information and research regarding the benefits of natural vitamins, herbs, and minerals.

■ EDUCATION

GreatSchools
www.greatschools.org
GreatSchools is a nonprofit organization with profiles of more than 200 thousand schools, pre-K through twelfth grade, featuring reviews from parents, teachers, and students. The website also provides information and support, including worksheets and videos, to help parents encourage learning at home.

Law Offices of Brad H. Rosken, PLLC
www.specialedcounselor.com
This website provides information on the current state of special education law, while also offering helpful links to organizations for children with developmental, learning, and behavioral disabilities.

Wrightslaw
www.wrightslaw.com
Wrightslaw is a website for parents, educators, and advocates. It provides information on special education law, education law, and advocacy groups for children with disabilities.

■ SUPPORT GROUPS

Autism Support Network
www.autismsupportnetwork.com
Autism Support Network is a free online support group for the ASD community. It includes chat rooms, resource listings, and useful information.

www.ldonline.net
This website contains numerous informative links to other websites regarding the definition, diagnosis, and treatment of ADHD and other learning issues.

www.millermom.proboards.com
These message boards provide people with an opportunity to ask questions, find answers, and discover information about education, special needs students, parenting, medication, resources, and treatments.

Roo's Clues
roosclues.blogspot.com
Roo's Clues is a very informative blog written by a mom who has decided to share the information she used to help her son recover from autism spectrum disorder. Like many of the other resources listed, this website adheres to the belief that many of the symptoms associated with ASD may be traced to another underlying issue that may be treated.

Talk About Curing Autism (TACA)
www.tacanow.org
TACA provides resource listings, education, and support for families affected by autism spectrum disorder. It espouses the idea that many children with ASD can improve greatly and even recover from their autistic symptoms with help from the right services.

■ VISION THERAPY

College of Optometrists in Vision Development (COVD)
www.covd.org
COVD is a nonprofit association of eye care professionals, including optometrists, optometry students, and vision therapists. This website provides information regarding behavioral and developmental vision care, vision therapy, and visual rehabilitation. It also is a good resource for finding local practitioners.

**The Optometric Extension
Program Foundation**
www.oepf.org
This organization offers information on visual health, prevention of visual problems, visual development, and vision training. It also is a useful resource for finding local practitioners.

APPENDIX C

References

Chapter 4

1. Wallis, Claudia, Hannah Block, et al. "Behavior: Attention Deficit Disorder: Life in Overdrive." *Time* 18 July 1994. Print.

2. Hancock, L. "Mother's Little Helper." *Newsweek* 18 Mar. 1996: 51–56. Print.

3. Sheedy Kurcinka, Philippa. *Raising Your Spirited Child.* New York, NY: HarperCollins, 1991. Print.

4. Daly, Matthew. "Connecticut Law Says Only Doctors—Not Teachers—Can Recommend Ritalin for Youngsters," *Associated Press* 17 July 2001. Print.

5. "Dear Ann Landers." *Newsday* 22 Mar. 1995. Print.

6. *Newsweek* 18 Mar. 1996: 52. Print.

7. Koplewicz, Harold S. *It's Nobody's Fault.* New York, NY: Three Rivers Press, 1996. Print.

8. *Newsday* 10 Mar. 1996. Print.

Chapter 10

1. Stevenson, Harold W., and James W. Stigler. *The Learning Gap.* New York, NY: Touchstone, 1992. Print; Sykes, Charles J. *Dumbing Down Our Kids.* New York, NY: St Martin's Press, 1995. Print.

2. *Newsday* 12 Jan. 1998: A6. Print; Hildebrand, John, and Jack Sirica. "Growing Costs, Growing Failure." *Newsday* 9 Nov. 1997: A4. Print.

3. Zito, Julie, Daniel Safer, et al. "Trends in the Prescribing of Psychotropic Medications to Preschoolers." *Journal of the American Medical Association* 283:8 (Feb. 23, 2000): 1025–1030. Print; Cantwell, Dennis P., James Swanson, and Daniel F. Connor. "Case Study: Adverse Response to Clonidine." *Journal of the American Academy of Child & Adolescent Psychiatry* 36 (1997): 539–544. Print; Swanson, J.M., D.A. Flockhart, D. Udrea, D. P. Cantwell, D. F. Connor, and L. Williams. "Clonidine in the treatment of ADHD: questions about safety and efficacy (letter)." *Journal of Child & Adolescent Psychopharmacology* 5 (1995): 301–304. Print.

Chapter 11

1. Koplewicz, Harold S. *It's Nobody's Fault*. New York, NY: Three Rivers Press, 1996. Print.

2. Rapp, Doris. *Is This Your Child?* New York, NY: William Morrow & Co, 1991. Print; Null, Gary. *Nutrition and the Mind*. New York, NY: Four Walls Eight Windows, 1995. Print; Block, Philippa Ann. *No More Ritalin*. New York, NY: Kensington Publishing Corp, 1996. Print; Stordy, B. Jacqueline, and Malcolm J. Nicholl. *The LCP Solution*. New York, NY: Ballantine Books, 2000. Print.

3. Freed, Jeffrey, and Laurie Parsons. *Right-Brained Children in a Left-Brained World*. New York, NY: Simon & Schuster, 1997. Print.

Chapter 12

1. Armstrong, Thomas. *The Myth of the A.D.D. Child*. New York, NY: Dutton, 1995. Print.

2. Savelsbergh, G.J.P., H.T.A. Whiting, and R.J. Bootsma. "Grasping Tau." *Journal of Experimental Psychology: Human Perception and Performance* 17:2 (1991): 315–322. Print.

3. Liberman, Jacob. *Take off Your Glasses and See*. New York, NY: Three Rivers Press, 1995. Print.

4. Stock Kranowitz, Carol. *The Out-of-Sync Child*. New York, NY: The Berkley Publishing Group, 1998. Print; Ayres, A. Jean. *Sensory Integration and the Child*. Torrance, CA: Western Psychological Services, 1979. Print.

Chapter 13

1. Breggin, Peter R. *Talking Back to Ritalin*. Monroe, ME: Common Courage Press, 1998. Print; Diller, Lawrence H. *Running on Ritalin*. New York, NY: Bantam Books, 1998. Print.

2. Mozlin, Rochelle. "The Use of Behavioral Parameters for a Visual Perceptual Evaluation." *Journal of Behavioral Optometry* 6:5 (1995): 115–116. Print.

Chapter 14

1. Zito, Julie, and Daniel Safer, et al. "Trends in the Prescribing of Psychotropic Medications to Preschoolers." *Journal of the American Medical Association* 283:8 (Feb. 23, 2000): 1025–1030. Print.

2. Vedantam, Shankar. "Study Finds Possible Link Between Childhood Deaths and Stimulants for ADHD." *The Washington Post* 16 June 2009. Print.

3. "A surge in women taking ADHD drugs." *Newsday* 13 Mar. 2014: A32. Print.

4. Reinberg, Steven. "More Kids Taking Antipsychotics for ADHD: Study." *HealthDay* 7 Aug. 2012. Web. 9 Oct. 2013.

5. "How Safe Is Methylphenidate in Preschoolers?" *The Brown University Psychopharmacology Update* 13(9) (2002): 2–3. Print.

6. Ibid.

7. Zito, Julie, Daniel Safer, et al. "Trends in the Prescribing of Psychotropic Medications

to Preschoolers." *Journal of the American Medical Association* 283:8 (Feb. 23, 2000): 1025–1030. Print.

8. Ibid.

9. Vedantam, Shankar. "Study Finds Possible Link between Childhood Deaths and Stimulants for ADHD." *The Washington Post* 16 June 2009. Print.

10. Ibid.

11. "Drug withdrawal weighs on Shire." *BBC News* 10 Feb. 2005. Web. 9 Oct. 2013.

12. Ibid.

13. El-Zein, R.A., S.Z. Abdel-Rahman, et al. "Cytogenetic effects in children treated with methylphenidate." *Cancer Letter* 230:2 (Dec. 18, 2005): 284–91. Print.

14. "FDA Warning of Fatal Risk with Drug for ADHD." *Newsday* 11 Oct. 2005: B13. Print.

15. *Newsday* 16 Oct. 2004: A7. Print.

16. *Newsday* 23 Mar. 2004: A7. Print.

17. *Newsday* 30 June 2005: A32. Print.

18. "British: Antidepressants Unsuitable for Children." *The Associated Press* 12 Dec. 2003. Web. 9 Oct. 2013.

19. Rossignol, Daniel. "Novel and emerging treatments for autism spectrum disorders: A systematic review." *Annals of Clinical Psychiatry* 21:4 (Nov. 2009): 213—36. Print.

20. "Parent Ratings of Behavioral Effects of Biomedical Interventions." *Autism Research Institute Publ.* 34 (Mar. 2009). Print.

21. Ibid.

Appendix A. What You Should Know

1. Koplewicz, Harold S. *It's Nobody's Fault*. New York, NY: Three Rivers Press, 1996. Print.

2. Stordy, B. Jacqueline, and Malcolm J. Nicholl. *The LCP Solution*. New York, NY: Ballantine Books, 2000. Print.

3. Connor, Tracy. "What's Causing the Rise in Autism?" *New York Post* 10 Oct. 2000: 8. Print.

4. Yeargin-Allsopp, Marshalyn, Tina Rice, et al. "Prevalence of Autism in a US Metropolitan Area." *Journal of the American Medical Association* 289:1 (Jan. 1, 2003): 49–55. Print.

5. Geier, David, and Mark Geier. "Early Downward Trends in Neurodevelopmental Disorders Following Removal of Thimerosal-Containing Vaccines." *Journal of American Physicians and Surgeons* 11:1 (Spring 2006): 8–13. Print.

6. Johnson, Carla K. "Government finds higher autism figure: 1 in 100." *The Associated Press* 5 Oct. 2009. Web. 9 Oct. 2013.

7. "Prevalence of Autism Spectrum Disorders—Autism and Developmental Disabilities

Monitoring Network, 14 Sites, United States, 2008." *Morbidity and Mortality Weekly Report Surveillance Summaries* Vol. 61: No. 3 (Mar. 30, 2012): 1–19. Print.

8. Kim, Young-Shin, Bennett L. Leventhal, et al. "Prevalence of Autism Spectrum Disorders in a Total Population Sample." *American Journal of Psychiatry* 168:9 (Sept. 2011): 904–912. Print.

9. Centers for Disease Control and Prevention. "Prevalence of Autism Spectrum Disorder Among Children Aged 8 Years—Autism and Developmental Disabilities Monitoring Network, 11 Sites, United States, 2010," *Morbidity and Mortality Weekly Report Surveillance Summaries* Vol. 63: No. 2 (Mar. 28, 2014): 1–21. Print.

10. Diller, Lawrence H. *Running on Ritalin*. New York, NY: Bantam Books, 1998. Print.

11. Eden, G.F., J.W. VanMeter, et al. "Abnormal processing of visual motion in dyslexia revealed by functional brain imaging." *Nature* 382 (1996): 66–69. Print.

12. Sanders, Stephan J., A. Gulhan Ercan-Sencicek, et al. "Multiple Recurrent De Novo CNVs, Including Duplications of the 7q11.23 Williams Syndrome Region, Are Strongly Associated with Autism." *Neuron* 70:5 (June 9, 2011): 863–885. Print.

13. London, Eric, and Ruth A. Etzel. "The Environment as an Etiologic Factor in Autism: A New Direction for Research." *Environmental Health Perspectives* 108:S3 (June 2000): 401–404. Print.

14. Ratajczak, Helen V. "Theoretical aspects of autism: Causes—A review." *Journal of Immunotoxicology* 8:1 (Jan.–Mar. 2011): 70. Print.

15. Hallmayer, Joachim, Sue Cleveland, et al. "Genetic Heritability and Shared Environmental Factors among Twin Pairs with Autism." *Archives of General Psychiatry* 68:11 (Nov. 2011): 1095–1102. Print.

16. Croen, Lisa A., Judith K. Grether, et al. "Antidepressant Use During Pregnancy and Childhood Autism Spectrum Disorders." *Archives of General Psychiatry* 68:11 (Nov. 2011): 1104–1112. Print.

17. Centers for Disease Control and Prevention. "Attention-Deficit/Hyperactivity Disorder (ADHD). Symptoms and Diagnosis." *CDC* 24 Sept. 2014. Web. 25 Sept. 2014.

18. *Diagnostic and Statistical Manual of Mental Disorders, Fourth Edition*. Arlington, VA: American Psychiatric Association, June 2000. Print.

19. Cross-Disorder Group of the Psychiatric Genomics Consortium. "Identification of risk loci with shared effects on five major psychiatric disorders: a genome-wide analysis." *Lancet* 381: 9875 (Apr. 20, 2013): 1371–1379. Print.

20. Sciberras, Emma, Kathryn L. Mueller, et al. "Language Problems in Children with ADHD: A Community-Based Study." *Pediatrics* Vol. 133 No. 5 (May 1, 2014): 793–800. Print.

21. Of note to this discussion is the fact that these new provisions still rely upon the subjective observance of symptoms to define the disorders. Indeed, the wording of the new ADHD provision is nearly identical to that of the DSM-IV.

22. Zito, Julie, Daniel Safer, et al. "Trends in the Prescribing of Psychotropic Medications to Preschoolers." *Journal of the American Medical Association* 283:8 (Feb. 23, 2000): 1025–1030. Print.

23. Schmidt, Rebecca, Robin Hansen, et al. "Prenatal vitamins, one-carbon metabolism gene variants, and risk for autism." *Epidemiology* 22:4 (July 2011): 476–485. Print.

24. Surén, P., Christine Roth, et al. "Association between maternal use of folic acid supplements and risk of autism spectrum disorders in children." *JAMA* 309:6 (Feb. 13, 2013): 570–577. Print.

25. Muggli, Reto. "Highly Unsaturated Fatty Acids in Nutrition and Disease Prevention." *The American Journal of Clinical Nutrition* 71:1 Suppl. (Jan. 2000): 169S–398S. Print.

26. Connor, William E. "Importance of n-3 fatty acids in health and disease." *American Journal of Clinical Nutrition* 71:1 Suppl. (Jan. 2000): 171S–175S. Print.

27. Crawford, Michael A. "The role of essential fatty acids in neural development: implications for perinatal nutrition," *American Journal of Clinical Nutrition* 57: 5 Suppl. (May 1993): 703S–709S. Print.

28. Innis, Sheila M. "Essential fatty acids in infant nutrition: lessons and limitations from animal studies in relation to studies on infant fatty acid requirements." *American Journal of Clinical Nutrition* 71:1 Suppl. (Jan. 2000): 238S–240S. Print.

29. Simopoulos, A.P. "Omega-3 fatty acids in health and disease and in growth and development." *American Journal of Clinical Nutrition* 54:3 (Sept. 1991): 438–463. Print.

30. Wauben, Ine P.M., Hua-Cheng Xing, and Patricia E. Wainwright. "Neonatal Dietary Zinc Deficiency in Artificially Reared Rat Pups Retards Behavioral Development and Interacts with Essential Fatty Acid Deficiency to Alter Liver and Brain Fatty Acid Composition, Biochemical and Molecular Action of Nutrients." *American Society for Nutritional Sciences* 129:10 (1999): 1773–1781. Print.

31. Foot, M., T. Cruz, and M. Clandinin. "Influence of dietary fat on the lipid composition of rat brain synaptosomal and microsomal membranes." *Biochemical Journal* 208:3 (Dec. 15, 1982): 631–640. Print.

32. Foot, M, T. Cruz, and M. Clandinin. "Effect of dietary lipid on synaptosomal acetylcholinesterase activity." *Biochemical Journal* 211:11 (May 1983): 507–509. Print.

33. Uauy, Ricardo, Dennis R. Hoffman. "Essential fat requirements of preterm infants." *American Journal of Clinical Nutrition* 71:1 Suppl. (Jan. 2000): 245S–250S. Print.

34. Willatts, P., J.S. Forsyth, et al. "Effect of long-chain polyunsaturated fatty acids in infant formula on problem solving at 10 months of age." *Lancet* 352:9129 (Aug. 29, 1998): 688–691. Print.

35. Uauy, Ricardo, Dennis R. Hoffman. "Essential fat requirements of preterm infants." *American Journal of Clinical Nutrition* 71:1 Suppl. (Jan. 2000): 245S–250S. Print.

36. Stevens, L.J., S.S. Zentall, et al. "Essential fatty acid metabolism in boys with attention-deficit hyperactivity disorder." *American Journal of Clinical Nutrition* 62:4 (Oct. 1995): 761–768. Print.

37. Horrobin, D.F. "Fatty acid metabolism in health and disease: the role of delta-6-desaturase." *American Journal of Clinical Nutrition* 57:5 Suppl. (May 1993): 732S–737S. Print.

38. Stevens, L.J, S.S. Zentall, et al. "Essential fatty acid metabolism in boys with atten-

tion-deficit hyperactivity disorder." *American Journal of Clinical Nutrition* 62:4 (Oct. 1995): 761–768. Print.

39. Horwood, John L, and David M. Fergusson. "Breastfeeding and later cognitive and academic outcomes." *Pediatrics* 101:1 (Jan. 1998): E9. Print.

40. Dettwyler, Katherine A. "When to Wean." *Natural History* 106:9 (Oct. 1997): 49; Horwood, John L, and David M. Fergusson. "Breastfeeding and later cognitive and academic outcomes." *Pediatrics* 101:1 (Jan. 1998): E9. Print; Kramer, Michael S., Frances Aboud, et al. "Breastfeeding and child cognitive development new evidence from a large randomized trial." *Archives of General Psychiatry* 65:5 (May 2008): 578—584. Print.

41. "Breastfeeding and the use of human milk: American Academy of Pediatrics. Work Group on Breastfeeding." *Pediatrics* 100:6 (Dec. 1997): 1035–1039. Print.

42. Ibid.

43. Kris-Etherton, P.M., Denise Shaffer-Taylor, et al. "Polyunsaturated fatty acids in the food chain in the United States." *American Journal of Clinical Nutrition* 71:1 Suppl. (Jan. 2000): 179S–188S. Print.

44. Ibid.

45. Ibid.

46. Stordy, B. Jacqueline, and Malcolm J. Nicholl. *The LCP Solution.* New York, NY: Ballantine Books, 2000. Print.

47. "Mercury Risk by the Sea." *Newsday* 26 Sept. 2005. Print.

48. United States Environmental Protection Agency. "What You Need to Know about Mercury in Fish and Shellfish." *EPA* 20 Nov. 2013. Web. 10 Oct. 2013.

49. U.S. Food and Drug Administration. "An Important Message for Pregnant Women and Women of Childbearing Age Who May Become Pregnant About the Risks of Mercury in Fish." *FDA* Mar. 2001. Web. 10 Oct. 2013.

50. Kris-Etherton, P.M., Denise Shaffer-Taylor, et al. "Polyunsaturated fatty acids in the food chain in the United States." *American Journal of Clinical Nutrition* 71:1 Suppl. (January 2000): 179S–188S. Print.

51. Stordy, B. Jacqueline. "Dark adaptation, motor skills, docosahexaenoic acid, and dyslexia." *American Journal of Clinical Nutrition* 71:1 (Jan. 2000): 323S–326S. Print.

52. Nidecker, A. "Fish Oil Fatty Acids May Soothe Some Disorders." *Clinical Psychiatry News* 26:11 (1998): 10. Print.

53. University of Oxford. "Increased intake of Omega-3 fatty acids improves children's reading and behavior." *Oxford University* 7 Sept. 2012. Web. 10 Oct. 2013.

54. Ibid.

55. University of Oxford. "Low Omega-3 could explain why some children struggle with reading." *Oxford University* 5 Sept. 2013. Web. 10 Oct. 2013.

56. Neufeld, K.M., N. Kang, et al. "Reduced anxiety-like behavior and central neurochemical change in germ-free mice." *Neurogastroenterology & Motility* 23:3 (Mar. 2011): 255–264, e119. Print.

57. Jyonouchi, Harumi, et al. "Dysregulated innate immune responses in young children with autism spectrum disorders: their relationship to gastrointestinal symptoms and dietary intervention." *Neuropsychobiology* 51:2 (2005): 77–85. Print.

58. Bingham, Max, and Glenn Gibson. "A gut feeling about autism." *The Autism File* 10 (2002): 25–28. Print.

59. Ibid.

60. Sandler, R.H., S.M. Finegold, E.R. Bolte, et al. "Short-term benefit from oral vancomycin treatment of regressive-onset autism." *Journal of Child Neurology* 15:7 (July 2000): 429–435. Print.

61. Campbell-McBride, Natasha. *Gut and Psychology Syndrome.* Amazon.com, 2003. Print.

62. Stanford University Medical Center. "Repeated antibiotic use alters gut's composition of beneficial microbes, study shows." *ScienceDaily* 13 Sept. 2010. Web. 10 Oct. 2013.

63. Ibid.

64. Rapp, Doris. *Is This Your Child?* New York, NY: William Morrow & Co, 1991. Print; Null, Gary. *Nutrition and the Mind.* New York, NY: Four Walls Eight Windows, 1995. Print.

65. Ibid.

66. McCann, Donna, Angelina Barrett, Alison Cooper, et al. "Food additives and hyperactive behaviour in 3-year-old and 8/9-year-old children in the community: a randomised, double-blinded, placebo-controlled trial." *Lancet* 370:9598 (Nov. 3, 2007): 1560–1567. Print.

67. U.S. Food and Drug Administration. "Background Document for the Food Advisory Committee: Certified Color Additives in Food and Possible Association with Attention Deficit Hyperactivity Disorder in Children." *FDA* 31 Mar. 2011. Web. 10 Oct. 2013.

68. Schnoll, R., D. Burshteyn, and J. Cea-Aravena. "Nutrition in the treatment of attention-deficit hyperactivity disorder: a neglected but important aspect." *Applied Psychophysiology and Biofeedback* 28:1 (Mar. 2003): 63–75. Print.

69. *Newsday* 22 Apr. 2003. A38. Print.

70. Ibid.

71. Resolution adopted at the National PTA Convention June 1999.

72. Sperling, Anne J., Zhong-Lin Lu, et al. "Deficits in perceptual noise exclusion in developmental dyslexia." *Nature Neuroscience* 8 (2005): 862–863. Print.

73. Ventura, R.H., D.B. Granet, and A. Miller-Scholte. "Relationship between convergence insufficiency and ADHD." *Strabismus* 13: 4 (2005): 163–168. Print.

74. Baron-Cohen, Simon, Donielle Johnson, et al. "Is synaesthesia more common in autism?" *Molecular Autism* 4:40 20 Nov. 2013. Web. 21 Oct. 2014.

75. Stevenson, Ryan, Justin Siemann, et al. "Multisensory Temporal Integration in Autism Spectrum Disorders." *The Journal of Neuroscience* 34(3) (15 Jan. 2014): 691–697. Print.

76. Ibid.

77. Chase, Marilyn. "New Behavior Therapy for Kids Uses Touch, Tones and Trampolines." *Wall Street Journal* 29 Oct. 1999: B1. Print; Stock Kranowitz, Carol. *The Out-of-Sync Child*. New York, NY: The Berkley Publishing Group, 1998. Print.

78. "Eye Patch Can Aid Reading." *Newsday* 7 Jan. 2000. Print.

79. Ibid.

80. Ibid.

81. Convergence Insufficiency Treatment Trial Study Group. "Randomized clinical trial of treatments for symptomatic convergence insufficiency in children." *Archives of Ophthalmology* 126:10 (Oct. 2008): 1336–1349. Print.

82. Atzmon, D., P. Nemet, A. Ishay, et al. "A randomized prospective masked and matched comparative study of orthoptic treatment versus conventional reading tutoring treatment for reading disabilities in 62 children." *Binocular Vision & Eye Muscle Surgery Quarterly* 8:2 (1993): 91–106. Print.

83. Ratey, John J., and Eric Hagerman. *Spark*. New York, NY: Little, Brown and Company, 2013. Print.

84. Siegel, Andrea C., and Roger V. Burton. "Effects of Baby Walkers on Motor and Mental Development in Human Infants." *Journal of Developmental and Behavioral Pediatrics* 20:5 (Oct. 1999): 355. Print.

85. American Academy of Pediatrics. "Media Education." *Pediatrics* 104:2 (1 Aug. 1999): 341–343. Print.

86. Ibid.

87. "TV Interferes with Infants' Language Development." *HealthDay* 2 June 2009. Web. 9 Oct. 2013; Christakis, Dimitri A, Jill Gilkerson, et al. "Audible television and decreased adult words, infant vocalizations, and conversational turns." *Archives of Pediatric & Adolescent Medicine* 163:6 (June 2009): 554–558. Print.

88. Owens, Judith, Rolanda Maxim, et al. "Television-viewing Habits and Sleep Disturbance in School Children." *Pediatrics* 104:3 (Sept. 1999): E27. Print.

89. Kelly, Yvonne, John Kelly, and Amanda Sacker. "Changes in Bedtime Schedules and Behavioral Difficulties in 7 Year Old Children." *Pediatrics* 14 Oct. 2013. Web. 20 Oct. 2013.

90. Gau, S.S-F, H-L. Chiang. "Sleep problems and disorders among adolescents with persistent and subthreshold attention-deficit/hyperactivity disorders." *SLEEP* 32:5 (May 1, 2009): 671–79. Print.

91. Herbert, Martha. *The Autism Revolution*. New York, NY: Ballantine Books, 2012.

92. Beam, Cris. "Babes in TV Land." *American Baby* Vol LXII: No 4. (Apr. 2000). Print.

93. Healy, Jane. *Failure to Connect: How Computers Affect Our Children's Minds and What We Can Do About It*. New York, NY: Simon & Schuster, 1998. Print.

94. Beam, Cris. "Babes in TV Land." *American Baby* Vol LXII: No 4. (Apr. 2000). Print.

95. Kubey, Robert, and Mihaly Csikszentmihalyi. "Television Addiction is no mere metaphor." *Scientific American* 23 Feb. 2002. Print.

96. Kubey, Robert, and Mihaly Csikszentmihalyi. "Television Addiction is no mere metaphor." *Scientific American* 23 Feb. 2002. Print; Beam, Cris. "Babes in TV Land." *American Baby* Vol LXII: No 4. Apr. 2000. Print; DeGaetano, Gloria. *Screen Smarts: A Family Guide to Media Literacy.* Boston, MA: Houghton Mifflin, 1996. Print.

97. Beam, Cris. "Babes in TV Land." *American Baby* Vol LXII: No 4. Apr. 2000. Print.

98. Koolstra, Cees M., and Tom H.A. Van der Voort. "Longitudinal effects of television on children's leisure time reading: a test of three explanatory models." *Human Communication Research* 23:1 (Sept. 1996): 4–35. Print.

99. Christakis, Dimitri A., et al. "Early Television Exposure and Subsequent Attentional Problems in Children." *Pediatrics* 113:4 (Apr. 1, 2004): 708–713. Print.

100. Grandjean, P, and P.J. Landrigan. "Developmental neurotoxicity of industrial chemicals." *Lancet* 368:9553 (Dec. 16, 2006): 2167–2178. Print.

101. Grandjean, P, and P.J. Landrigan. "Neurobehavioural effects of developmental toxicity." *Lancet Neurology* 13:3 (Mar. 2014): 330—338. Print.

102. Bouchard, Philippase F., and David Bellinger, et al. "Attention-deficit/hyperactivity disorder and urinary metabolites of organophosphate pesticides." *Pediatrics* 126:6 (June 2010): e1270–e1277. Print.

103. Centers for Disease Control and Prevention. "Factsheet Phthaltaes." *CDC* 16 July 2013. Web. 25 Sept. 2014.

104. Kim, B.N., S.C. Cho, Y. Kim, et al. "Phthalates exposure and attention-deficit/hyperactivity disorder in school-age children." *Biological Psychiatry* 66:10 (Nov. 2009): 958–963. Print.

105. Bouchard, Philippase F., and David Bellinger, et al. "Attention-deficit/hyperactivity disorder and urinary metabolites of organophosphate pesticides." *Pediatrics* 126:6 (June 2010): e1270–e1277. Print.

106. Froehlich, Tanya E., Bruce P. Lanphear, et al. "Association of tobacco and lead exposures with attention-deficit/hyperactivity disorder." *Pediatrics* 124:6 (Dec. 2009): e1054–e1063. Print.

107. Volk, Heather E., Fred Lurmann, et al. "Traffic-related air pollution, particulate matter, and autism." *JAMA Psychiatry* 70:1 (Jan. 2013): 71–77. Print.

108. Roberts, Andrea L., Kristen Lyall, Jaime E. Hart, et al. "Perinatal air pollutant exposures and autism spectrum disorder in the children of Nurses' Health Study II participants." *Environmental Health Perspectives* 121:8 (Aug. 2013): 978–984. Print.

109. Ibid.

110. James, S.J., et al., "Metabolic biomarkers of increased oxidative stress and impaired methylation capacity in children with autism." *American Journal of Clinical Nutrition* 80:6 (Dec. 2004): 1611–1617. Print; Kirby, David. *Evidence of Harm.* New York, NY: St. Martin's Press, 2005. Print.

111. James, S.J., et al., "Thimerosal Neurotoxicity is Associated with Glutathione Deple-

tion: Protection with Glutathione Precursors." *Neurotoxicology* 26:1 (Jan. 2005): 1–8. Print; Kirby, David. *Evidence of Harm*. New York, NY: St. Martin's Press: 2005. Print.

112. Kennedy, Robert F. Jr. "Tobacco Science and the Thimerosal Scandal." Robert F. Kennedy Jr. 22 June 2005. Web. 20 Oct. 2014

113. Meador, Kimford J., Gus A. Baker, et al. "Fetal antiepileptic drug exposure and cognitive outcomes at age 6 years (NEAD study): a prospective observational study." *Lancet Neurology* 12:3 (Mar. 2013): 244–252. Print.

114. Christensen, Jakob, Therese Koops Grønborg, et al. "Prenatal Valproate Exposure and Risk of Autism Spectrum Disorders and Childhood Autism." *JAMA* 309:16 (Apr. 24, 2013): 1696–1703. Print.

115. Depakoteer. Web. 20 Oct. 2013.

116. Liew, Z., et al. "Acetaminophen Use During Pregnancy, Behavioral Problems, and Hyperkinetic Disorders." *JAMA Pediatrics* 168:4 (2014):313–320. Print.

117. Divan, H.A., et al. "Prenatal and postnatal exposure to cell phone use and behavioral problems in children." *Epidemiology* 19:4 (July 2009):523–529.

118. Aldad, Tamir S., et al. "Fetal Radiofrequency Radiation Exposure From 800–1,900 Mhz-Rated Cellular Telephones Affects Neurodevelopment and Behavior in Mice." *Nature: Scientific Reports* 2: 312. 15 Mar. 2012. Web. 20 Oct. 2013.

119. Haley, Graham, and Rosemary Haley. *Haley's Hints*. New York, NY: New American Library, 2004. Print.

120. Stordy, B. Jacqueline, and Malcolm J. Nicholl. *The LCP Solution*. New York, NY: Ballantine Books, 2000. Print.

121. Herbert, Martha. *The Autism Revolution*. New York, NY: Ballantine Books, 2012. Print.

122. McGinnis, J. "Attention Deficit Disaster." *The Wall Street Journal* Sept. 18, 1997: A14. Print.

123. Ibid.

124. Briggin, Peter R. *Talking Back to Ritalin*. Monroe, ME: Common Courage Press, 1998. Print; Diller, Lawrence H. *Running on Ritalin*. New York, NY: Bantam Books, 1998. Print.

About the Authors

Robert J. Stevens is a graduate of Brown University and New York University School of Law. Inspired by his son, Robert became an educational consultant in 1998. While helping to shape and refine various curricula for learning centers and in-school programs, Robert has accumulated thousands of hours of hands-on experience with children struggling in school. Along with other educational and developmental experts, Robert created the Spark Development & Learning Program for children with attention, learning, and behavioral issues.

Catherine E. Stevens, MS, received her BA in biology from Boston University and her BS in cardiorespiratory technology from Stony Brook University. After seeing the positive impact dietary and nutritional intervention had upon her son, she returned to college for her master's degree in clinical nutrition from New York Institute of Technology. In addition to her work as a cardiac catheterization technologist at North Shore Long Island Jewish Hospital, Catherine specializes in working with children who demonstrate learning, attention, and behavioral issues. She resides with her husband, Robert, in Garden City South, New York.

Index

Dry scalp. *See* Cradle cap.

Ear
    infection, 10–11, 26, 127, 133
    tubes, 10–11, 26, 127
Evaluation, 24, 36–41, 48, 101–102
Eye contact, 14

Formula, baby, 10

GABA, 142
Gamma-aminobutyric acid. *See*
    GABA.
Growth, suppression of, 75–76

Hyperactivity, 16, 20, 24–26, 35,
    38, 41–43, 45, 55, 61, 77, 79,
    91, 116, 123–124, 134

IEP. *See* Individual education
    program.
Individual education program,
    62, 178

Luvox, 118–120, 132

Medication, 174–177. *See also*
    Adderall; Antidepressants;
    Catapres; Clonidine;
    Dexdrine; Luvox; Prozac;
    Ritalin; Strattera; Tenex.
Mood swings, 44, 75, 80, 86, 92,
    107, 129, 171
Nausea, 79–80
Networking, 39, 50

ODD. *See* Oppositional defiance
    disorder.
Omega-3 fatty acids, 141
Oppositional defiance disorder,
    41–43, 50, 55, 61, 79, 144
Optometry, developmental, 148, 150
Organic food, 128–129

PDD. *See* Pervasive developmental
    disorder.
Pervasive developmental
    disorder, 94, 173
Phenylalanine, 141
Phosphatidylserine, 142
Positive reinforcement, 20
Prozac, 95–97, 101, 104–108, 112,
    115–120, 175, 185

Ritalin, 44, 46, 49, 58–59, 71–79,
    81–87, 90–92, 94–97, 105–108,
    115, 117–118, 132, 134,
    141–142, 147, 153–154, 173,
    175–177, 185

Sensitivity
    to noise, 14, 87, 95, 134, 145–146
    to touch, 14, 145–146
Sensory integration, 144–145, 147,
    149, 165
SEPTA. *See* Special education
    parent-teacher association.
Sleep, loss of, 75
Spanking, 15–17, 19, 31
Special education, 39–40, 45, 48–50,
    53, 55, 62, 91, 97–98, 101, 110,

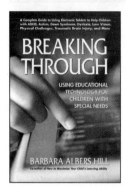

BREAKING THROUGH
Using Educational Technology for Children with Special Needs
Barbara Albers Hill

For many years, the techniques used to teach special needs children evolved slowly, with some approaches having more success than others. Some children progressed well, while others painfully struggled or failed to react at all to the methods being used. Then—seemingly overnight—a quiet revolution occurred. With the introduction of the electronic tablet came a new and surprisingly effective way to engage and help kids with autism spectrum disorder, ADHD, language impairment, intellectual disability, and many other learning differences. The tablets' small size, portability, bright colors, sounds, music, and responsive touch screen attracted all kids from the start, enabling them to immediately play, explore, and learn. Suddenly, kids who had never before responded to teachers and parents were enraptured, and children who had long struggled found the process of learning not only easier, but actually *fun*. Technology was breaking through the barriers caused by psychological and physical challenges.

Electronic tablets have been proven to enable communication, socialization, and the acquisition of new skills. Whether you're a parent, a teacher, or a caretaker, let *Breaking Through* guide you in using this technology to lessen life's challenges for your special children.

$16.95 • 160 pages • 6 x 9-inch quality paperback • ISBN 978-0-7570-0395-0

CREATIVE THERAPY FOR CHILDREN WITH AUTISM, ADD, AND ASPERGER'S
Using Artistic Creativity to Reach, Teach, and Touch Our Children

Janet Tubbs

Thirty years ago, Janet Tubbs began using art, music, and movement to reach children with low self-esteem and behavioral problems. Believing that unconventional children required unconventional therapies, she then applied her program to children with autism, ADD/ADHD, and Asperger's syndrome. Her innovative methods not only worked, but actually defied the experts. In this book, Janet Tubbs has put together a powerful tool to help parents, therapists, and teachers work with their children.

Creative Therapy is divided into two parts. Part One begins by explaining the author's creative approach to balancing a child's body, mind, and spirit through proven techniques. Part Two provides a wide variety of exercises and activities that are both fun and effective. Each is designed to reduce hyperactivity, increase focus, decrease anger, develop fine motor skills, or improve social and verbal skills while helping children relate to their environment without fear or discomfort.

$18.95 • 336 pages • 7.5 x 9-inch quality paperback • ISBN 978-0-7570-0300-4

THE IRLEN REVOLUTION
A Guide to Changing Your Perception and Your Life

Helen Irlen

After decades of revolutionizing the treatment of dyslexia through the use of colored lenses, Helen Irlen has turned her attention to children and adults who suffer from light sensitivity, headaches, attention deficit disorder, and other visual perception-related conditions and learning disabilities. Here, finally, is hope for everyone who has been misdiagnosed and needs real help for a real problem.

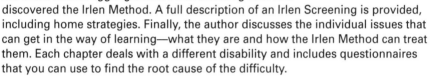

The book begins by sharing Helen's journey, focusing on her work with struggling readers and detailing how she discovered the Irlen Method. A full description of an Irlen Screening is provided, including home strategies. Finally, the author discusses the individual issues that can get in the way of learning—what they are and how the Irlen Method can treat them. Each chapter deals with a different disability and includes questionnaires that you can use to find the root cause of the difficulty.

Problems in processing visual information can cause physical symptoms and fragmented vision that affect attention, concentration, and performance. Thankfully, there is an easy, cost-effective solution—the Irlen Method.

$17.95 • 224 pages • 6 x 9-inch quality paperback • ISBN 978-0-7570-0236-6

REVERSING DYSLEXIA
Improving Learning & Behavior Without Drugs

Dr. Phyllis Books

Although dyslexia is often accompanied by social, psychological, and even physical issues that can make many everyday tasks seem unmanageable, mainstream treatment focuses on compensatory techniques, often leaving dyslexics feeling hopeless. In this book, Dr. Phyllis Books offers a new approach that can actually reverse dyslexia in a large number of cases.

The author begins by redefining dyslexia and its associated conditions. It goes on to explain how the brain develops and how an improperly functioning brain can be rewired and repaired through therapy. It then shows how important nutrition, exercise, play, and music are to learning ability. This lays the groundwork for significant improvements not only in reading but also in general learning ability, emotional stability, and psychological well-being. Dr. Books has spent over twenty-five years disproving the idea that dyslexia is a permanent condition, and *Reversing Dyslexia* can teach you how to disprove it as well.

$16.95 • 160 pages • 6 x 9-inch quality paperback • ISBN 978-0-7570-0378-3

WHAT TO DO ABOUT YOUR BRAIN-INJURED CHILD

Glenn Doman

In this updated classic, Glenn Doman—founder of The Institutes for the Achievement of Human Potential and pioneer in the treatment of brain-injured children—brings real hope to thousands of children who have been sentenced to a life of institutional confinement.

In *What To Do About Your Brain-Injured Child,* Doman recounts the story of The Institutes' tireless effort to refine treatment of the brain-injured. He shares the staff's lifesaving techniques and the tools used to measure--and ultimately improve--visual, auditory, tactile, mobile, and manual development. Doman explains the unique methods of treatment that are constantly being improved and expanded, and then describes the program with which parents can treat their own children at home in a familiar and loving environment. Included throughout are case histories, drawings, and helpful charts and diagrams.

$18.95 • 336 pages • 6 x 9-inch quality paperback • ISBN 978-0-7570-0186-4

THE A.D.D. & A.D.H.D. DIET!

Rachel Bell and Howard Peiper, ND

Every day, children are diagnosed with attention deficit disorder (ADD) or attention deficit hyperactivity disorder (ADHD). Addressing the causes of ADD and ADHD should be the first step in any treatment, but unfortunately, conventional drugs such as Ritalin deal with only the symptoms.

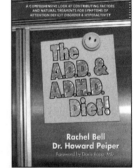

In their new book, *The A.D.D. & A.D.H.D. Diet!,* authors Rachel Bell and Dr. Howard Peiper take a uniquely nutritional approach to treating ADD and ADHD. The authors first address the causes of the disorders, from poor nutrition and food allergies to environmental contaminants. They discuss which foods your child can eat and which foods he should avoid. To make changing your child's diet easier, the authors also offer their very own healthy and delicious recipes. Final chapters examine the importance of detoxifying the body, supplementing diet with vitamins and nutrients, and exercising regularly in order to achieve good health.

With *The A.D.D. & A.D.H.D. Diet!,* you'll learn that a simple change in diet may be the most effective treatment for your child.

$10.95 • 112 pages • 6 x 9-inch quality paperback • ISBN 978-1-884820-29-8